Snowshoeing and Cross-Country Skiing in the Western Maine Mountains

Snowshoeing and Cross-Country Skiing in the Western Maine Mountains

Rangeley-Saddleback;
Flagstaff-Bigelow;
Carrabassett Valley-Sugarloaf;
Weld-Tumbledown;
and Farmington-Foothills Regions

34 Outings
Accessible from Franklin County

Doug Dunlap

Camden, Maine

Down East Books

An imprint of The Rowman & Littlefield Publishing Group, Inc.
4501 Forbes Blvd., Ste. 200
Lanham, MD 20706
www.rowman.com

Distributed by NATIONAL BOOK NETWORK

British Library Cataloguing in Publication Information available

Library of Congress Cataloging-in-Publication Data available

ISBN 978-1-60893-707-3 (paperback)
ISBN 978-1-60893-708-0 (e-book)

∞™ The paper used in this publication meets the minimum requirements of American National Standard for Information Sciences—Permanence of Paper for Printed Library Materials, ANSI/NISO Z39.48-1992.

Dedication

Becky, Ben, Anna, Matt

For all the good childhood times in—and on—the snow.

And thanks for shoveling!

Books in This Series

Day Hiking in the Western Maine Mountains, 2nd Edition
27 day hikes in the High Peaks and Foothills, ranging from 2.0 to 6.0 miles round-trip, and including level, moderate, and high elevation terrain. *(2015)*

Paddling in the Western Maine Mountains
22 lake, pond, river, and stream flat water day trips, from short outings of an hour or so, to all day adventures. *(2015)*

Snowshoeing and Cross-Country Skiing in the Western Maine Mountains
34 forest and lakeside routes, groomed trail systems, mountain ascents—and tips for winter travel on foot. *(2016)*

Waterfall Walks in the Western Maine Mountains
39 outings—waterfall adventures, foothills and forest hikes, and streamside and lakeside rambles. Most between distances of a half-mile to 2 miles. *(2017)*

Walking Trails in the Foothills of Western Maine
20 outings—lakeside, riverside, hillside and forest rambles, with waterfalls, mountain views, wildlife watching areas, and choice routes for daily walks. Most distances under 1 mile, many with options to extend. *(2018)*

Meet the Author

Greetings! Heading into the outdoors on foot in winter has been a joy for most of my life! I welcome you heartily to that enjoyment!

I began my winter travels breaking trails in the snow-covered hayfields behind my childhood New Hampshire home. My equipment back then was a pair of wooden skis attached to my boots by a single leather-strap. Growing up in a small town in New Hampshire meant spending much time around snow—playing in it, sliding on it, shoveling it and traveling over it by skis and snowshoes.

When our own children were growing up in Maine they would clamor to go outside in the first snowstorm of the winter, and preferred time in the snow to most any other activity one could name. Later they all skied cross-country and downhill, and took up snowshoeing. We truly look forward to winter in our family! Every winter I pack snowshoe and ski trails in the woodlot behind our farmhouse, and I am out in those woods, or on one of the many trips described in this book, almost daily.

My pursuit of winter on-foot travel has opened me to some remarkable places in North America. I have skied in the Alaska Range, and made my way on snowshoes to peaks north of Fairbanks in interior Alaska. In the West I have skied cross-country or hiked by snowshoe in the high desert country of northern Arizona and Utah and up on the Western Slope of Colorado. Closer to home, I have enjoyed winter days in the Adirondacks of New York, Green Mountains of Vermont, White Mountains of New Hampshire, and in Quebec—along with the Western Mountains of Maine. I have skied across Maine's Baxter Park multiple times, and completed a winter ascent of Mount Katahdin.

My outdoor experience includes working as an Outward Bound Instructor; and hiking the complete length of the Appalachian Trail, the Long Trail in Vermont, portions of the Pacific Crest Trail, and extensive regions of the Canyonlands country in the Southwest. I am a Registered Maine Guide.

It is a joy for me to introduce others to the wonder and simple beauty of wild waters, high peaks, and our expansive forests—especially in winter! I do hope to see you on the trail!

I have personally hiked or skied every snowshoe or ski route described in this book—most of them, many times.

— Doug Dunlap

3

Table of Contents

Dedication 1

Meet the Author 3

Acknowledgements 6

Be Prepared 7

Welcome, Winter Travelers!. 8

Rangeley-Saddleback Region 26

Rangeley Lakes Trail Center 28

Rock and Midway Ponds/Upper Fly Rod Crosby Trail 32

Hatchery Brook, Rangeley Lake North Shore. 38

Hunter Cove, Rangeley Lake North Shore 42

Bonney Point Trails to Smith Cove, Rangeley Lake North Shore . . 46

South Bog Stream Trail to South Bog, Rangeley Lake South Shore . . 52

Bald Mountain – Oquossoc 56

Low Aziscohos Mountain 62

Piazza Rock, Ethel and Eddy Ponds via the Appalachian Trail . . . 68

Fly Rod Crosby Trail/Reeds Mill 74

Orbeton and Hardy Streams Oberton Conservation Area Trail. . . 78

Flagstaff-Bigelow Region 84

Flagstaff Lake East Shore and Flagstaff Hut   Maine Huts and Trails . 86

Dead River, Grand Falls, and Grand Falls Hut
    from Long Falls Dam Road Maine Huts and Trails 90

Dead River and Grand Falls Hut from West Forks 98

Flagstaff Lake South, Round Barn Area, and Bigelow Lodge . . . 104

Little Bigelow Mountain. 110

Cranberry Peak. 114

Carrabassett Valley-Sugarloaf Region 118

Sugarloaf Outdoor Center 120

Oak Knoll and Stratton Brook Hut, Maine Huts and Trails . . . 126

Poplar Stream and Poplar Hut, Maine Huts and Trails. 134

South Poplar Stream Falls 140

Narrow Gauge Pathway 144

Crommett Trail. 150

Weld-Tumbledown Region 154

Center Hill Ski Trails Mt Blue State Park 156

Center Hill Snowshoe Trails Mount Blue State Park 162

Mt. Blue Road to Mt. Blue Trailhead, Mount Blue State Park . . . 166

Mount Blue, Mount Blue State Park 170

Bald Mountain 174

Tumbledown Pond and Parker Ridge 178

Little Jackson 184

Blueberry Mountain 192

Farmington-Foothills Region 198

Titcomb Mountain Trails 200

Powder House Hill Trails, Flint Woods 204

Sandy River Intervale. 208

Make-Your-Own Routes. 211

A Favorite Snowshoe Hike – Using Snowmobile Trails 213

Snowshoeing on an Abandoned Woods Road 216

Night Travel 218

Your Own Field and Forest Route 221

Long Distance Trail Systems 222

Recommended Reading 223

Trail Maintaining Organizations Mentioned in This Book: 224

One More Time – Be Safe! 227

Acknowledgements

I thank, with deep gratitude, Michael Höhne and Angela Werner of Höhne-Werner Design in Wilton, Maine. Their encouragement led me first to write *Day Hiking in the Western Mountains of Maine: Rangeley-Saddleback, Carrabassett Valley-Bigelow, and Weld-Tumbledown Regions,* published in 2012. Next have come *Kayak and Canoe Outings in the Western Mountains of Maine,* published in 2015; and the Second Edition, expanded and updated, of *Day Hiking in the Western Mountains of Maine,* 2015.

As I have said often, and cannot say enough, Michael and Angela are people of exceptional skill and experience, keen eye and ear, and high art. They treasure the Western Mountains as I do, and welcome the particular joy that comes with being out on foot in winter. I am privileged to know them and to have the benefit of their wisdom, insight, and skill.

A succession of editors of the *Franklin Journal,* our twice-weekly, county-wide newspaper, have provided encouragement for my column *Foot and Paddle,* which formed the basis for this guidebook and its hiking-oriented predecessor. Those editors include Mike Petersen, Bobbi Hanstein, Greg Davis, and the current editor, Barry Matulaitis. I thank them for their commitment to serve our regional community, and for their own particular appreciation of our remarkable mountain and foothill setting in Western Maine.

Be Prepared

Winter travel can be exhilarating and rewarding—but there are risks associated with the winter season. Be prepared—not surprised—with regard to emergencies. You are responsible for your own safety. Have the skills, experience, and gear for *Self-Rescue*.

When a mishap occurs immediate response is required. Persons warmed by moving on snowshoes or skis may quickly become chilled—dangerously so—when stopped because of a mishap. It could take considerable time for outside help to arrive, even when on groomed trail. Mishaps in outlying areas could necessitate an overnight stay in winter conditions.

The author and publishers expressly state that we assume no liability for the use of this book, including, but not limited to, accuracy of descriptions of terrain and trails, mishaps or accidents that may occur, or the completeness of lists of suggested items to bring or safety preparations to make, or any other information provided.

The descriptions herein are good faith accounts of the author's personal experience. The experiences of others will vary. Some outings in this book are at commercially-operated areas, State Parks, and not-for-profit clubs—all of which may change trail locations, trail openings and closings, services and amenities, and fee structures. Weather events can change the nature of a route or trail, and in winter, quite quickly. Inquire locally about current conditions before undertaking a winter outing.

Inform a responsible person in writing of where you are going and when you will return.

Welcome, Winter Travelers!

The magnificence of a long view of peak after snow-covered peak against the sharp blue sky of a bright winter day … the supreme quiet of a snowshoe trek through snow-draped fir and spruce forest … the low, horizon-hugging sun slanting in on the coppery leaves of a beech tree with a rich glowing light … bobcat tracks in fresh snow … a red squirrel chattering from a pine branch lookout … a Blue Jay's scolding call … a Black Capped Chickadee singing out its name …. Welcome to winter in the Western Mountains of Maine—the High Peaks and Foothills region that reaches from the Farmington-Wilton-Jay area northward through the mountains to the border with Quebec.

Enjoy!

What This Book Contains

- 34 day outings for snowshoeing, cross-country skiing, or both, in the High Peaks and Foothills Region of Western Maine.
- Maine Huts and Trails huts-lodges and access trails: Stratton Brook, Poplar, Flagstaff Lake, and Grand Falls.
- Regional Outdoor Centers with groomed trail, rentals, lessons, day lodge and food: Sugarloaf Outdoor Center, Rangeley Lakes Trails Center; Titcomb Mountain Trails.
- Bigelow Preserve, Mount Blue State Park, and Maine Public Lands; Rangeley Lakes Heritage Trust land and trails.
- Backcountry snowshoe hikes—some to open peaks with long views; others through quiet forests or by ice-sculptured rivers, lakes, and ponds.
- Make-your-own-route opportunities on snowmobile trails, old roads, and local forests—even description of a moonlight hike!
- Winter safety information.
- Practical tips: How to select snowshoes or skis; clothing and gear lists; how to dress for warmth and comfort in winter; food and water on the trail; children; dogs!
- Map recommendations, and reading suggestions—winter birds, tree identification, animal tracks, and winter weather.

Franklin County—Access to the High Peaks

Franklin County is home, or provides major access, to Maine's High Peaks Region, where rise 10 of Maine's mountain peaks over 4000 feet in elevation. This mountain country is dotted further with dozens of mid-elevation peaks, foothills, and with great valleys providing unending possibilities for outdoor travel.

Major foot trail systems in this High Peaks and Foothills Region, include the Appalachian Trail, the Maine Huts and Trails System, the Bigelow Preserve, Maine Blue State Park and Weld-Tumbledown trails; Rangeley Lakes Heritage Trust Trails; and the north-south Fly Rod Crosby Trail. Local trail systems may be found in or nearby most Franklin County towns.

Maine Huts and Trails System provides an 80-mile groomed trail network and four full-service lodges, and makes possible a wide variety of day and overnight outings. Three commercial outdoor cross-country skiing and snowshoeing centers may be found here: Rangeley Lakes Trail Center, Sugarloaf Outdoor Center, and Titcomb Mountain Trails. All three offer groomed trails, lessons, rentals, and food. Mount Blue State Park provides many miles of groomed cross-country ski trails and marked snowshoe trails in an historic hiking locale—the Weld Valley.

The region remains pristine, with long views of the great northern forest available from mountain tops and ridgeline look-out points, and from valley pathways that offer panoramic exposure to the high-rising mountains beyond.

Franklin County—Getting Here

Franklin County is located in West Central Maine, with its southern boundary approximately 90 minutes drive north of Portland, 90 minutes west of Bangor, and 45–60 minutes from Augusta, Waterville, and Lewiston-Auburn.

The northernmost region of Franklin County shares the international border with Quebec, and is about 2.5 hours from Quebec City, and 3 hours from Montreal.

US Route 2, a major east-west highway crosses the southern region of the county near the County Seat of Farmington. The major north-south highways are Maine Highways 4 and 27.

Maine Highway 156 provides access to the Weld region. In the northern region Maine Highway 16 enters Maine from New Hampshire west of Rangeley, connects to the Stratton area, and coincides with Highway 27 until it leaves the county east of Kingfield.

County Towns

Farmington is a college town with a population of 7500. Motels, bed and breakfast establishments, and campgrounds, may be found here, along with grocery stores, pharmacies, outdoor clothing and equipment retailers, bookstores, and automobile sales and repair. Franklin Memorial Hospital is the regional medical center.

Other Franklin County towns of Wilton, Weld, Rangeley, Phillips, Strong, Kingfield, Carrabassett Valley and Stratton-Eustis offer supplies, lodging, and automotive services. In addition, smaller communities in and near the county provide gas stations and convenience stores. The major ski and snow-sport resorts of Saddleback and Sugarloaf USA also offer lodging and food services.

Trailheads and snowshoe/ski centers described in this guide are within a 30 minute drive of one or more towns, unless specifically described otherwise.

Words to the Wise

Travel properly: with appropriate clothing, supplied with food and water, prepared for winter emergencies, safety conscious, and appropriately equipped.

Traveling Safely in Winter

Some of the outings described are on well-used winter trails, not far from assistance in the event of an illness or injury. But many are in remote locations. The following points on *Self-Rescue, Common Emergencies,* and *Gear and Clothing* include pointers I have learned over the years.

This is introductory information only. *Obtain up-to-date winter first-aid and other emergency instruction before heading out on a winter trek.* If new to winter outings, consider retaining the services of a Registered Maine Guide for your first few trips.

Self-Rescue

All parties who undertake winter outings must be prepared for Self-Rescue.

Self rescue is the concept that a party has the skills, experience, and equipment to care for an ill or injured person for many hours in cold conditions until rescue resources may be notified and arrive. *In some remote locations the wait time could require an overnight bivouac on trail.* Cell phone coverage may not be reliable in mountain country.

Most trails described in this book, including those at commercial snowsports areas and state parks, are not patrolled.

Trailhead Parking in Winter

Parking is both a practical and a safety matter in winter. Some trailheads are plowed throughout the winter. Other are plowed occasionally—or not at all. Plowing policies may change from year-to-year, such that a trail that is readily accessed one year may not be so in another.

Where a trailhead is not plowed, finding a safe place to park will add to the length of an outing. It is recommended to inquire locally at an outfitter, Chamber of Commerce, Town Office, or other source, about trailhead access and parking.

Extreme caution must be used when parking along any road. Highways and woods roads are regularly traveled by logging trucks and equipment, and by commercial vehicles. Snow banks narrow the useable width of a road. Snow and ice on road surfaces may make maneuvering past parked vehicles difficult. Plow trucks may travel at any time of the day or night, both to clear roads in stormy weather, and in good weather to scrape and sand, and set back snowbanks. Vehicles in the way may be towed.

Never block a road that leads to a trail, no matter how remote the area. You may be blocking the route for a rescue vehicle.

If in a group, leave extra vehicles in town and combine passengers to limit the number of vehicles. For safety's sake, be prepared to park at a distance from the trailhead, then walk single file to the trail.

If parking does not appear to be safe—have an alternate destination in mind. One day I had a hike planned for the Rangeley area, but upon arrival, did not like the parking situation (or lack thereof). I changed my plans to hike Bald Mountain in Oquossoc, which has a plowed parking lot on the Carry Road. I had a great day!

Winter Emergencies

Be prepared for the following emergencies—among others—by obtaining competent *winter* first aid training. Know the symptoms. Have the clothing, food, water, and gear, to respond. Remember it may take many hours, including an overnight in the back-country, for help to arrive.

I call attention to the following common winter emergencies. I make no attempt to provide complete diagnostic or treatment information. That is beyond the scope of this book. Complete a winter first aid course for that information and skill-set.

Hypothermia: Hypothermia is life threatening and may occur when the body is unable to maintain proper body temperature. It can develop when damp clothing has an air conditioning effect. It may also occur because clothing does not provide proper insulation for the weather conditions. Dressing in wicking fabric layers that may be removed or added as the body heats up or cools down, is one way to reduce chances of hypothermia. Hypothermia may occur at temperatures *above* freezing as well as *below.*

Dehydration: At cold temperatures, there is a risk that winter travelers may not drink adequate fluids. Dehydration may contribute to hypothermia, fatigue, and disorientation. Avoid dehydration by scheduling water stops, such as once per hour. Carry water for the trip in and return. Pack water inside a pack to avoid freezing. Designate a person in your party to call out water break times.

Frostbite: Exposed skin may become injured in low temperatures. Members of the party should check one another periodically for frostbite, such as at water breaks. Even if not needed at the start of an outing, items such as neck warmers, winter hats, ear protection, mitts, and wind-blocking clothing such as shell parkas and wind pants, may be essential when reaching an exposed mountain top, or when the weather changes during an outing.

Ankle or knee injury: Certainly not limited to winter travel, such injuries require particular response in winter because affected individuals may be unable to travel. Keeping the person warm is essential, as a person who is not active will have a reduced ability to generate heat.

Every back-country party should have the clothing and equipment to keep an injured person warm, fed, and hydrated (if it is safe to take in food and liquid), until the trailhead is reached or a rescue team might arrive—which could be several hours.

Headlamps with spare batteries are essential equipment on all winter outings—even when night travel is not expected.

Rivers, Streams, Lakes, Ponds, Bogs

Use great care when crossing any snow or ice-covered water, whether a lake, pond, river, stream, or even a swamp or bog. Carry trekking poles or ski poles that may be used to test the weight-bearing nature of ice.

Be aware that even at sustained cold temperatures, the stability of ice varies considerably with very local conditions—such as spring holes on the bottom, currents, and wind condition—that can weaken the ice.

I once went up to my knees in water after breaking through thin ice, covered by snow, while snowshoeing across a high mountain bog in February. Our party built a fire to warm my chilled legs and feet, and I was carrying spare socks and other clothing—so this story turned out well.

Use care when crossing streams that appear completely snow-covered or have snow bridges. Test the snow before proceeding. Be alert to weather forecasts and check with local authorities if your plans call for travel over frozen bodies of water.

Do not cross unfamiliar bodies of water after dark.

Private Land

Through the generosity of private landowners, Maine has a long tradition of public recreational access to privately held timberlands. Some of the routes in this book pass through private lands. Hikers are asked to keep these lands free of litter, practice "Leave No Trace", and not cut or damage live trees. Please park in a manner that does not block a road or a gate, no matter how remote the area.

Timber harvesting may occur at any point in the year, which could limit or close access for a period of time. For this reason some trail routes may not be considered as permanent, but may change in accord with harvesting or other owner use. For personal safety, and the safety of wood harvesting crews, hikers and skiers should not enter active timber harvest areas.

Winter Clothing and Gear: Suggested Checklist

Choose what to bring based on forecasted weather, length of outing, nature of terrain, and remoteness of location. Pack for the scenario in which a member of the party has a mishap and is unable to proceed.

Clothing

___ Long underwear separate top and bottom of wicking material: synthetic, wool, or silk.

___ Wind resistant pants. Not cotton.

___ Insulating upper layer, such as a fleece top.

___ Jacket or shell parka, breathable, wind-resistant.

___ Cap that covers the head: fleece or wool.

___ Ear protection: earmuffs or cap with ear covering, or both.

___ Neck-warmer or neck gaiter, and/or balaclava.

___ Gloves or mitts of fleece or wool. Mitts are usually warmer than gloves. One pair may become wet from perspiration, rain or sleet, or falling snow. Carry a spare pair.

___ Winter footwear. Summer footwear is not sufficient. Snowshoers should have winter boots designed to be worn with snowshoes. Ski boots must fit the bindings on your skis. For extreme cold, bring or wear over-boots.

___ Socks: woolen or wicking synthetic material. Bring a spare pair.

___ Gaiters to keep snow out of boots and away from lacings and ties.

___ Spare clothing: Extra inner layer and/or outer layer for chilling conditions.

___ "Puff jacket" of down or synthetic material, preferably with a hood, for when stopped, and for exposed terrain such as mountain and ridge tops, or windswept valleys and open fields.

___ Lightweight sandals to wear inside Maine Huts System huts—no outside footwear allowed beyond the vestibules.

Gear

___ Trail Map, up to date, to establish location at all times.

___ Compass; if using a GPS, carry spare batteries and a separate compass.

___ Snowshoes and/or Nordic skis. These should be fitted prior to departure from home. Make certain that all bindings work, and may be adjusted readily. *Check all screws, rivets, and other fastening points.*

___ Trekking poles with snow baskets (and spare baskets) for snowshoeing; or poles designed for snowshoeing.

___ Cross-country ski poles.

___ Flexible boot crampons for icy terrain.

___ Tie-down straps to attach snowshoes (or skis) to pack when switching to crampons.

___ Day pack, preferably with a waist belt and a chest belt. Attachment points for snowshoes or skis (or sleeves for skis).

___ Whistle (one for each member of the party).

___ Water—sufficient for the hike up or out, *and the return.* A one liter container will usually suffice. Carry more for long outings. (Also leave water in your vehicle for all members of the hiking party at the end of the hike.) Carry a water purification means (filter, or chemical treatment, for example) if your hike will be near water, and one liter may not be enough. (Remember that water sources may be frozen.)

___ Sun protection: lip balm, sun screen.

___ Sunglasses; spare pair for extended trips.

___ Biodegradable toilet paper and hand sanitizer.

___ Headlamp with fresh batteries *and* spare batteries, even if you do not expect to be out after dark. For trips with overnight stays carry a spare headlamp.

___ First aid supplies: Band-aids, antiseptic, blister treatment.

___ Heat reflecting rescue blanket or bivouac bag.

___ Notebook, sketch pad, pen.

___ Guides to birds, trees, animal tracks.

___ Fire starter: waterproof matches, lighter, or other fire device.

___ Square of closed-cell foam for sitting during a break.

___ Repair kit for snowshoes or skis. Carry some extra screws of the proper size and a screwdriver or other tool for repairs in the field. If you have 3-pin bail-style bindings on skis, bring an extra bail. If skis are of wood, bring a spare tip.

___ Ski wax, scrapers, cork, for waxable skis.

Food and Drink

Food and drink needs will depend upon length of the outing. Some of the outings described are at commercial snowshoe or ski centers that offer food. Maine Huts and Trails sells hot lunches during most of the winter season—but do check ahead, especially during the "shoulder seasons" of early winter and late winter-into-spring. Even if you plan to purchase a lunch, carry sustaining foods in case of delay or emergency.

Nutritional demands are high for winter travel. Avoid "empty calorie" foods and drinks. These will usually be insufficient for your sustained energy needs. Consider the following.

____ Hearty sandwiches, fruit, bagels, cheese, nuts, and the like for lunch.

____ Trail snacks of fruit, cheese, nuts, trail mix.

____ Water—enough for the trip out and back. (Carry water bottle in the pack in a wool sock to prevent freezing.)

____ Soup, broth, or decaffeinated tea in an insulating bottle.

____ Food in your vehicle. Leave food that can sustain freezing temperatures. Upon your return your body may be hungry for recovery from your work-out. Waiting until you reach home or a place to purchase a meal delays the recovery process. Go ahead and have that bagel or PBJ sandwich at your vehicle. You will still have an appetite for supper later.

Selecting Snowshoes

Purchase or rent snowshoes from a source knowledgeable about snowshoeing. A good pair of snowshoes will last for decades. Two of the most important considerations are (1) Correct length and "flotation" for the *total weight* of yourself and your pack; and (2) Ease of binding adjustment in the field, when your fingers may be cold and bindings stiff.

There are many styles of snowshoes. In recent years metal shoes, usually of aircraft aluminum, have become popular. Most of these shoes have a design resembling the traditional Green Mountain Bear Paw shoes, although that term is rarely associated with these newer metal shoes. The snowshoes have a slight taper towards the back, and an uplift at the toe. They are of a width that allows a person to walk with a normal gait, without a "waddle", and without the shoes bumping into one another. The uplifted toe lifts the front of the shoe in the snow ahead. The tapered tail keeps the shoe in a straight line.

Metal snowshoes often come with built-in crampons. These are teeth-like metal edges underneath the snowshoe, which provide a grip on slippery surfaces. Use care when descending steep slopes lest the crampons grab, causing a pitch forward. Some shoes come with a heel lift that can be raised on steep ascents to keep the foot level.

Newer bindings may be adjusted and closed by pull straps. Traditional H-pattern leather bindings, if not fastened properly, can become loose over time, and allow side-to-side motion that can be tiring. Make sure the wearer can demonstrate how to adjust the bindings *before* leaving the store or rental shop.

Newer snowshoes have a "Right" and a "Left". This is determined by which side of the binding is the location for the adjustment straps for the heel. Some shoes are marked as Right or Left. The first time a person puts the shoes on, it should be apparent which side is which. If you are twisting in a contortion to reach the strap, switch shoes.

Size of snowshoes determines flotation. The term *flotation* refers to the capacity of the shoe to limit the wearer from sinking into the snow. *Combined weight* of the person and gear determines the size. Too small, and the person sinks unduly. Too large, and the snowshoeing becomes awkward and tiring. That is why it is good to be fitted by a knowledgeable person.

Another consideration in snowshoe choice is whether travel will be on packed trail, or by bushwhacking. Packed trails do not require the same flotation as unpacked conditions. On packed surfaces a shorter shoe may suffice. But do be prepared for changing conditions.

No snowshoe will keep a person entirely above the snow in all snow conditions.

The snowshoe gait should resemble a normal walk. Advertisements showing people running in snowshoes or people lifting their shoes high in the air with each step are, well, advertisements.

If what you have are the old style wooden snowshoes with rawhide bindings, those can be fine. After all, people have used them for centuries! Just be sure that the bindings are in good shape, fit your boots, and can be adjusted in the field.

Snowshoe Poles

I recommend using snowshoe poles or trekking poles equipped with snow baskets. These poles should have baskets wide enough to prevent the poles from sinking well into the snow. For this reason, most Nordic racing ski poles and summer trekking poles are not suitable. Alpine poles are usually too short, and lack loop grips.

I use trekking poles fitted with snow baskets designed for those particular poles. It is possible to buy snowshoe poles. Another option is to look for old-style alpine or cross-country ski poles that have wide baskets. Desired length is usually armpit height to chin height. Poles shorter than that will result in an awkward gait and are of little use.

Yard sales are a great place to pick up this old-style pole.

Cross-Country Skis

Cross-country skis (also referred to as Nordic Skis) fall into one of three categories: (1) Classic, also called "Touring'; (2) Skate; and (3) Back-Country. Those on Classic skis usually ski on a groomed parallel track, but some break trail with classic skis. Skate skis are used on wide, packed trails, and are not suited for ungroomed routes or deep snow. Back country skis are the choice for bushwhacking, and for ascending un-groomed mountain terrain—or for icy conditions, because they are usually equipped with steel edges.

Classic or "Touring" skis come in waxable or no-wax design. Skate skis require wax to achieve optimum glide. Waxable skis require application of ski waxes selected for temperature, structure of the snow, and water content of the snow. The correct wax enables a ski to glide forward, but not slip backward on level to gently rising terrain.

No-wax skis have a raised pattern on the bottom, often referred to as "fish-scales", that have the same effect. Some newer no-wax skis have a fiber base under the foot, and this functions similarly to the fish-scale design. No-wax ski performance can be optimized by applying glide wax to the tips and tails of no-wax skis. Wax also serves to protect the base of the ski, which can become worn or "burned" over time without such protection. For this reason "no wax" skis should be base-prepped with wax—tips and tails.

Waxing is not difficult to learn, and skiers are encouraged to become familiar with how to do it.

I recommend renting skis before buying, and having one or more lessons to learn both the classic and skate techniques.

Crampons

For mountain ascents by snowshoes and for travel over uneven terrain with steep pitches or icy stretches, boot crampons will be essential. Off come the snowshoes. On go the crampons.

I carry elastic cord or rope to affix the snowshoes to my pack when I am using crampons.

Even if snowshoes come equipped with built-in crampons, boot crampons offer better grip on steep terrain.

Flexible crampons designed for hiking may be pulled onto a boot by stretching the rubber structure over the toe and heel, then closing a strap.

These boot crampons are *not* the "grippers" sold for walking on icy sidewalks! The "grippers" usually lack points and are not suitable for angled surfaces.

The flexible crampons differ from "platform crampons" used in mountaineering. Platform crampons have a stiff lattice-like base. This type of crampon may certainly be used for winter hiking, but are typically more expensive than the flexible crampons.

I may put on crampons for one short pitch, then remove them—or I may hike for the better part of a day wearing them. Until I am in the field I may not know the extent to which I will need them—therefore I routinely carry crampons in my winter pack when on snowshoe outings.

On the Day of Your Outing

_____ Inform each person in the party where the trip is going, how much time will be involved, and what time you expect to return.

_____ Check the gear, clothing, food, and water that each person is carrying.

_____ Inform a responsible person (who is not on the outing) *in writing*: where you are going; time of your return, and whom to contact if you do not return when expected.

_____ Agree on water breaks, food breaks, frost-bite checks, and whistle use.

_____ Carry two or maps within the party.

_____ Cell phones: save for emergency. Stow "off" in a warm place, usually an inside pocket.

Water

All backcountry water should be purified by filter, chemical, or other effective means. The fact that water is clear or cold, does not indicate that it is safe to drink.

Most outings in this book are day hikes for which parties should be able to carry enough water for the day. Maine Huts and Trails huts provide safe drinking water for day visitors at no cost. Ski areas such as Rangeley Lakes Trails Center, Sugarloaf Outdoor Center, and Titcomb Mountain, have snack bars with drinking water. Mount Blue State Park does *not* have a water source for winter users, at this writing.

Sanitation

Please step well off the trail for toileting. Cover the remains. Be considerate of those who will follow you. What else is there to say?

Lost?

Parties who consult a map prior to starting a trip, keep track of progress, and stay together will minimize the likelihood of becoming lost.

If you should become lost, stay in one place in order that others may find you. Put on the extra layers of clothing you have brought in your backpack. To maintain warmth, ski or snowshoe in a circle. Eat and drink.

Use your whistle.

One blast = "I am here."

Two blasts = "Come to where I am."

Three blasts = "Emergency! Get here by the quickest means."

Try cell phone. Text feature may work when voice does not. Be prepared to give your position as best you can. Minimize battery use.

If it is likely that extended time may pass before others locate you, or if you must prepare for the night, prepare shelter from the wind, and use emergency bivouac gear for warmth. Make a fire for signal and warming purposes.

Right of Way: Courtesy and Safety

Most Cross-country ski trails are two-way. Some trails may be traveled by both skiers and those on snowshoes.

Snowshoes: The usual courtesy is for the downhill hiker to yield to the uphill hiker. The uphill hiker is "under load"—or to use nautical terminology, "burdened".

Cross-country skiing: The *Skiers Responsibility Code* applies to Cross-country skiing as well as to Alpine skiing.

A key provision: *Ski under control at all times.* Yes, it is a well-earned joy to zip down a long descent after climbing your way to a high point. But there may be slower skiers below—or those on snowshoes. You must be in sufficient control to avoid a collision. Cross-country trails are usually two-way *with traffic heading towards you, as well as with you.*

And this: *Never stop so as to block a trail.* This is also part of the Skier Responsibility Code, and common sense for those on snowshoes. To take a water or lunch break, step off the trail, or well to the side so there is ample room to pass.

Snowmobile Trails

When using a snowmobile trail, proceed as you would along a highway—hike or ski on the left, single file. Wear visible clothing, particularly in low light conditions, and wear a headlamp after dark.

Do not assume that you will hear a snowmobile approaching with sufficient warning to gather your group and move to the side. Snowmobile engines have become markedly quieter in recent years, and the sound they do make does not travel far ahead of a machine.

Although snowmobilers have a responsibility to be watchful for pedestrians, you will reduce the chances of an accident by making yourself visible, and leaving room on the trail.

I add that I wave hello to those on snowmobiles as they pass. If they are stopped I also stop—for conversation about trail conditions, weather information, and points of interest.

When on a snowmobile trail, be aware that snowmobile club volunteers build and maintain trails year round. They remove blown-down trees, cut brush, and install bridges and culverts. They groom the trails in season. It would be a nice courtesy to thank snowmobilers for their efforts. I send a donation to my local snowmobile club out of appreciation for the trail work.

Cell Phones

Certainly cell phones have become part of every-day life for many people. But cell phone service may be unreliable in mountain country. At cold temperatures most rechargeable batteries, such as those in cell phones, lose power rapidly, even when turned off. Carry a spare battery.

As for talking on cell phones, please understand that many people enter pristine mountain country to enjoy the sounds of the forest, the wind, the call of birds, the rush of wind in the tree-tops. If you must make a call, please step out of earshot of others.

Save the phone for emergencies. I know of one party who chatted away on their phones throughout a trip, checked email and so forth, until their batteries all died. Then one of the members of the party had an equipment failure. With no battery power, the group had no way to notify their families of their plight. Save battery power.

After Your Trek

As noted earlier in the Food section, leave some food in your trailhead vehicle—food that will be minimally affected by freezing. Eating some healthy replacement foods soon after exercise may reduce some of the burden on your body as it seeks to recover. I leave some water as well, wrapping it in a fleece blanket, or putting in an insulated cooler. It may freeze, but as the vehicle warms, some of the ice will thaw. It is worth the attempt.

Children

Children love the outdoors, and they do love snowshoeing and skiing.

As with summer hiking, it is a good idea to start modestly with short trips, then extend the length and degree of difficulty as skills and confidence develop—which is usually fairly quickly.

The same rules for clothing apply as for adults. Dress in layers, with wicking clothing next to the skin. Avoid bundling up so fully that children become uncomfortable or overheat. That heavy winter coat they wear while waiting for a school bus back home will ordinarily be unsuited for activity on skis or snowshoes.

To monitor the comfort level of a child, announce at the outset that there will be a clothing check every 15 minutes, or at some other reasonable interval. Most winter travelers achieve a comfortable heat status in 15-20 minutes into the hike or ski outing.

Accompanying adults: Carry spare mitts and neck-warmer, and other layers depending upon the weather. Adults will need to have a backpack large enough to carry children's spare clothing—or the layers they remove when they warm up. But children do like to carry their own packs, and it may work well to start children early at carrying a pack, even if it is small and the weight is minimal.

Pay attention to water and food needs.

If toileting in the outdoors will be a new experience, talk about this before the trip.

Bring along a sketchbook, a guide to animal tracks, tree-identification chart, a winter bird guide. Encourage children to make a collage, binder, or electronic journal of their outings.

Oh yes—tell children beforehand where the trip is going and how long it is expected to take. (Are we there yet?)

Dogs

I enjoy bringing our Chocolate Labrador Retriever on many outings, but I am very selective in winter. Wildlife is particularly vulnerable to dogs in winter.

Many of the routes in this book pass near deer yards. When deer detect a dog in the vicinity, they may flee the yard, expending precious energy. Whether or not a dog gives chase, flight through deep snow could be life-threatening for deer.

Other considerations are for the sanitary and aesthetic nature of winter routes when a dog is present. Dogs also may damage set tracks on Nordic trails.

Commercial cross-country areas and snowshoeing areas vary in their dog policies. Some allow dogs on certain trails, and on certain days of the week. In all such cases dogs must be under immediate control. Others may prohibit dogs entirely. Check with the ski or snowshoe area.

Prohibited Trail Systems: Maine Huts and Trails prohibits dogs on its groomed trail system during the winter season, and dogs are not allowed at the huts. Mount Blue State Park also prohibits dogs on both snowshoe and ski trails.

Please clean up after dogs as you would on a neighborhood walk or run at home.

As for snowmobile trails, think as you would when walking a dog along a highway. Dogs should be leashed and well under control.

Our Chocolate Lab and I enjoy bushwhack outings on snowshoes. (I am on snowshoes; she follows in my track.) We are out on snow 3-4 times a week, sometimes every day, but I do not bring her to groomed trails or on mountain ascents in winter. See the entries in this book on "Make your own routes" for you and your dog to enjoy.

Canine Health in Winter

Winter conditions can be quite taxing for a dog. Carry food and water. Frostbite to the ears and frozen feet are winter dangers, and are difficult to observe in a dog until it is too late and tissue damage has occurred.

Watch for behavior changes in the dog which signal discomfort. Be prepared to abandon your outing immediately to avoid permanent injury. Do not bring the dog when temperatures plunge well below freezing, when there are strong winds, or in freeze-thaw-freeze conditions when there is risk for hypothermia.

On the Trail

Now the fun begins! Watch for tracks—pointed track of deer, broad moose tracks, the 2+2 track of hare or red squirrels, straight line of a fox, feather marks in the snow left by an owl swooping down for prey. If you are fortunate, you will come across the trail of a bobcat or fisher. Watch for the half-pipe trough-trail of porcupine or beaver. Do pack a tracking book in your pack. Pack a bird book as well—the winter birds will be about.

Keep to regular water breaks—checking for frostbite in particularly cold and windy weather. Fuel your party with food breaks. I usually have something to eat every hour and a half.

Cold temperatures and steady movement burn energy.

A small closed-cell foam pad can be useful to sit on at breaks.

If some members of the party are moving slowly, keep the party together. Slower moving individuals usually move more steadily in the company of others, than when left alone.

Dividing a party can be dangerous in event of an emergency. (Have this understanding before you begin the trip—that you will stay together.)

Guide to Entries

Ski or Snowshoe. Fee/no fee. Rentals/lessons

Overview: Distance; Terrain; Points of Interest; Views; Brief Historical Information. *Note:* Distances as depicted on trail signs and maps, and in various guidebooks, may differ because different methods may be used to compute distance—including measuring wheel, estimate, map measurement, and GPS. When there are such differences they are ordinarily not significant.

Trailhead: Location of trailhead; parking; driving directions. For developed ski and snowshoe areas, "Trailhead" will usually be the main lodge or central trail departure area.

Nearest Town: For gas, lodging, food.

Map Recommendations: Delorme *Maine Atlas* map #; US Geological Survey topographic map; and/or local maps—such as available through by Maine Huts and Trails System; Rangeley Lakes Heritage Trust; Maine Bureau of Public Lands; Maine Appalachian Trail Club; and the developed ski/snowshoe areas.

Elevation Gain: An estimated figure for the vertical rise from trailhead to destination. For long distance outings a figure may be provided for cumulative gain.

On Trail: Account of one or more trips I have enjoyed at this location.

Locator Map: Map to identify the trailhead and route. Not intended for navigation on foot.

Easy? Difficult?

This book does not rate trails or routes for level of difficulty. What may be easy for one person may be difficult for another, and vice-versa.

Instead, I provide distance and elevation gain, and a detailed description of the terrain—which I expect will be more helpful than a rating.

Winter conditions can change the nature—and difficulty—of terrain. A level trail that ices over becomes difficult. A boulder field that is strenuous to cross in summer might become a fairly easy snowshoe route when the rock is covered in 6′ of snow.

Study map and description before undertaking a winter outing, and seek latest local information on trail conditions and weather.

Locator Map Legend

This is the legend for the maps in this book:

═══════	Paved Road	▬▬▬▬	Unpaved Road
──────	Main Trail	------	Alternate Trail
P	Parking Area	🛖	Hut

Rangeley-Saddleback Region

  Winter on-foot options in the Rangeley Region cluster in four locations: (1) Rangeley Lake shores and nearby mountains; (2) Saddleback Mountain; (3) Reeds Mill-Orbeton Stream region in Madrid, on the south side of Saddleback; and (4) Outlying mountains to the west and north of Rangeley.

  All locations offer extraordinary experiences on snow—whether looking across the lake at the looming Saddleback Range, making one's way through snow-blanketed mountain forest, or a three-state, two-nation view from from a remote mountain summit.

Rangeley Lakes Trails Center	28
Rock and Midway Ponds	32
Hatchery Brook, Rangeley Lake	38
Hunter Cove, Rangeley Lake	42
Bonney Point, Rangeley Lake	46
South Bog, Rangeley Lake	52
Bald Mountain, Oquossoc	56
Low Aziscohos Mountain	62
Piazza Rock, Ethel and Eddy Ponds by the Appalachian Trail	68
Fly Rod Crosby Trail: Madrid-Saddleback	74
Orbeton Stream Conservation Area	78

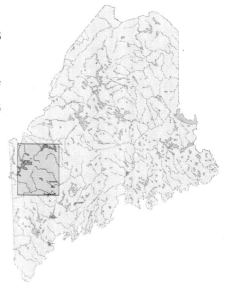

Dead River, Grand Falls - West Forks
Dead River & Grand Falls Hut - LFD

Flagstaff Hut & Flagstaff Lake East Shore
Flagstaff Lake Round Barn
Little Bigelow Mtn.

Cranberry Peak
Stratton Brook Hut & Oak Knoll
Crommett Trail
Poplar Hut & Poplar Stream Falls
Narrow Gauge Pathway

Bonney Point
Hunter Cove
Hatchery Brook

Sugarloaf Outdoor Ct.

Long Falls Dam Road

Rangeley Lakes Trail Ctr.
Rangeley
Bald Mt.
Rock & Midway
Ponds
South Bog Trail
Piazza Rock
Low Aziscohos

Oberton & Hardy Streams
Fly Rod Crosby Trail

Little Jackson Mt.
Blueberry Mt.
Tumbledown Pond & Tumbledown Mt.
Byron Road
Center Hill

Mount Blue

Sandy Rvr
Intervale
Powderhouse Hill
Farmington
Titcomb Mt.
Bald Mt.
Wilton

27

Rangeley Lakes Trail Center
Dallas Plantation

Ski or Snowshoe; Fee; Equipment rentals; Lessons

Overview: The Trails Center is a Four Season facility with over 55 kilometers of snowshoe and cross-country ski trails, on the lower north slope of Saddleback Mountain, adjacent to Saddleback Lake. xcskirangeley.com. (207) 864-4309

There are fine views of the peaks of the Saddleback Range to the south, cone-shaped Potato Nubble to the northeast, and Redington Peak and the Crocker Range farther to the northeast. When the ice is safe the trail system includes a route across Saddleback Lake just off the south shore, connecting two woods trails. *Check at the RLTC lodge for ice conditions before going onto the lake.*

The ski trail system includes novice, intermediate, and advanced terrain, with plenty of options for those seek the ease of level or gently rolling terrain, or those who enjoy the work of hill climbing followed by downhill runs. New trails are being developed.

For those on snowshoes, a distinctive feature of RLTC is machine grooming of nearly 6 kilometers of trail for multi-use by either snowshoes or skis. This includes Geneva Loop, Tote Road, and the Lake Trail.

There is also an extensive network of snowshoe-only trails. The Center has a group of volunteer snowshoe trail packers who take to the trails following snowstorms to pack additional trail routes.

Dogs: On selected trails on certain days, dogs are welcomed—usually not on weekends. Ski-joring is welcomed on designated trails and days. Contact the Trails Center ahead of time for current dog policies.

A yurt-style lodge has the ticket counter, rentals of snowshoes and cross-country skis, and food. Lessons can be arranged. Hot soup and baked goods are daily staples. Nestled in the woods, the trail system is fairly sheltered from the wind—making this area a choice for days when brisk winds make outdoor venturing elsewhere a bit dicey.

Other features of interest: bird-watching trails, gnome-houses (constructed by local school children) on certain trails, and two memorial

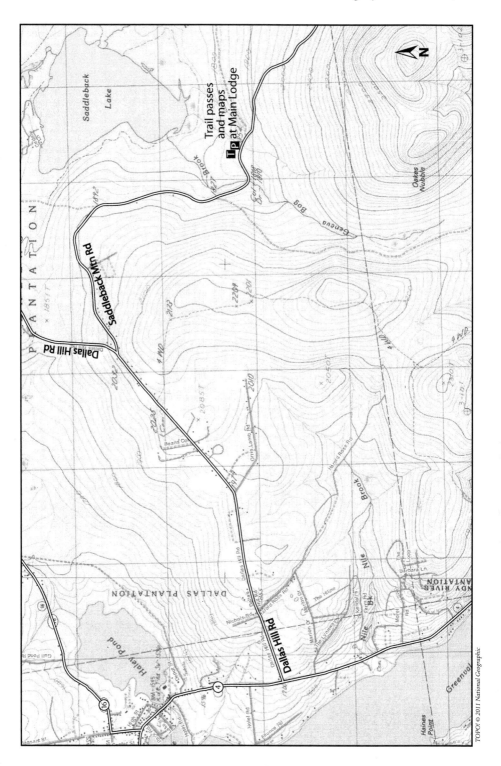

Saddleback
Lake

Trail passes
and maps
at Main Lodge

Oakes
Nubble

Geneva Bog

P L A N T A T I O N

Saddleback Mtn Rd

Dallas Hill Rd

Nile Brook

DALLAS PLANTATION

Dallas Hill Rd

Haley Pond

Gull Pond Rd

Nile Bk

SANDY RIVER
PLANTATION

Haines
Point

Greenvale

16

4

bridges in the trail system: Wounded Warrior Bridge and Boston Strong Bridge.

Trailhead: 524 Saddleback Mountain Road, off Dallas Hill Road, east of Rangeley Village. On Maine Highway 4, watch for signs for Saddleback Mountain Ski Area. Dallas Hill Road is opposite a prominent viewpoint above the east end of Rangeley Lake.

Proceed towards the alpine area. RLTC is on the left side of Saddleback Mountain Road, before reaching the alpine parking area.

Nearest Town: Rangeley

Maps: Delorme *Maine Atlas* Map #29, 1-E; RLTC map available at lodge.

Elevation Gain: Varies with trail system choices, which include level, gently rising, and steady ascending trails.

On Trail

I start my Rangeley Lakes Trails Center outing on one breezy day by skiing the Geneva Loop, 3.27 kilometers in length—about 2 miles. This route traverses Geneva Bog, crossing Geneva Bog Stream twice on wide bridges built wide enough for skate-skiing. A one-inch layer of fresh powder lies atop well-groomed trail—perfect conditions!

I ski clock-wise, on a gentle downhill slope for most of the way. The trailside bog and forest are thick with cedar and fir, well-sheltered from wind. This is pure fun, gliding down, down, down, through the woods. Eventually what goes down, must go up, and in the latter half of the route the trail ascends in the direction of the Lodge, but moderately so. Near the end of the Geneva Loop there is a convenient intersection with the Lake Trail, and I ski down this dual use route for a visit to Saddleback Lake.

The gently descending ski trail ends at a cove in the southwest corner of the lake. To the east the symmetrical cone of Potato Nubble rises prominently on the ridgeline that drops down from Saddleback Mountain. One accounting for the name is that Native Americans cached potatoes on the mountain.

My lakeside spot offers a view of Saddleback Mountain itself, rising over 4000 feet in elevation, the main peak at center on the summit ridge, and the companion peak, The Horn, also a four thousand footer, to the east. The pristine lake, snow-covered, stretches before me. All is quiet, save for the sound of my own breathing. Quite a moment.

On either side of the trail junction where the ski trail ends at the lake, snowshoe trails branch—one heads north along the lake shore about one mile to Picnic Point, where a picnic table sits under a high red pine. The other goes east toward a section of forest known for birding, where it connects to another snowshoe trail that leads to another lakeside viewpoint.

Although I am on skis, and not snowshoes, I opt for the route to Picnic Point. Snow conditions make this quite do-able. Those on snowshoes have packed the trail by their passage earlier in the winter. Fresh snowfall has smoothed out the bumps. I ski along the lakeshore, pass a snowshoe trail that connects with Geneva Loop, and, after one mile of travel, reach Picnic Point. The views of Saddleback Range are all the better here, one mile farther out from the base of the mountain. The picnic table is cake-layered with snow. I brush off a corner, have a seat, and take in that view.

OK, back on trail. I reverse direction, return to the cove, then ski the lake Trail uphill toward the lodge. At the broad area known as the stadium, I turn east on the Zapolsky Trail, eastward over gently rolling terrain, connect to Tote Road, and continue on the Bridge Trail as it crosses Haley Brook. I ski to the eastern perimeter of the Trail Center system by Junction Rock. There are more stretches of trail at this east end, which I save for another day.

On Tote Road fresh moose tracks punctuate the trail—so fresh that hoof-stirred snow dust kicked up as this great creature passed along, still lies scattered by the tracks. Might I catch up to the moose? I ski a bit faster, but it remains out of sight. Ungainly in appearance, moose move quickly!

On the return I ascend the Upper Pipeline Trail steadily for 1.5 miles with Saddleback Mountain well in view through the gap opened by the trail cut. This is work—a long, steady uphill! It does generate warmth! When I reach the Larry Hall Trail, just below the end of Upper Pipeline, I take this route to reach the Lodge. The Hall Trail passes through a rock maple and fir forest, westward over rolling terrain, with a good mix of downhill glide and warming short ascents.

On other days my wife and I have spent the day snowshoeing, returning to Picnic Point, and then exploring the birding trails. I have also headed out on the far perimeter trails. There are many choices here: snowshoes vs. skis, touring vs. skating, easy, level trail to climb and swoop down. Enjoy!

Rock and Midway Ponds/ Upper Fly Rod Crosby Trail

Sandy River Plantation

Snowshoe primarily; Skiing possible to Rock Pond; No fee

Overview: Rock and Midway ponds are two pristine mountain ponds midway up the north slope of Saddleback Mountain. The hike is short and the terrain fairly easy to travel. Beautiful at any time of day, they are particularly so in the dawning light of early morning or in the alpen-glow of late afternoon.

The trail is known locally as the Rock Pond Trail, though it continues to Midway, to a spur that leads to two fine Overlooks off Oakes Nubble (Not to be confused with Oak Knoll in Carrabassett Valley). This route also forms part of the north-south Fly Rod Crosby Trail between Rangeley and Phillips. Crosby Trail diamond markers mark the route directly to a trail junction (sign) just before Midway Pond. At that point the Crosby Trail turns left as it continues towards Reeds Mill and Phillips. Midway Pond is straight ahead 0.1 miles.

Short snowshoe hike of 0.5 to 1.0 mile one-way (1.0–2.0 miles round-trip) depending upon whether hiking to one or both ponds, and whether taking side trails to overlooks. Terrain is level to gently rising, with a short descent to Midway Pond, and short, steady ascents on the viewpoint side trails. There may be blow-downs, which are more readily maneuvered on snowshoes than on skis.

When the ice is safe for foot travel, the two ponds offer more territory for snowshoeing. This is a quiet, set-apart place. The fairly level terrain makes it a good choice for those new at snowshoeing. The trail is sheltered from most wind. I enjoy the solitude and simple beauty here.

I come here often when in the Rangeley area. A 10-15 minute drive from town brings me to the trailhead. In another 15 minutes I am at the edge of Rock Pond on snowshoes. Another 15 minutes and I am up at the overlooks—sighting distant Mount Blue through a gap in the ridge beyond Midway Pond, or looking over City Cove at Rangeley Village, then across the length of the lake toward Bald Mountain. Yet another

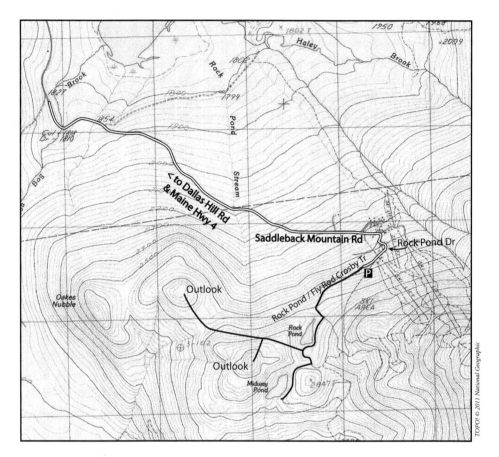

5 minutes and I reach Midway Pond, set in a small bowl cradled on the edge of the Saddleback Range.

Pack some hot chocolate or tea. Bring a foam pad to sit on. Hang out here for a while. Take it all in.

Trailhead: End of Rock Pond Road, 0.4 miles above Saddleback Mountain Base Lodge parking area. Usually plowed.

Drive to end of Saddleback Mountain Road, to the Alpine area. From the Base Lodge drop-off loop by the flagpoles, continue right toward the upper parking lots. Keep to the left of the parking lots, to take the Rock Pond Road through the condominium area. At the top of the S-turn, continue straight west to where the plowed road ends. The end of the vehicle road is marked by boulders, but will be obvious as the plowing of the road ends here. To the left is a small parking area, usually plowed. If parking on the road, do not block the road.

The road continues, unplowed, to become the Rock Pond Trail. There are trail signs—3 of them—on the left, just past the parking area. The trail continues for 0.8 miles to Midway Pond, passing Rock Pond, trail-right, in 0.4 mile. Marked side trails lead right (north) just beyond Rock Pond, to overlooks toward Midway Pond and Rangeley Lake. Watch for pointed signs that read "Overlook".

The Rock Pond Trail trailhead is also the trailhead for the Fly Rod Crosby Trail, which extends south to reach Reeds Mill in Madrid, about 13 miles distant. Part rough woods trail, part multi-use route with snowmobiles, the Crosby Trail should be taken in winter only by experienced parties. It passes through remote country. Sections through thick woods often have blowdowns which slow travel. The terrain and distance work against a round-trip.

Nearest Town: Rangeley

Maps: Delorme *Maine Atlas* Map #29, 1-E;
Saddleback Mountain Ski Area Trail Map, available at the lodge. A summer hiking version of this map is also available.

Elevation gain: <100′

On Trail

I book-end one particular winter with two snowshoe hikes to Rock Pond and beyond.

On a bright, sunny December morning my wife and I break a trail on our way to Rock Pond. The following March, on a sharply cold but equally bright day, a snowshoe buddy and I set out on a hike to Rock Pond, the two Overlooks, and Midway Pond. Once we arrive at Midway we will explore that pond from end to end.

On the first hike my wife and I break trail in fresh snow. Early snows had been heavy and wet, freezing fast in great mounds on the conifers. Fresh powder snows followed. The effect is magical! We are at a modest elevation—yet the white-laden trees resemble the rime-frost-covered scrub found on the slopes of Mount Katahdin and Mount Washington.

We clamber over the snow bank pushed up by snowplows near the parking area, pass the three signs for the Rock Pond Trail, and head west up a gentle slope. In 50 yards, after passing an alpine ski trail, we come to a Trail Register for the Fly Rod Crosby Trail (FRCT). The Crosby Trail and the Rock Pond-Midway Pond Trail coincide up to Midway, where FRCT bears left on a narrower route to parallel the east shore of the pond, then curves to the southeast, eventually joining the multi-use (snowmobile, snowshoe, ski) Black Fly Loop 1.0 mile past Midway.

Past the Register the trail continues through a wide cut, as the remnant of an old road, now well grassed over (under the snow). There are blow-downs already, this early in the season, but ample room to tramp out a route around them. The air is still. It is a supremely quiet winter day in the Maine woods.

We reach Rock Pond in 15 minutes, hiking down a short spur trail to the edge of the frozen, snow-blanketed water. I examine the ice by digging away some snow. We have had many days of single digit temperatures. The ice is solid. We notice a line of tracks running the full length of the pond, hike to them, then follow them. A discovery. Near the far end of the pond a flat boulder rises 3–4' high. The tracks go from the pond up onto the boulder—then continue across its 6' flat top, and down the other side. They look big for a red fox. My guess is coyote. I imagine what it would be like to watch that maneuver—a coyote trots across the pond, jumps to the top of the boulder, has a look around, sniffs the air, then jumps down the other side!

Pause for some hot tea and muffins—then we snowshoe around the pond, the only people out at this time. Not a cloud in the sky. Such a time and place! We spend about an hour on this short hike, an hour well spent!

Let us pick up the story with the March hike. My buddy and I hike to Rock Pond, explore a bit, then continue on the main trail in the direction of Midway Pond. Just past the last view of Rock Pond through the trees, we come to a trail junction for the Overlooks—and a primitive campsite.

Straight ahead the Fly Rod Crosby Trail continues to Midway Pond. Turn right to reach the Overlooks. The nearer look-out point is high above Midway Pond, facing south; the farther point looks west over the length of Rangeley Lake. We head for the Overlooks, ascending the thickly forested southeast slope of Oakes Nubble. In 0.1 mile there is another junction: right to the Overlooks, straight and angle left to return to the Fly Rod Crosby Trail without having to backtrack.

We turn right, following a route well-packed by others on snowshoes, towards the Overlooks. There are no evident trail markers. In summer an occasional blue blaze or weather square marker, indicates the route. I see neither—which may be a factor of snow 4–5' deep, or snow crusted on trees.

Blowdowns on this trail slow us, but we reach a short spur to the first Overlook in 15 minutes. The striking view is from a promontory over Midway Pond. Beyond, to the southeast, through a gap in the lower end of Saddleback Ridge, rises Mount Blue. In the middle view lies Eddy Pond. At our feet, as the promontory falls away, lies Midway Pond, snow-covered, trackless, rimmed by fir and spruce.

In under 10 minutes we reach the westward overlook, in a clearing near the high point of Oakes Nubble. Beyond the length of Rangeley Lake rises Bald Mountain, and beyond that the double peaks of Aziscohos Mountain. The sky is cloudless, and the view goes on all but forever, until the pale blue of the mountains of northern New Hampshire, and Vermont, merge with the thin blue sky. Quite a sight.

We descend, pass the spur to the first Overlook, reach the junction with the shortcut to Fly Rod Crosby Trail and Midway Pond, and soon arrive at a 4-way junction. Left is the Fly Rod Crosby Trail North back to Rock Pond and the Trailhead. Behind us, of course, is the route to the Overlooks. Right is a 0.1 mile descending trail to the upper end of Midway Pond. Straight, or slightly angling to the right, is the Fly Rod Crosby Trail South towards Eddy Pond, and, eventually, Reeds Mill.

However, this intersection may be confusing to first-time visitors because a double-pointed arrow sign indicates Midway Pond either to the right, *or* on FRCT south. The sign is correct. The closest route to Midway is that 0.1 mile right turn. But the far end of the pond may be reached by continuing on the FRCT south for about 0.3 mile. This is the route that we take. We intend to hike the trail to the end of the pond, then hike out onto the pond, hike its full length, then pick up the short trail at the upper end to return towards Rock Pond. Which we do!

Important note: The FRCT map, and the USGS topo map show the FRCT route paralleling the south shore of the pond; but some other maps incorrectly show a straight-south, discontinued ski trail, leading uphill, as the route. The Crosby Trail, as marked by signs and diamond-shaped markers, passes within 100' of the southeast shore of Midway Pond.

Wind has packed the snow on the well-frozen pond. We snowshoe without sinking unduly into the winter's accumulation. Discovery! Bobcat tracks nearly circle the pond, a few feet in from the irregular shoreline. At one point these intersect with the tracks of snowshoe hare. We see no signs of an encounter. Who passed here first? A story here.

A small cove offers a lunch spot. sheltered from a brisk northwest wind. We pull out mats for sitting on the snow. We eat surrounded by an immense, bright, quiet.

It is often with reluctance that I take the first steps in the direction of the trailhead. This gentle pond, snowbound with a pack that will refresh its waters in spring, storied with bobcat and hare, soundless except for the occasional wind—it all makes for a remarkable day in the Maine mountains in winter.

We reach the upper end of Midway Pond, ascend to that 4-way trail junction, stay straight on the Fly Rod Crosby Trail North to pass Rock Pond, and reach the Trailhead. Even here the views extend north towards the East Kennebago Range, east towards Potato Nubble and the Redington Range, southeast to the great mass of the Saddleback Range, looming large above us. It is the rare hike that offers such a long and broad view from the trailhead!

Not bad for a round-trip hike of about 2 miles!

Hatchery Brook
Rangeley Lake North Shore
Rangeley

Snowshoe or Ski on ungroomed trail. No fee.

Overview: Rangeley Lake Heritage Trust. 1.0 mile forest loop, marked by white trail blazes, over essentially level terrain, leading to three openings onto Rangeley Lake. Views east from lakeside toward Dallas Hill, Oakes Nubble, and the Saddleback Range beyond. Closest to downtown Rangeley of all routes in this book (0.5 mile from center of town), but still a quiet place apart. Forested nature of the trail provides shelter on windy days. When ice conditions are safe, it is possible to continue the outing onto Rangeley Lake.

Trailhead: Manor Road off Maine Highway 4, just past the western edge of downtown Rangeley. Heading west towards Oquossoc, pass the bowling alley on the right, cross Hatchery Brook, and make a left turn, across from the cemetery on right. If coming from Oquossoc on Highway 4, when descending the long hill immediately west of Rangeley, with the downtown area coming into view, the Manor Road is a right turn at the bottom of the hill. Rangeley Lakes Heritage Trust sign for Hatchery Brook Preserve. Drive 0.1 mile on Manor Road. Parking area on left is kept clear by volunteers; it may be a day or two following a storm before it is plowed. Information kiosk with a trail map display.

Maps: Delorme *Maine Atlas* Map #29, 5-E;
Rangeley Lakes Heritage Trust Hatchery Brook Cove Preserve Trails <www.rlht.org>.

Elevation gain: Negligible

On Trail

The temperature is in the balmy 30°s as I set out to hike the Hatchery Brook one mile loop, by the shore of City Cove on Rangeley Lake. I come here year-round—to hike, or to snowshoe or ski, depending upon the season. Today the calendar reads early winter, and I had a snowshoe trip in mind, but early

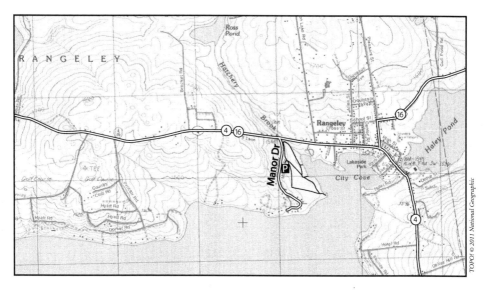

snowfall has melted back in recent days. No need for snowshoes—I find that my winter hiking boots will work well today. I step readily through snow less than 3″ deep, to seek an hour or so of lakeside quiet, a 5-minute drive from town.

Just beyond the trailhead sign, the route passes through the browns and tans of dried golden-rod, raspberry, and marsh grass, near a stand of white birch. I quickly reach the Loop Trail junction. Left or right, the distance to Loon Landing, farthest point, is the same, 0.5 mile. My choice is to the left, clockwise. I am underway, hiking through the balsam fir and white birch forest that characterizes much of the Hatchery Brook terrain. This area is shoreline lowland interspersed with wetlands. Fir do well on such ground, at least at this latitude!

In less than five minutes of travel over ground that essentially is level, I see the inlet bog of Hatchery Brook on my left, and beyond, through the trees, the waters of Rangeley Lake. A sign-post, minus a sign, stands at the junction to a short spur trail that leads 30 feet to the lakeshore. A wooden ramp lies entangled with the lake ice. This is not one of the named landings of the Hatchery Brook lands, and I know that better lake views lie farther along the route.

I move on to Heron Landing, 100 yards up the trail. Logs placed across the trail indicate a short re-route, and the Loop Trail makes a sharp left to reach the landing.

I have no difficulty finding the way. The distances are short in the Hatchery Brook Preserve. Heron Landing, with its picnic table, opening to the water, and prominent sign, is in view from this turn.

The trail continues southward, about 40 feet in from the shore, to reach the short spur to Mallard Landing. There is a sign here, but no picnic table. As I hike on I catch movement in the trees ahead—a Hairy Woodpecker lands on a fir, hammers a time or two, and quickly takes off. On other winter days I have spotted Blue Jays and Black Capped Chickadees along this trail, but today this lone woodpecker is the only creature with which I share these quiet woods.

A junction with the MCC Trail offers a choice of trails. Turn right on the MCC Trail to head back to the parking area, bypassing Loon Landing, and the southwest quarter of the Loop Trail. This southwest section passes through wetland crossed by bog bridges of split cedar logs. The MCC Trail itself rejoins the Loop Trail 0.25 miles from the trailhead and parking area, after passing through a fairly dry slight upland where windstorm-damaged trees have been cut and left to decompose into the forest soil. An interpretive sign describes a 2008 storm and subsequent forest management activity to maintain healthy tree stands.

The MCC Trail is a good choice in very wet conditions, such as in early spring or following heavy rains. In low-snow conditions snowshoeing or skiing over thin snow cover on bog bridges on the Loop Trail can be slow-going. When the woods are fairly dry, or when the snow is deep—no problem. Or, explore both the full Loop Trail and the MCC Trail, with some doubling back. Why not? There is no rush!

I continue on the Loop Trail to Loon Landing, which I reach after 25 total minutes of walking from the parking area and trailhead. The trail is in good condition and, as I have noted, essentially flat. Loon Landing is located near the mouth of City Cove on Rangeley Lake. The name of the cove is a curiosity! The nearest Maine cities of Augusta, Waterville, and Lewiston are each 80 miles away! However, the term "city" was applied at times to logging camps in the Maine woods—maybe therein lies the origin? Or perhaps in the early logging days Rangeley seemed like a city to loggers who had spent winter months in the back country. I have inquired in Rangeley about the derivation of "city" in the name, but have yet to find someone who knows. Certainly the cove is not very city-like today.

Loon Landing has a picnic table and a trailhead sign with map for visitors approaching by water. In summer, kayakers and canoeists pull in here for a lunch break, or to stretch the legs, usually after launching at the Town Landing one-half mile east on the lake.

The views from Loon Landing are the best from any of the three landings. Saddleback Junior, elevation 3655', rises on the eastern horizon, saddled itself by a bank of clouds that obscures its taller neighbor, 4041' Saddleback Horn. Here I stand at the edge of Rangeley Lake, looking over a shimmering cover of early ice that ends at deep blue open water a few hundred feet off shore. A southwest wind beats across the lake, driving lake water against the ice. By my shoreline spot, the thin ice undulates and cracks. Water runs over the top of the ice to lap on the snowy shore. Wavelets sparkle in the low-lying winter sun. Quite a sight!

What's next? I decide to hike the full Loop Trail. A few moments of travel brings me to wetland crossed by bog bridges. "Bridge" is a bit of exaggeration; they sit only a few inches above the wet ground or standing water. They function to save wet soil from the compacting that comes with foot traffic—and to keep footwear dry (or at least less wet!) I have no trouble making my way over the bog bridges in the thin snow cover.

Just before the end of the last bog bridge the MCC Trail enters on the right, coming in from the direction of Loon Landing. Options here—return directly to the parking area and trailhead by continuing on the Loop Trail; or follow the MCC Trail back to the lake, then retrace steps in either direction on the Loop Rail to extend the hike a bit. It is a 10-minute walk back to the parking area from this point.

No snowshoe hike this day, and no ski outing either—but most definitely a good outing! The snows will return, and once again I will have the opportunity to tramp out a snowshoe trail, or perhaps ski loops on my cross-country skis. There is much to be said for the Hatchery Brook trails—at 0.5 mile from the edge of town, the trail system is easy to reach; the wooded trails are protected from prevailing winds; and the lake and mountains views are well worth the short hike!

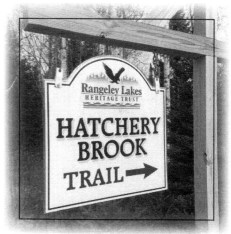

Note: Many days of freezing temperatures will have to pass before travel of any kind on the lake will be safe. As this article describes, strong winds can weaken the ice, and the effect may not necessarily be visible. Check in town with knowledgeable authorities about ice conditions. Hikers who bring a dog on lakeside hikes should be vigilant during thin-ice conditions. Dogs may trot onto ice too thin to support human weight, and break through. Rescue would be extraordinarily difficult if not impossible. One more reason to hike with a leash.

Hunter Cove

Rangeley Lake North Shore

Rangeley

Snowshoe. Skiing possible on ungroomed route. No fee.

Overview: Rangeley Lakes Heritage Trust. 1.0 mile snowshoe loop over level, variably-forested terrain, reaching upper region of quiet Hunter Cove on Rangeley Lake. Three short cross-trails cut across the loop route, providing options. A good choice on blustery days, as the surrounding woodland offers protection from wind. Opportunity for tree study, as the route passes through a stand of Norway Pine; marshland alder thickets; hardwood stands of maple, beech, and birch; and cove-side cedar.

Trailhead: 3.0 mile west of Downtown Rangeley, off south side of Maine Highway 16 (sign). Parking area (plowed) with trail kiosk. The Red Trail loop *west* leaves from the kiosk. The Red Trail loop *east* departs from the southeast (Rangeley Village direction) corner of the parking lot, about 50 feet to the left of the kiosk.

Nearest Town: Rangeley

Map: Delorme *Maine Atlas* Map #28, 4-E;
Hunter Cove Conservation Area Map, Rangeley Lakes Heritage Trust.

Elevation Gain: Negligible.

On Trail

So many times over the years I have passed the sign for Hunter Cove Conservation Area when driving west of Rangeley towards Oquossoc. One bright winter afternoon, with the sun lowering to the southwest, I finally stopped to have a look, after I had completed a snowshoe ascent of Bald Mountain. I am glad that I did. This is a peaceful spot—good place to stretch legs after a longer hike, or come simply for an hour or so of solitude. I now come by here often, year-round.

The woodland between the highway and Hunter Cove itself was once farmland, much of it serving as pasture. Imagine the days when those who tended this land looked out over Rangeley Lake toward the Four Ponds Mountain

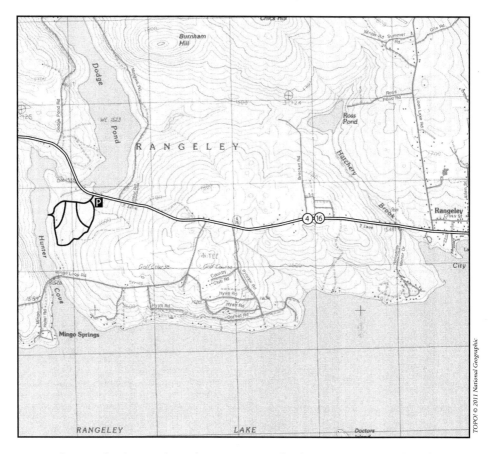

Range that marks the southern horizon. Now the forest provides shelter for bird and animal life, and a getaway location for hikers and those on snowshoes.

The trail system has colored metal markers to designate the way. The outer loop is the Red Trail. A Green Trail, Blue Trail, and Yellow Trail cut across the loop. I start on the Red Trail, heading east, following a well-tracked snowshoe path. Soon I enter an alder-bordered area, which I expect to be wet in the summer, but today I travel on a 2′ snowpack, and traverse it easily. At various points on the loop trail I see the outline of snow-buried bog bridges that would keep hikers out of the mud in season.

Tracks of deer, fox, snowshoe hare, and red squirrel cross the path. I move readily over the flat terrain, reaching Hunter Cove itself in 15 minutes. The cove is hard-frozen and snow-packed on this day, well into mid-winter. I step out onto the cove and trek about, passing a wood duck box, enjoying the quiet of this sheltered spot.

As I continue on the Red Trail loop, I soon return to the parking area. But all too soon!

So… I check the kiosk map to note the location of each of the three cross-trails, and head out again to hike each one. The beauty of the trail system is that I could spend a quick half-hour here, or be out for an hour or more—perhaps bring lunch to eat by the shore of Hunter Cove, or hike here on a moon-lit night.

Simple gifts await at Hunter Cove!

Bonney Point Trails to Smith Cove
Rangeley Lake North Shore
Rangeley

Snowshoe. No fee.

Overview: Rangeley Lakes Heritage Trust. 1.0 mile loop snowshoe hike, descending to north shore of Rangeley Lake at the mouth of Smith Cove, just east of Bonney Point. Steady ascent on the return. The yellow-blazed trail system includes the loop on the wooded slope above the lake, and a 0.2 mile spur to the cove. Fine views across the lake in the direction of Rangeley Lake State Park, with Beaver Mountain and Four Ponds Mountain commanding the skyline beyond.

Caution: The inlet stream to Smith Cove may create unsafe ice conditions in the cove.

Enjoy this route for its access to a pristine cove, and good views, in a place-apart quiet corner of Rangeley Lake.

Trailhead: Bonney Point Road, south off Maine Highway 16, 5.0 miles west of downtown Rangeley, and 1.5 miles east of Oquossoc Village. A prominent white and green sign displaying *Bonney Point Conservation Lands* stands on the south side of the highway at the entrance to the road, which is a gravel road.

The trailhead (signed) is in a meadow on the left (east) side of the road, 0.5 miles from Highway 16. The parking lot may not be plowed, but the Bonney Point Road is usually plowed wide enough by the trailhead for cars to parallel park. Be careful not to drop a wheel into the ditch. In a high snow year the trailhead kiosk may be hidden from view by the snowbank. Climb over the bank to reach the trailhead.

Nearest Town: Rangeley; Oquossoc Village

Maps: Delorme *Maine Atlas* Map #28, 4-E;
Bonney Point Map, Rangeley Lakes Heritage Trust

Elevation gain: 200′ on the return ascent.

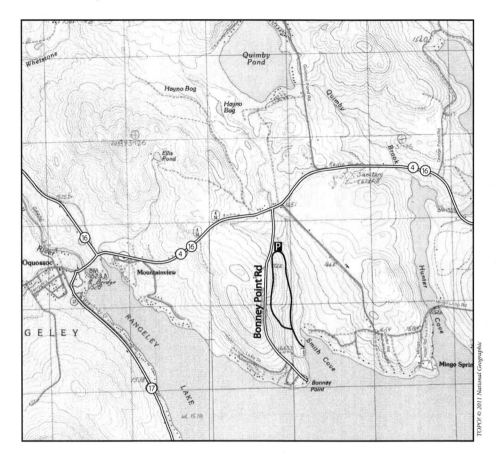

On Trail

I stand on snowshoes near the mouth of Smith Cove off the north shore of Rangeley Lake, with an expansive view across the ice-locked, snow-covered waters toward the wooded southern shore, and the peaks and ridges beyond that separate the Rangeley valley from the Sandy River and Swift River drainages to the south. Beaver Mountain, 3160′ in elevation, tops the eastern end of that high ground, and Four Ponds Mountain, 2910′ rises at the western end.

Midday sun beams through a break in the cloud cover so brightly that I pull out sunglasses. In a moment, high elevation clouds block the sun, the lake and hills turn gray-velvet. The cycle repeats—and repeats. A brisk northwest wind whips across the lake. In the shelter of the cove, I am out of the direct force of the wind, but some gusts make a way around Bonney Point to whirl fresh powder into the air right before me. For a moment I stand as in a snow globe—flakes tumbling all about me.

There are more discoveries to be had on this late-winter day. In my peripheral vision, as I stand in silence looking over the lake, I catch movement amidst the trees on the far side of the cove. Four deer leap across a clearing between camps deserted at this time of year, and into the woods beyond. I spot more deer standing under lakeside cedar and fir, and I wait—not making a move, not making a sound. The deer do—or not do—the same as I. We take our measure of one another, separated by about 200 yards of open snow. A doe and two yearlings. I blink first, taking the first step, moving at an angle to the deer that keeps me in plain sight, but putting some distance between us to avid spooking them. They step out from their cover, the doe first, then the yearling, to trot, but not run, in the direction of the other deer I had spotted only a few minutes earlier. Quite a sight—these dark brown forms in their gracefulness the only movement in sight, save my own, and the snow-scatter working of the wind.

A map I had obtained from Rangeley Lakes Heritage Trust <www.rlht. org>describes the trail as a 1.0 mile loop. The trail is roughly a north-south oval with a spur at the lower end of the oval leading to the lakeshore on Smith Cove. On this March day recent snowfall of about 16" covered a significant snow base that had accumulated over the winter. A breaking-trail day! That means exertion. It also means that I enjoy a pristine snow cover, with all the sheer beauty that offers. Fresh snow also affords the opportunity to have a look at animal tracks before winds obliterate them, or the thaw-freeze cycle alters them beyond recognition.

At the trailhead sign there is the option to head either left (north) or right (south). An arrow on a trail marker points left, and with no preference I head in that direction, making my way through unbroken snow. My snowshoes are 30" and I move fairly readily. I do sink into the snow 2-3 inches, sometimes a bit more, for the recent snowfall was a dry, light powder. No snowshoe keeps a person entirely on top of such soft cover. But I pass over the snow well in the conditions, heading on a downward slant from the trailhead clearing into a forest largely of fir, spruce, maple, and white birch.

There are deer tracks aplenty as I descend along the upper arc of the loop trail, then turn southward. The trail occasionally crosses some twitch trails—old logging trails once used for wood harvesting—then re-enters the woods. The trailhead signboard indicates that this area was once known as Sheep's Hill, because sheep were pastured here. It is possible that some of the twitch roads date back to days of the farm, but more likely they are recent developments. In the sheep days this hillside would have been open ground.

When I pass near thickets of fir, I see abundant tracks of snowshoe hare. Much life in these woods, even in winter! I am not alone. At the southern end of the loop trail, a yellow-blazed trail leads approximately 0.2 miles to the lake, and the main trail makes a right turn on its way back to the trailhead clearing to complete the loop. My destination is the lake. Here a picnic table sits under a grove of softwoods—with a foot of snow on the table top. By the shore, a small dock drawn up onto dry ground for the winter offers a narrow snow-free edge just the right size for me to sit for lunch. Kayak and canoe paddlers access this quiet site during the open water season.

I take in the view across the cove, and beyond that, well across the lake. Straight away on the south shore lies Rangeley Lake State Park, unbroken forest reaching from the hills down to the lake. Though there are camps on much of Rangeley Lake, and in the Bonney Point area, from my particular vantage point there is hardly a human-made structure in sight. It is good to sit, and to take in this pristine view.

Sitting in the chill air, I soon cool off. Shouldering my daypack I hike out onto the lake, testing the ice with my trekking poles. At this point in the winter the ice beneath the snow is thick and hard. I always bring trekking poles for such conditions. Local currents and spring holes can create weak ice at any time. Care must always be used. I trek through the cove towards the broad white expanse of the lake. There I make my deer sighting, and enjoy the dance of the snow squalls. My turn-around point is a spot from which I see Saddleback Mountain far to the east, where a new line of snow squalls punctuates the view, but the high peak rises above the blustery snow-flinging clouds at its base. To the west rises Bald Mountain, a fine hike any time of year, and one that I have made on snowshoes a number of times. From its summit tower there unfold striking views of Rangeley Lake on one side, Mooselookmeguntic Lake to the other. In the southwest runs the distant long ridge of Bemis Mountain.

I turn back, retracing my steps to the shoreline and my lunch spot, to pick up the Bonney Point Trail for the return hike. On the way across the lake I notice a set of tracks I had overlooked—probably while watching the deer. With a span of about three feet I think bobcat tracks. Another discovery. What do you think, Rangeley dwellers—bobcat along the north shore?

Looking up the cove to where it ends at a marsh I see a beaver lodge a hundred yards off, so buried by the deep snow that I had not seen it earlier—and beyond the lodge I see snow significantly disturbed by what appears to be a trail of tracks. Passing the lodge, whose occupants are likely snoozing at mid-day, I discover the tracks to be a well-worn deer trail that leads to open water where the marsh stream meets the cove. This open water, where the stream runs with discernible swift current even on a cold winter day, is a watering spot for deer. The snow lay trampled all around it. I stay well clear of the open water, and the lodge, both to keep my human presence away from it, and to avoid going through ice weakened by the current! I did linger, imagining deer coming day after day to this spot for life-sustaining water throughout the long Maine winter.

From this tranquil spot I head back to the point, the trail, and the route home. At the trail junction of the spur trail with the loop trail, I choose the western side of the loop, which I have not yet traveled, breaking trail once more. This section rises a bit more steeply than the route I took when I began my hike from the trailhead, but not unduly so, and I make good time. I see the tracks of a red squirrel, and then the peculiar track of a porcupine—as though someone had dragged a cylinder through the snow, but with some claw marks visible as well. These creatures are built low to the ground, and leave a distinctive trail! I scout for signs of their feeding. Sure enough—gnaw marks on a number of trees. The one solitary beech tree I saw on the entire hike, still bearing its coppery leaves from the previous fall, had been well chewed—a sweet taste for a hungry porcupine.

Back at the trailhead I enjoy an apple and some community bake-sale cookies I bought earlier in the day at a local store. Then—time to head for home. My outing has lasted just under three hours, including my hike of the trail loop, trekking out onto the lake, and exploring Smith Cove. If I had not been breaking trail, and I had not explored the lake and shoreline, my time would have been less—but what is the rush, and what is time for? Bonney Point is a fine location for a snowshoe hike—or a hike in any season. Enjoy!

FIELD NOTES

South Bog Stream Trl. to South Bog
Rangeley Lake South Shore
Rangeley Plantation

Snowshoe. No fee.

Overview: Rangeley Lakes Heritage Trust. 3.0 mile (approximate) forest snow-shoe hike, one-way, 6 miles round-trip, first bordering South Bog Stream, then in mixed growth forest, crossing a wet area on bog bridges, passing a 10 year old harvest area, ascending and descending a knoll, to end at a picnic table on the shore of Rangeley Lake near the delta of South Bog Stream. Eastward views from the knoll, through the bare hardwoods. Extensive views northward over Rangeley Lake to the high ground beyond, in the direction of Ephraim Ridge and Spotted Mountain.

A good choice for a windy day, as most of the route is fairly sheltered. Even the lakeside point where the trail ends offers some protection from the wind.

Trailhead: South Shore Road, Rangeley Plantation, 0.5 miles west of Rangeley Lake State Park entrance. This road connects Maine Highway 4 to Maine Highway 17, south of Rangeley Lake. The trailhead is on the north side of the road by a bridge crossing South Bog Stream. There is a parking area, kiosk, and sign for South Bog Conservation Area, maintained by the Rangeley Lakes Heritage Trust.

Note: There are *two trails*, a shorter, Interpretive Trail, leading from the parking lot, and ending streamside in 200 yards; and the longer one, described here in detail, that leaves west of the parking area, on the other side of the stream. To reach the trail that extends to Rangeley Lake, park, walk across the bridge over South Bog Stream on the South Shore Road, and look for a white "South Bog Trails" sign and a second, brown, sign on the right about 50 feet past the bridge. (The Interpretive Trail is worth a visit, too. I usually walk it before or after a hike in to the lake.)

The parking area may not be plowed in winter. If parking on the road, park close to the snow banks. Do not obstruct traffic.

If using the *Maine Atlas*, the trailhead parking area is on the edge of two maps, #18, 4-A; and #28, 4-E; west of Rangeley Lake State Park.

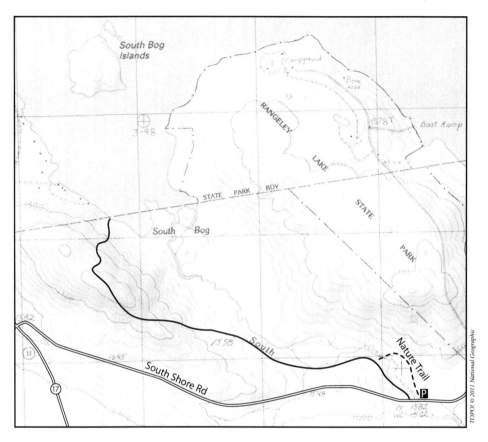

Nearest Towns: Oquossoc Village, Rangeley

Maps: Delorme *Maine Atlas* #18, 4-A; and #28, 4-E;
   South Bog Conservation Area Map, Rangeley Lakes Heritage Trust;
   USGS: Rangeley

Elevation Gain: ca. 100′

On Trail

South Bog Stream Trail on the south side of Rangeley Lake offers a fine three-hour round trip snowshoe hike. Here is the opportunity to explore a classic Maine mixed hardwood-softwood forest, a small bog crossed by plank bridges, and of course the clear-running stream itself, on the way to one of the most pristine coves of this magnificent lake. There is one small hill—more knoll than hill—otherwise the terrain is mostly flat or gently rolling. Good snowshoe terrain.

One of the great joys of a Maine winter is to be in the woods on snowshoes. Make it a day when the south-riding sun slants rich light on new snow, the bare hardwoods glow, and the pine, fir, spruce, and hemlock wave deep green in the northwesterly winds, and there are few places I would rather be. So it is that after one of the winter season's first snowfalls, I head out on the South Bog Stream Trail.

There is a choice of trails, as there are actually *two* trails. On this near side (east), the broad Interpretive Trail heads north for 200 yards, then ends at a pool in the stream—snow and ice covered on this day. The lake trail passes through the woods on the far side, but there is no footbridge. Crossing the stream in winter is not advised—not the time of year for wet feet—so I retrace my steps to the road. The Interpretive Trail is worth exploring, however. It is well-marked by four foot high brown wands, and there are informational signs along the way about trees, wildlife, and wildflowers. (Return in the spring for the wildflowers!)

A major attraction on the Interpretive Trail is a metal plaque set into a flat boulder stream-side about one hundred feet from the road, and just past the first of a number of picnic tables. (You may need to brush some snow off boulders to find the right one, but it is worth the search.) The boulder honors Franklin County resident Forrest R. Bonney, retired Fisheries Biologist with the Maine Department of Inland Fisheries and Wildlife (DIFW).

Under Forrest's guidance, South Bog Stream, a vital headwater for the region's trout fishery, has been restored following years of erosion. Carefully reconstructed pools provide locations for fish to weather dry periods, and are a beauty to behold on this winter day as water tumbles over boulders, and ice reaches lacey fingers toward the center of the stream. I have had the privilege of fly-fishing with Forrest, and taking canoe trips with him. Certainly, I am pleased for him and his colleagues at DIFW that his dedication to the South Bog Stream and Rangeley Lake fisheries is recognized in this way.

The second trail—the one to the lake—leaves from the west side of the bridge, marked by white paint blazes. There is a sign here as well. For the first quarter mile this trail to Rangeley Lake and this second section of the Interpretive Trail coincide. Look here for rock maple and yellow birch sharing the forest floor with balsam fir and red spruce. Soon the Interpretive Trail diverges to the right, and drops down to the water's edge. There is a fine view up the stream. On this day butter-colored ice had formed under the rushing water, and fresh snow sparkled in the sunlight. Quite a sight.

Returning to the trail to the lake I make my way through a forest crossed by tracks of snowshoe hare and squirrels, and the tiny footprints of white-footed mice. At a cedar swamp the trail zigzags on cedar planks just wide enough for my snowshoes. When I emerge I discover much bigger tracks than those of any rabbit—a moose has been by, and not long ago. More tracking discoveries lie ahead, as I find that a red fox has crossed the trail.

A half-hour of hiking brings me to where the trail coincides with a snowmobile trail on an old tote road, and then follows it for about 0.4 mile. If time is short, this could serve as a turn- around point for a fine forest hike of about one hour. I continue on, destination, Rangeley Lake. The trail skirts an old log yard, and selective cutting area, then climbs gently up a knoll before departing from the snowmobile route to head over the high ground in the direction of the lake.

Through the trees I enjoy fine views of the Saddleback Range, and beyond that the stunning uplift of the Bigelow Range with its two sets of snow covered twin peaks—the Horns on the west end, West Peak and Avery Peak beyond them. The four thousand foot Crocker Peaks and Redington Mountain rise to the northeast. To the north of Rangeley Lake stands the Spotted Mountain Range. To the northwest lies Bald Mountain in Oquossoc, a fine snowshoe hike in itself, with an observation tower at the summit. In summer, when the hardwoods are leafed-in, the mountain view from this point are limited. Winter has its benefits!

The trail slabs down the far side of the hill, leaves the harvested area, and drops back into thick woods for a hundred feet or so to emerge at a point on the lake where there is a picnic table. I dust off the snow, have a seat, break out lunch—including a container of hot tea. Before me lies the delta of South Bog Stream. Yellow marsh grass pokes through the snow. An occasional low cedar rises out of the snow cover, rooted in soil carried down out of the hills and down the stream for centuries. This is a very peaceful spot.

But it is winter, and I linger only for so long before I cool down. Time to hit the trail again. I warm quickly, trekking back up the high ground to enjoy the mountain views one more time, then follow my tracks back to the South Shore Road.

South Bog Stream is quite striking on a sunny day. But there is no need to stay indoors when the wind blows and the snow falls. I have taken this sheltered hike on days when high winds made more open terrain a bit inhospitable, and when snow is falling. It offers good introductory terrain for those learning to hike on snowshoes, and a long enough round-trip for winter hikers seeking a half-day outing.

Bald Mountain – Oquossoc

Rangeley

Snowshoe. No fee.

Overview: Maine Bureau of Public Lands and Rangeley Lakes Heritage Trust. From Bald Mountain Road trailhead to summit, 1.3 miles one way (2.6 miles round-trip). From the alternate Carry Road trailhead the distance is approximately 2.0 miles one-way (4 miles round-trip).

Summit observation tower provides long views west towards the Presidential Range in New Hampshire, and east toward Maine's High Peaks. Bald Mountain rises on the isthmus between Rangeley and Mooselookmeguntic Lakes, with fine views of these two expansive lakes.

From either the Bald Mountain Road or Carry Road the route ascends gradually until reaching the base of the summit cone. At this point there is a steep scramble, sometimes icy, of about 50 feet. Snowshoes with crampons, or even flexible boot crampons to switch to from snowshoes, might be handy here. The route continues upward as a steep mountain trail for 0.3 miles, passing a west-facing overlook toward Mooselookmeguntic Lake before reaching the summit tower.

Trailheads: *Bald Mountain Road,* 0.8 miles south of Haines Landing area on Mooselookmeguntic Lake (Delorme *Maine Atlas* Map # 28, 3-E). From Oquossoc Village, head west towards Haines Landing on the Carry Road. Bald Mountain Road is 0.9 miles on the left. There is a prominent blue sign designating the area as Maine Public Reserve Land. The parking lot may not be plowed, but there is usually ample room to park roadside. The Bald Mountain Trail leaves from the east end of the parking lot, and is marked by a trail kiosk. Distance to the summit: 1.3 miles.

Carry Road trailhead, 0.8 miles west of Oquossoc Village, on the left, before the Bald Mountain Road, at a parking area (large blue sign) used by snowmobilers in winter, boaters in summer. The trail leaves from the south end of the lot, where there is a trail kiosk. The distance listed on the kiosk is 2.2 miles to the summit. However, 10 yards into the woods on the trail, a smaller, older, sign lists that distance as 1.8 miles. Call the distance approximately 2.0 miles. This route heads north to join the trail from the Bald Mountain Road Trail described above.

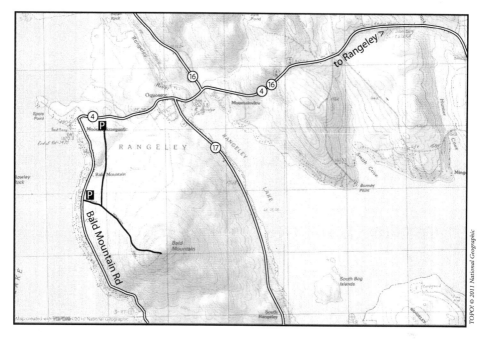

TOPO! © 2011 National Geographic

Nearest towns: Oquossoc, Rangeley

Maps: Delorme *Maine Atlas* Map #28, 2-E;
  Rangeley Lakes Heritage Trust, Bald Mountain; Maine Bureau of Public
  Lands, Bald Mountain Unit.

Elevation Gain: 1000′

On Trail

When asked to recommend a good "starter" winter mountain ascent I think of Bald Mountain in Oquossoc, on Maine Public Reserve Land. However, do note that Bald Mountain *is* a mountain, with a significant elevation gain over a short distance, but the approach trails to the base of the summit are gradual in ascent. The final, sometimes-icy, pitches on the summit cone do make for a bit of scrambling, thereby giving a taste of what may be encountered on higher peaks. I come here often for the two-state, two-nation views (west to New Hampshire, north to Canada).

The trail is well marked with blue paint blazes. Thanks goes to the Rangeley Lakes Heritage Trust for trail maintenance. and for the observation tower at the summit. The view from the top is one of the very best in Maine for a mountain of this height—2443′.

Bald Mountain Road Route: One bright winter day, when I had some matters to attend to in downtown Rangeley in the morning, I brought along my snow-shoes and daypack, with the hopes of climbing Bald Mountain in the afternoon. What better way to spend a winter afternoon? I had climbed Bald Mountain previously in summer and fall conditions, and wanted to enjoy the winter view.

There is a foot of snow in the parking lot, but I am able to make my way readily enough in my four-wheel drive vehicle. A picnic table, mounded with snow this day, and a vault toilet, are located at this trailhead.

The trail heads east, climbing gradually for the first mile through a mixed hardwood forest of yellow birch, beech, and maple. Beech distinguish them-selves by their parchment-like leaves, some of which remain throughout the winter until spring budding. Blue paint blazes mark the trail. When the trail takes a sharp turn I see a double blaze—two blue stripes, one above the other. In 10 minutes I come to the junction with the trail that comes in from the north, where the trailhead is at the Carry Road parking area near Oquossoc.

Carry Road-Oquossoc Route: I first take this route on a snowy day that is giving way to clearing skies after a snowfall. It is so soon after the snowfall that I doubt that the Bald Mountain Road route parking area has yet been plowed— but also I wish to explore this alternate route. As it is, this parking area has not yet been plowed for this storm, either, but it had been throughout the winter. I am able to drive in, using a four-wheel drive vehicle to maneuver through the 8" fresh snowfall.

The trail leaves from the south end of the lot, where there is a large sign, indicating 2.2 miles to the top. Curiously, about 50 feet along the trail a second, older, sign, lists a distance of 1.8 miles. Consider these distances to be approxi-mate!

I hike with a friend, and we agree to take turns breaking trail in our snow-shoes. We can see the trail depression in the snow left by other winter travelers earlier in the season, but we do have our work to do. There appear to have been a few storms since the most recent hikers passed this way. The surrounding for-est is predominantly fir, with growth I estimate at about 15 years following a harvest. At one point I pass the blowdown of a white pine, about 2' in diameter, remnant of the previous older growth in this forest.

There is a bit of a winter wonderland feel to the woods this day, as trailside firs droop, heavy with new snowfall. An occasional gust sweeps the snow off the trees, scattering mini snow showers. Tracks of snowshoe hare disappear into the thick fir growth.

In about 10 minutes we come to a 90 degree left turn (east) at the top of a small rise. The blue-blazed route follows an old twitch road for about 150 yards, then turns 90 degrees to the right (south). Watch for the blue blazes. We swap positions, and I break trail, as we continue south entering more mature forest predominantly of maple, with an occasional yellow birch and beech. Deer tracks cross the trail. I see more tracks—red squirrel. A raven cries a drawn "ca-rock!". We are not alone.

We slab the low west slope of the mountain, with occasional ascent, cross a snowmobile trail, then a short bridge, before ending at the junction with the trail from the Bald Mountain Road trailhead, which comes in from the right (west). This junction is well signed.

The joined routes head east in a steady but not steep ascent, swinging through some long S-turns, and we reach the base of the wooded summit cone. I look back over the route I have traveled and am a bit surprised at how much elevation gain we have achieved, with moderate effort. We are now well above the shore of Mooselookmeguntic Lake, visible through the trees in the distance. The trail has gained this elevation steadily but without sharp elevation changes to this point.

At the base of the cone, still very much in the woods, the trail swings south, then east once more, climbing more steadily. The forest changes from hardwood to fir, spruce, and an occasional errant white pine remnant of the predominantly pine forest that once grew here. One steep pitch requires some clambering, or scrambling—choose your own word for this short stretch. This is a natural drainage point, and sometimes is icy. The snow is deep enough this day for me to kick some steps. My snowshoes have built-in crampons, which help. In my pack are flexible boot crampons, which I can change to from snowshoes if the route is too icy, but I do not need these on this day. I make my way without undue difficulty. This is a short scramble, something to expand about to friends upon the return.

About 100 yards below the top a short side trail leads northwest to an overlook. There are good views of Mooselookmeguntic Lake to the west, and Cupsuptic Lake, above it and connected to it, to the northwest. Of course, on this winter day, the lakes are snow and ice-covered—broad expanses of white bordered by the deep green of the northern forest.

The best lies just ahead! We emerge from the woods at the base of the four-story tower, which rises from the summit ledges. Here my hiking companion and I remove our snowshoes, and pull out hooded down jackets from our packs, as the wind is brisk—and of course, once we stop, we are not generating heat as we did on the approach. We climb the stairway to the platform at the top.

The view is surely one of the finest in Maine! To the far west rise Mount Washington and the Presidential Range in New Hampshire, riding on the horizon like a great sailing ship at sea. To the northwest and north I could see the double peaks of Aziscohos Mountain, then Deer Mountain, Cupsuptic Mountain, and the ranges of West and East Kennebago Mountains. To the northeast and east rise the peaks of the Bigelow Range. The Crockers, Sugarloaf, Spauld-

ing Mountain, and, of course, the greater Saddleback Range of Saddleback Junior, Saddleback Horn, and Saddleback itself. To the south I have a glimpse of the tip of Jackson Mountain in Weld, and the long Bemis Ridge beyond the south end of Mooselookmeguntic Lake.

We stay at the top for a while, savoring the view, taking in the vast expanse of the northern forest, and the striking side-by-side view of the great, snow-covered, expansive lakes of the Rangeley Lakes Chain, and the neighboring High Peaks. Quite a sight! Your turn!

FIELD NOTES

Low Aziscohos Mountain

Lincoln Plantation

Snowshoe. No fee.

Overview: 1.7 miles one-way (3.4 mile round-trip) steady mountain ascent, in remote country west of Rangeley near the settlement of Wilson's Mills. Upper portion is steep, where rocky trail and summit ledge may be ice-covered, and four-point hiking (using both hands and feet) may be required for steep pitches.

The views are among the finest in Western Maine, extending to New Hampshire, Vermont, and Quebec, along with the High Peaks Region of Maine. Aziscohos overlooks the Rangeley Lake Chain, including Rangeley, Mooselookmeguntic, Richardson, and Umbagog Lakes.

Aziscohos Mountain is located on private land. At this time the owners welcome considerate pedestrian use, consistent with a long-standing tradition in Maine by which many woodland owners make private lands available for such public use. However, timber harvesting may occur at any point in the year, which could limit or close access for a period of time. For this reason the Low Aziscohos Trail routes may not be considered as permanent, but may change in accordance with harvesting or other owner use. For personal safety, and the safety of wood harvesting crews, hikers and skiers should not enter active timber harvest areas.

Trailhead: The trailhead is 16 miles west of the junction of Maine Highways 4 and 16 east of Oquossoc Village. Follow signs toward Wilsons Mills. A small parking parking area—more a turn-out than a parking lot—is on the south side of Maine Highway 16, 1.0 mile east of the Azisochos Dam; and 1.6 miles west of the Lincoln Pond Road.

Note that some maps depict the discontinued Fire Warden's Trail that began across Highway 16 from the Aziscohos Lake Dam. The current route is as I have indicated—1.0 mile east of the dam.

Towns: Rangeley, Maine; Errol, New Hampshire

Maps: Delorme *Maine Atlas* Map #28, 1-E;
USGS: Richardson Pond, Wilson's Mills.

Elevation Gain: 1700'

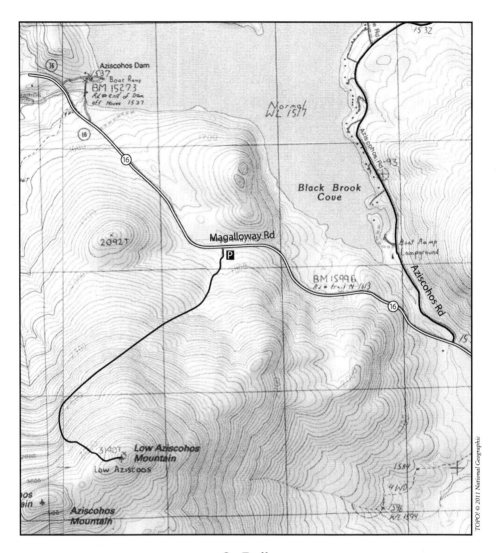

On Trail

So taken was I by the striking long views from Aziscohos that I enjoyed on a recent summer hike, that I put it on my "to do" list for winter. There are particular summits in the Western Mountains that I keep in mind for winter hikes, watching the weather for the right combination of a clear day and manageable wind. That day arrived, I called a hiking friend and we headed for Aziscohos.

Aziscohos is a double-peaked mountain. The higher summit is wooded. It is the lower peak, Low Azizcohos, 3190′, that offers one of the finest viewpoints to be had in Maine. Not surprisingly, it is a former fire watch peak.

How far are those views? Before this day is over, I would look out at Mount Washington and the Presidential Range of New Hampshire in the west, to Boundary Peaks in Quebec to the northeast, and 11 of Maine's 14 mountains over 4000′ elevation.

It is said that the mountains at the upper end of Vermont's Long Trail—Jay Peak and Belvedere Mountain, among them, can be seen from here. I can attest that in every direction, beyond the peaks I could name, stretched yet more mountains, running to the horizon.

The thermometer reads 5 degrees F. as we enter the woods 50 feet east of the plowed area. The start of the trail may be difficult to see from the highway. A small, arrow-shaped, red-lettered sign among the firs simply reads "Aziscohos". I had expected to be breaking trail, but we find a well-packed snowshoe track, fresh enough that someone has traveled here within the past day or two. The elevation gain is estimated at 1700′—equivalent to 100 feet per 0.1 mile. We will get our exercise today.

We ascend steadily through a fir and spruce forest, passing a second sign that also indicates 3.4 mile round trip mileage. Up we go to gain the height of a low shoulder just above the highway. Soon the grade moderates a bit, and the growth changes to a hardwood forest where rock maple and beech predominate, with a few yellow birch. Bright sun that rides just above the higher of the two peaks of Aziscohos shines full in our faces. There is no wind. It is cold, for certain, but we warm quickly as we move. The conditions truly are excellent.

The route follows a small stream in this section. In summer, this area is often muddy, but with 2–3 feet of snow on the ground, there is no mud to contend with this day! Sometimes winter travel makes a summer route easier to negotiate—though the reverse is also true—and today we travel over obstacles that might slow our progress in summer. The route continues its ascent to cross a harvest area and some twitch trails, where views open up to the west and north. The broad meadows of Wilson's Mills lie to the northwest. More directly north stretches Aziscohos Lake, and beyond that, Bosebuck Mountain.

Deer tracks have been crossing the trail up to this point—on the drive in I spotted three on a side road. There are tracks of red fox—and I saw two of those roadside on the drive as well.

After 1.0 mile the work truly begins. The route leaves the old cut, and ascends steeply toward the summit ridge. We climb steadily, now in thick fir, with some pitches requiring the use of hands and feet. Snowshoe hare tracks are here aplenty.

A recent thaw-freeze cycle has iced trail-bed rocks. I carry boot crampons in the event that I need to switch out of snowshoes. However, I find just enough untracked snow around steep and icy sections to tramp out a new route with good purchase underfoot. In spots I squeeze my way through the thick cover—a few contortions required—using hands and feet but manage. Still on snowshoes! I may need the crampons later, but not here.

The exertion keeps us warm. We reach the intersection of the main trail with the abandoned Fire Warden's Trail, which heads west passing the higher of the two Aziscohos summits. That higher peak is wooded with limited views. The old trail is blocked at many spots along its length by blow-downs and thick, encroaching growth. It is quite difficult to travel, as it has become obscure. In its day, this formed part of the route from Wilson's Mills, where a hotel, the Aziscohos House, was a popular place to stay the night for those who wished to hike the mountain.

A sign post at this junction relates some of the history of the area—including the fact that Low Aziscohos was once a fire watch peak. The first lookout post was a cabin on cement piers. The second was atop a 27-foot tower. Both are long gone.

In the final 0.2 miles to the open summit of Low Azizcohos, I discover the true benefit of the tramped-out snowshoe trail. As the thick growth gives way to low *krumholtz*—stunted, twisted, high fir that bears the full force of the mountain wind, I opt to step off the packed trail to make my own way to the top.

"Ca-thump!" I sink half-way up my shins—wearing snowshoes! I wade for a few yards, think better of my trial-trail, and return to the main route.

Above, at the very peak, rises a triangular ledge, snow and ice covered, neighbored by the old cement piers that once supported the fire lookout structures. I ascend that high-point ledge and—wow! The south side of the mountain falls away toward Upper Richardson Lake, and Mooselookmeguntic Lake beyond. Far to the east, beyond Bald Mountain in Oquossoc, runs Rangeley Lake. To the west lies Umbagog Lake, straddling the Maine-New Hampshire border.

The day is completely clear, the view unobstructed. Mount Washington rides the far western skyline. To the north rise mountains in Quebec. The seldom visited peaks of northern Franklin and Oxford Counties extend to the northeast: Deer, West Kennebago, Snow Mountain Cupsuptic, Kennebago Divide, among them. Some of these appear on the list of the One Hundred Highest Peaks in New England, yet aside from a few hikers who aim to reach the top of every one of these mountains, they are little known.

Old Speck and the Baldpates, Elephant Mountain, Bemis and Four Pond Mountains—on northward to the Saddleback Range and the High Peaks in the Sugarloaf Region and on to the Bigelow Range. To the south I look upon the Tumbledown-Jackson Range in Weld. All in view from this one spot!

Now on ledge, we park our trekking poles, step out of our snowshoes, and break out lunch—which includes hot tea. The view is stunning. I make a 360 degree turn, then turn again, and again. The country near and far is dearly familiar. Our family has enjoyed many a canoe trip in the Rangeley Lakes Chain, hikes all throughout the High Peaks, fly fishing on the rivers that flow through the valleys.

The wind stirs. I feel a chill. One of my first moves when we reached the top was to pull out wind-blocking layers to retain the well-earned warmth. Now I am cooling off, and it is time to move on. One more circle turn, one last view, and we head down the trail. The route is now all the more packed from the ascent, and gravity works in our favor.

That said, in very steep sections I turn around and face the mountain in a "down-climbing" technique in order that my snowshoes not catch on a downward pitch and send me head over heels. Even with caution on the steeps, we cover the 1.7 miles to the highway in one hour flat.

The current route to the summit of Low Aziscohos Mountain is over private land managed by Seven Islands Land Company. According to a company spokesperson, Seven Islands welcomes recreational foot-travel use by the public. However, prospective hikers should be aware that timber harvesting may occur at any point in the year, which could limit or close access for a period of time, and that the route of the trail is not considered permanent, but may change in accord with harvesting or other owner use.

Through the generosity of landowners, Maine has a long tradition of public recreational access to privately held timberlands. Hikers should keep these lands free of litter, practice "Leave No Trace", not cut or damage live trees, and stay away from areas where harvesting operations are active.

This is a remote area. Winter hikers who are well-prepared for a steep ascent, varying trail conditions to be expected in winter, and who carry supplies for self-rescue—consider putting Aziscohos Mountain on the "to-do" list!

Piazza Rock, Ethel, and Eddy Ponds
via the Appalachian Trail
Sandy River Plantation

Snowshoe. No fee.

Overview: Appalachian Trail. Piazza Rock is a geological curiosity—a great angular boulder jutting out of the forested western mountainside of Saddleback Mountain. It is located on a short 0.1 mile blue-blazed trail from Piazza Rock campsite on the Appalachian Trail. From Highway 4 to Piazza Rock is 1.8 miles, largely wooded, with one outlook south into the valley of the Sandy River. The Rock, campsite, and surrounding woods offer their own attraction. Those seeking a longer hike may continue on the AT 1.0 mile to Ethel Pond, and beyond that, an additional 1.0. Mile to Eddy Pond—both attractive mountain ponds, well worth a visit.

Trailhead : Appalachian Trail crossing of Maine Highway 4, north of Madrid, south of Rangeley. *The Appalachian Trail parking lot off the west side of the highway may not be plowed.* Parking along the highway is not advised, as this section of highway is hilly, with curves, and narrow at high snow depths. One option is to be dropped off, with an agreed pick-up time, but parties must watch the time carefully. Cell phone service may not be reliable in this area.

I have hiked to Piazza Rock, and beyond on the AT, in late fall and in late spring, when snow levels were low enough that I could enter the parking lot with a four-wheel drive vehicle. However light the snow at roadside, snow was deep enough in the woods that my hike still required snowshoes.

You are advised to scout the trailhead parking before committing to this hike. Have an alternative hike in mind if safe parking is not available here.

Nearest Town: Rangeley

Maps: Delorme *Maine Atlas* Map #28, 1-A;
Maine Appalachian Trail Map #6, Maine Highway 27 to Highway 17;
USGS: Saddleback Mountain

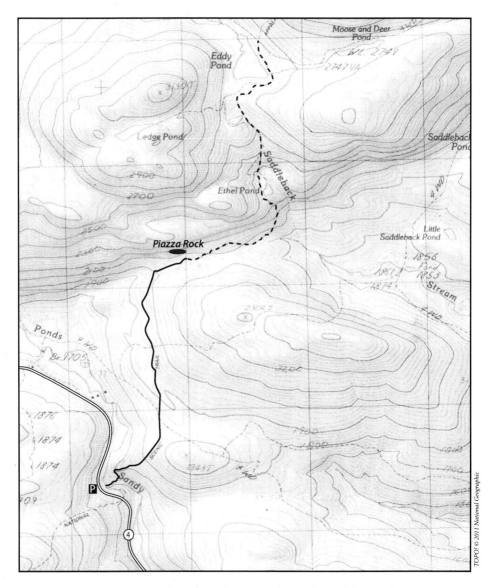

Elevation Gain: Estimated 100′ to Piazza Rock, 300′ to Eddy Pond.

On Trail

This popular summer hike on the Appalachian Trail (AT) to the distinctive Piazza Rock formation is 1.8 miles one way, and 3.6 miles round-trip. Most of the route is gently rolling or nearly level. If the parking matter can be resolved, this is a fine snowshoe hike.

The hike to Piazza Rock was the very first hike I ever took in the Western Maine mountains. My wife and I were visiting the Farmington area in preparation for a move from our Northern Maine home. As we discussed where to stay for the night, we decided to forego a motel room, and instead hike in to Piazza Rock on the Appalachian Trail to pitch a tent. It was April, over 30 years ago, and we had the trail and the Piazza Rock campsite to ourselves. We found snow in April and frozen streams—and we had a fine time.

Since then I have hiked to this spot in all four seasons, including trips on snowshoes in deep snow. I have also passed through on multi-day hikes of 50-100 miles or more, on my way to, or from, Saddleback Mountain. While the Rock is certainly worth seeing, I also enjoy the setting: intertwined brooks, broad coniferous forest, and the great scattering of elephant-sized glacial erratic boulders across the forest floor at the base of Saddleback Mountain.

I choose an April day for a return visit to Piazza Rock, following a period of very warm days with temperatures reaching well above freezing. Much of the winter snowpack had melted across the region, and I looked forward to the first hike of spring. Enter a spring snowstorm the day before my hike—and a half-foot of fresh snow covers the mountains!

But to quote an old north-country expression, "There is no such thing as bad weather—only poor clothing choices." I set out anyway, on a clear, bright morning that is markedly cold and windy. Instead of hiking shorts, for this spring day with its winter conditions, I choose instead, water-repellent hiking pants, top layers of long-sleeve wicking material, a waterproof shell, a wool cap and a fleece neck-warmer, and gaiters to keep snow out of my boots. The boots are double-duty—sturdy enough for hiking, but warm and snowshoe-compatible. I carry flexible crampons in my pack.

In the course of the hike I shed some of those outer layers, as the sun warms the day. But I was mighty glad to have cold weather gear with me at the start. When I hike in spring and fall, I always have extra layers in my pack, just in case. On another occasion I set out to climb Saddleback on a sunny day in October, when the weather changed and I waded through fresh knee-deep snow on the summit ridge. In my pack I carried winter-grade clothing, gaiters, mitts, wool hat, and balaclava. Before the day was over, I was wearing it!

The trail, marked by white paint blazes of the Appalachian Trail, descends an old roadway to a crossing of the Sandy River by a metal footbridge. The bridge is only about 10' long, and essentially is a sheet of metal placed across the narrow gap between old cribwork. I find this short metal bridge to ice over in winter, forming a mound of ice. Although the distance is short—just 2–3 steps to cross over the river—there is no sense in taking the chance of slipping here. The drop to the water is considerable, and the water itself drops in a chute. A fall here would be more than an inconvenience—it could cause serious injury.

Instead, I step back from the bridge to explore the narrow river for a crossing point upstream of the bridge. There is considerable snow cover remaining here. I test the snow for firmness with my trekking poles, find a safe crossing spot, and get over on snowshoes. Use care here.

After the river crossing the trail turns a sharp left (north) to climb steeply out of the ravine to gain high ground. Wooden steps have been placed on the hillside to stem erosion and to help with the ascent. I see their outline under the snow. (There is a plan to replace these, possibly with rock steps.) At the top of the ravine the trail swings right, and proceeds through stands of spruce and fir, with occasional hardwoods: rock maple, yellow birch, beech, and here and there, ash. Bog bridges in this section, constructed from eastern white cedar by volunteers, may be visible in outline under the snow.

Watch for a look-out point on the right side of the trail. You may get a view west through the trees of Big Jackson Mountain, and to its left, Blueberry Mountain. Directly below this viewpoint is drainage that reaches the Sandy River on its way to the Kennebec River, and then to the sea.

A Hiker Register box stands at a point 1.5 miles along the trail. From here 0.3 mile remains to Piazza Rock. Once I reach the Piazza Rock Campsite there is a sign board with a map of the area, showing the side trail to Piazza Rock itself. The trail is blazed in blue and climbs steeply 0.1 mile, passing the outcrop to the right as it circles behind the rock. It is possible to access the top, with a bit of a scramble. Watch the footing! The top is usually icy from the thaw-freeze cycle. It is a long way down!

Back at the trail junction, I have options. The campsite, with an Adirondack-style three-sided shelter, and tent sites, is rarely occupied in winter. But there are winter hikers who pass here on their way to hike all of Maine's Four Thousand Foot peaks in winter, and a few who are hiking the Appalachian Trail in winter.

Seeking to hike a bit farther, I continue north on the Appalachian Trail for another 1.0 mile to Ethel Pond, a quiet, pristine, shallow pond. The trail passes to the left of the pond. The trail to this point from Piazza Rock is steeper than what I have traveled to this point, as the route once again makes a major elevation gain on the way to the main peak of Saddleback Mountain.. On my snowy April hike I see the tracks of moose, deer, and snowshoe hare.

Ethel Pond is a good turn-around point. It is 2.8 miles back to Highway 4 from here.

I have had an early start, and am comfortable with my energy level—and choose to continue 1.0 mile, to Eddy Pond. This pond is larger and more wide-open than Ethel Pond. I make my way to the shore at the north end of the pond—a short distance from the AT, where there is a campsite used by summer hikers. I look over the pond at billowing powder snow whipped up by the wind, scattering across the landscape. Above me, on the well-forested mountainside, fresh snow glows in the spring sunlight. Cloud shadows race across the snow and ice-covered surface of the pond. Quite a place to be, indeed, on this wintery spring day.

The trail continues north 0.1 mile to an unsigned junction with the Fly Rod Crosby Trail, approximately 10 miles north of Reeds Mill and Madrid. This junction is 3.9 miles from Highway 4. From this point the Appalachian Trail crosses the Crosby Trail, and begins the long northward climb of Saddleback. That is not my plan for this day, and I do not suggest that route unless you are an experienced and well-provisioned hiker prepared for an all-day round trip hike of 10 hours of more. Eddy Pond, Ethel Pond, Piazza Rock, and the great and graceful woods along the Appalachian Trail route have certainly made my day! For that matter, to Piazza Rock and back from Highway 4 is a magnificent 3.8 mile journey in itself—and makes for a fine day's outing.

As I begin my hike out, the mid-day sun has already melted the light snow cover off south and west facing portions of the trail. The warmth feels good on my face. I remove my hat and gloves, and my shell layer, and enjoy what moment-by-moment becomes a spring-like day. Off come the snowshoes, which I strap to my daypack. But the trail is slippery, still. I switch to flexible boot crampons for the hike out.

Note: Immediately beyond Eddy Pond the AT intersects the Fly Rod Crosby multi-use trail—as I indicate. From this intersection it is approximately 0.6 mile to the left (north) on the Crosby Trail to a junction (signed) where the Crosby Trail turns 90 degrees right (east) and continues on an ascending, forested route to the Rock Pond Trail. This route ends at the Rock Pond/Fly Road Crosby Trailhead near the Rock Pond condominium area above Saddleback Mountain Lodge. This hike could be made in either direction. However, because parking on Highway 4 is problematic, a party might be dropped off at Highway 4, then hike to the Rock Pond Trailhead to be picked up.

Only hikers skilled in map and compass should attempt this extended hike. A USGS topological map and a Fly Rod Crosby Trail map are essential. Hikers must avoid the mistakes of unintentionally heading south on the Crosby Trail toward Reeds Mill (10 miles); of hiking up Saddleback Mountain on the AT; or missing the Crosby Trail turnoff towards Rock Pond. Note that cell phone service may not be available in this area.

Flexible boot crampons (l) and platform crampons (r).

Fly Rod Crosby Trail/Reeds Mill

Madrid

Snowshoe. No fee.

Overview: Snowshoe hike 1.8 miles (3.6 miles round-trip) ascending the west ridge above Orbeton Stream, then descending to the stream. Ridge views of Mount Blue to the south, and Big Jackson Mountain to the west, through leafless hardwoods. Ascent to the ridge, and the descent to the stream are over steep terrain, moderated by switchbacks, and for the descent over a wide, abandoned woods road. View of the bare Middle Peak of Mount Abraham from the woods road portion of the trail. Ice formations and wind-sculptured snow on Orbeton Stream are an attraction. Open water pools at midstream serve as winter water holes for wildlife. Tracks abound.

Trailhead: Fly Rod Crosby Trailhead at Reeds Mill is 4.4 miles east of Madrid Village on the Reeds Mill Road. Turn from Maine Highway 4 to the Reeds Mill Road, immediately crossing a one-lane bridge. The road is paved to a point just beyond the trailhead, where it crosses Orbeton Stream by a vehicle bridge. Cross the bridge and you have passed the trailhead by 0.2 mile.

The trailhead is on the left on Reeds Mill Road, 0.1 mile past a farmhouse with two barns on the hillside to the left. Trail kiosk is at the back edge of a small field which serves as a parking spot in summer. In winter park well to the side of the road. Room for a vehicle or two may be found in the vicinity of the bridge beyond—but do not block driveways, and do not block snowmobile trail ITS 115 beyond the bridge.

Maps: Delorme *Maine Atlas* Map #19, 3-A;
Fly Rod Crosby Trail Map (kiosks and Internet);
USGS: Redington

Nearest Towns: Phillips, Rangeley

Elevation Gain: 200' one-way (Ascent to bluff above Orbeton Stream, followed by descent to stream.) Round-trip adds 200' for total of 400'.)

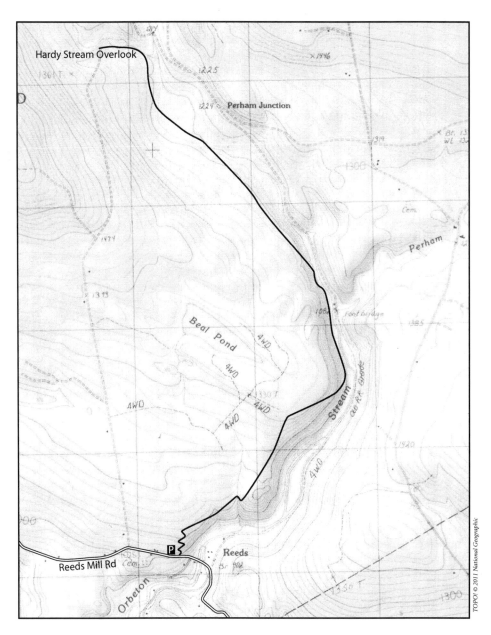

On Trail

I return for the latest in my 4-season hikes on the Fly Rod Crosby Trail on a bright March day when the snowpack lies deep after a stormy winter. The latest storm of a day or two ago has buried whatever tracks might have remained from the most recent hiker. I am breaking trail today. That means a bit more work. But there is something compelling, refreshing about being the first on trail in a while, making my own way over unbroken snow.

The trailhead on Reeds Mill Road is in a small field at the edge of a sharply rising bluff that extends northward along the west side of Orbeton Stream. The trail is marked by blue paint blazes. I begin with a work-out, climbing that bluff over a series of switchbacks. Soon well-warmed, I pause at the top to remove one layer, stuff it in my pack, and hike on. With the leaves of the hardwoods dropped for winter, I enjoy long views back towards Mount Blue, and to Big Jackson, both in the Weld region.

I tromp along, soon reaching the junction of a trail that leads 0.2 miles west to the former Star Barn Bed and Breakfast. To the west of the trail rises an intriguing stand of conifers—Norway Spruce. On my first few hikes here something about these trees caught my attention—needles a cross between hemlock and balsam fir, but the bark did not fit. After a few inquiries I learned that a former landowner, a native of Germany, had planted Norway Spruce in what was then open field, in an effort to create a local version of the Black Forest. Now it stands in the midst of Maine native trees—white pine, balsam fir, rock maple, white birch, beech, ash. No Black Forest, but a curiosity for this hiker.

Am I out here by myself? Perhaps in the moment, yes, but tracks abound, including those of moose. The Fly Rod Crosby Trail runs along the rim of the bluff, which falls off steeply to the gorge of Orbeton Stream below. A moose has chosen the same route, keeping remarkably to the trail, perhaps on the watch for a way to the river? Who knows the mind of a moose?

Then there are the bobcat tracks! These enter from the woods to the west of the trail, and then these, too, follow the trail for a considerable distance. The rim of a gorge provides a good vantage point to take in the sights and smells of prey below.

The trail runs roughly southwest to northeast in this section, a good angle for the south-riding winter sun to light up the woods. That light falls on the coppery leaves of beech trees, one of my favorite trees in winter—thin, parchment-like leaves flittering in the wind, a rare bright sight against fresh new snow, hardwood grays, coniferous deep greens. On close inspection I observe new pods that will yield fresh leaves in the spring season, only a few weeks away.

More tracks: fox, snowshoe hare, squirrel. Busy place! After a long level stretch, the trail meets an old woods road, grassed over in summer, snowpacked now like the rest of the woods. The road drops down to Orbeton Stream, and the trail follows its route. I take exaggerated steps, just short of leaps, having a bit of fun on the way down. On some winter slopes I can do a ski technique on snowshoes, aided by the use of my trekking poles with their snow baskets. I try a bit of that here, too.

At the bottom the trail continues north along the west side of Orbeton Stream for 0.3 mile, then moves away from Orbeton Stream to enter the watershed of Hardy Stream, and from there swings west to cross a gap in the low western reach of the Saddleback Range near Eddy Pond. All of that is far beyond my plan for this day, which is simply to break trail hiking to the stream, then return for a round-trip of 4 miles.

I make my way to the edge of Orbeton Stream, across from the confluence of Perham Stream to the east. Here the mix of waters has made an opening amidst the thick ice of late winter. The waters gurgle and rush, the only sound about. I position myself where I can see from a safe distance the clear water flowing swiftly on this sharply cold day. Discovery! Leading to that opening—tracks of deer, and that bobcat. How about that!

A lunch and water break, then time to turn around, and to climb that hill. I trudge deliberately upward, and am surprised at how little time it seems to take for me to reach the rim of the gorge. Back I trek, this time following the tracks I set on the way in. As the trail nears the far end of the bluff I climbed at the start of my hike, I see once again Mount Blue and the Jackson Range against the western sky-line. One good outing!

Orbeton and Hardy Streams
Oberton Conservation Area Trail
Reeds Mill, Madrid

Ski or snowshoe. No fee.

Overview: Orbeton Conservation Area. Ski or snowshoe trip of 5.0 miles one-way (10 miles round trip) to a ridge-top viewpoint towards the Saddleback Range to the northwest, the Mount Abraham (Abram) three-summit ridge to the northeast, and neighboring foothills. There are options for shorter, out-and-back trips, as there are many viewpoints toward high ground along the way, and the various streams—Orbeton, Hardy, and Perham—are points of interest.

The multi-use trail passes through the Orbeton Stream Conservation Easement, officially designated in February 2015. The Easement conserves 5500 acres for recreation use and sustainable timber harvesting.

Orebeton Stream portion of the trail is over the lower portion of the former Sandy River and Rangeley Lakes Railway. The Hardy Stream section is over unplowed logging roads. These factors make for a wide trail, with plenty of room and good visibility, considering its use by both foot travelers and those on snowmobiles. The route is level to gently rising in the Orbeton portion, and more steadily rising, with some hill ascents, in the Hardy Stream portion.

Trailhead: Reeds Mill Road, Madrid, 100' east of the road bridge over Orbeton Stream, 4.6 miles east of Maine Highway 4. The trailhead is well-signed, as it serves as the Moose Loop ATV trail in summer, and the Black Fly Snowmobile route in winter. (See Delorme *Maine Atlas* Map #19, 3-A) It is marked as ITS 89 (Interconnected Trail System route 89) on snowmobile trail maps, and by signs along the route.

Nearest Town: Madrid has a small store and diner at this writing. Nearest gas and outdoor supplies are in Rangeley, north on Highway 4. Phillips, south on Highway 4, has gas, a grocery store, and a diner.

Maps: Delorme *Maine Atlas* Maps #19, 3-A; #29, 2,3-E);
Fly Rod Crosby Trail Map;
USGS: Redington, Saddleback Mountain

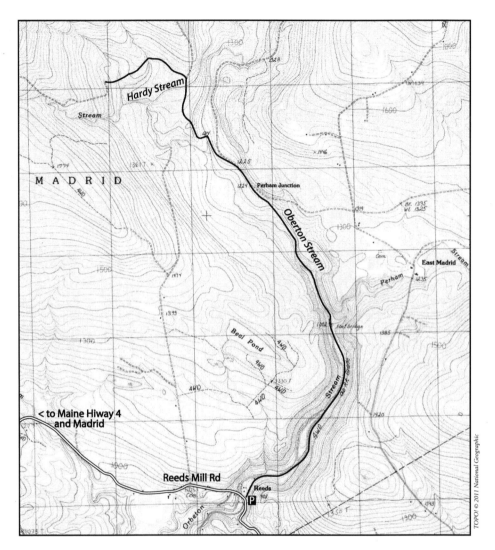

Elevation Gain: 550′ to the 5.0 mile viewpoint.

On Trail

After trekking numerous times on the Fly Rod Crosby Trail north out of the settlement of Reeds Mill, by snowshoe in winter, hiking in other seasons, I decide to ski the route on the other side of Orbeton Stream—the former rail bed now turned multi-use recreation trail. The Orbeton Stream area had been formally designated a Conservation Easement area, in 2015, making the great sweep of land to the southeast of the Saddleback Range a protected area for recreation use, wildlife habitat, and sustainable timber harvesting. I have hiked much of the route in summer, and am here today to explore it in winter. On a bright, cloudless, late winter day, snow 3 feet deep in the surrounding woods, but well-packed on the trail, I set out on skis, destination to be determined—but hopeful of reaching high ground for long views towards Saddleback and Mount Abram.

First impression? This is cross-country ski "candy"—broad, well-groomed trail, easy grade!

In the first quarter-mile the trail passes stream-side seasonal camps, some accessed by snowmobile in winter, then passes a sign indicating the end of summer vehicle passage. Orbeton Stream, on my left, is largely snow-blanketed. Occasional open-water pools reveal the ice-strata that has built up in the course of the winter. Clear water splashes against stream boulders and against the ice itself—some water music on a winter day.

In 10 minutes I draw parallel to the lower end of an island in the stream, then reach the upper end in another 5 minutes. I cross a number of bridges that pass over small streams running down off the lower slopes of Mount Abram. The largest of these crosses Perham Stream 1.8 miles from my starting point. Perham Stream is fully snow-covered, with no open water. I stop on the bridge to look, and to listen. Under the snow Perham Stream offers up a low-pitched, marbles-in-a-drawer rumbling sound, as its waters rush to meet Orbeton Stream—just 50' beyond from where I stand. The confluence produces a short stretch of open water at Orbeton Stream, and a higher pitched, slapping-splashing tune.

Stop to listen in the outdoors! Always a discovery! There are discoveries in the snow, too. Moose tracks cross the trail. Bobcat tracks. The track of a solitary grouse. Red squirrel. Snowshoe hare. Busy place!

I classic-ski up the gentle grade, occasionally breaking into a skate technique. Two snowmobilers pass. I wave and they wave back. A trailside log offers a spot for a break, and I stop for water and the first-half of lunch. The sun is bright and warm. This day is as good as it gets!

Back on my skis, I note that the stream and the trail diverge such that the water is now out of sight. I pass prominent Perham Junction, once a railway junction for a spur that accessed timber harvest ground on Mount Abraham. Now it is the junction for east-running ITS 84 which heads towards Kingfield. This junction is well signed.

Under a half-mile beyond Perham Junction the trail angles west at a point where the Orbeton Valley railway route continues straight ahead. This junction is signed. My route is over the main trail (Moose Loop, Black Fly Loop, ITS 89/84) and I head west. Another day I will return to explore the upper reaches of the old railway, as it climbs towards Orbeton Canyon and far Redington Pond—but not today.

I cross a bridge over Orbeton Stream, to enter the high ground above Hardy Stream—which is just out of sight to my left. There is continuous ascent ahead—and with it the opening up of views towards Saddleback and Mount Abram. There are two bridge crossings over tributaries to Hardy Stream, as the trail draws closer to the Saddleback Range just under 3640′ Saddleback Junior. To the right, between the Range, and the long, east-lying Mount Abram ridge lies 2556′ Potato Hill.

For most of the way I *ski* the ascents, that is, my skis provide enough grip that I ski up using classic technique. I have chosen "fish scale" skis for today's conditions, expecting frozen, crusty snow in the morning, but above freezing temperatures with soft, wet snow, later in the day. It is difficult to wax for grip when there is a wide temperature range, below and above freezing. My skis are referred to as "no wax" skis, but I wax the tips and the tails with glide wax in order to have both glide, and grip, when needed.

At some points along the way the angle of ascent is a bit steep to ski, and I switch to herring-bone technique to make the climb—then switch back to the classic stride when the steepness moderates. Technically not difficult—I just have to work harder. Very much on my mind is the long downhill that awaits me when I turn around. Should be a good run—more ski "candy"!

Two more sets of snowmobilers pass, once from behind me, another coming towards me. I wave to them as well. There is plenty of room on this wide trail, but I am careful to avoid "blind spots" on corners and hills where a snowmobiler heading toward me may not see me coming. Usually I ski on the left side of the trail, facing on-coming traffic—as I would if walking or running along a road. But when the line of sight is limited, I move to the far right of the trail. In this way I am out of the lane of the snowmobile coming at me, and remain visible to a snowmobile coming from the rear. Did I mention I am wearing a visible yellow-green jacket?

The trail swings to a point just above the main branch of Hardy Stream, barely in sight through the trees, crosses a level area, then begins a long uphill climb. Do I do this, or turn around here? Behind me the Mount Abraham ridge rises in nearly full view, with a few high maples in the foreground. If I climb higher I may get an even better view, and that much longer a downhill run on the return. Up I go, up, nearly to the height of land where the trail next turns west. I find a good look-out point and pull up.

Saddleback Junior hovers overhead, its main, bare summit just north of a lower, unnamed twin summit. In the east, the three peaks of Mount Abraham form the horizon along a 5 mile ridge. The bare main and middle peaks are bright, snowfields lying in full sun. The wooded southern peak, a dark hunter green, trails off in the direction of the southern Franklin County foothills. Quite a sight! The main peak of Mount Abraham is a former Maine Forest Service fire tower peak. Fire watch days by tower are long gone, replaced by aircraft surveillance.

Beyond (above) my 5 mile destination the route continues more westerly, crosses the Fly Rod Crosby foot trail twice, then coincides with the Crosby Trail to reach a 9.0 mile viewpoint over the Onion Valley. Elevation gain between mile 5 and Mile 9 is 1000'. This would be a very long out-and-back ski or snowshoe hike from Reeds Mill in Madrid (18 miles round trip), and therefore should be considered only by well-experienced and well-conditioned parties, equipped for contingencies in a remote area.

The Crosby Trail continues, farther still, beyond the Onion Valley Overlook, reaching the Rock Pond area near the Saddleback Ski area in another 4 miles (total 13 miles one-way from Reeds Mill; 26 miles round-trip). Portions of this route on un-groomed, ascending, rough ground where progress on skis or snowshoes would be markedly slower than on the groomed trail section described here. (See the Rock and Midway Pond entry in this book for information on the Rock Pond area.)

Today's 5-mile ski sits well with me—especially because I have the return 5 miles ahead, for a total outing of 10 miles. That is plenty of ski time, on a bright see-forever day!

Turn-around time. I designated my turn-around time expecting that I would have benefit of gravity on my way back, and I am not disappointed. I finish the second half of lunch, enjoying the view. Now, I turn the skis toward home, and let them run!

Down, down, down, High Peaks above, and Hardy and Orbeton Streams heading in the same direction that I am. Surprise! On the way back I look up to see Mount Blue in the distance, framed by high fir on either side of the trail. That Mount Blue view had been behind me on my way up—I was so focused on the unfolding view of the Saddleback Range ahead of me, that I had not turned around to look back. Out and back trips are like that—the view is never the same in both directions.

I check my speed, stop for a water break, have another close-up look at the winter-sculptured contrasts in Orbeton Stream. Open water and broken ice strata stand a few feet from boulders mounded with deep snow. At the Perham Stream bridge I pull up to listen to the dueling stream sounds one more time—then cover the final two miles to the trailhead.

My time up to the viewpoint from Reeds Mill was 2½ hours. Coming out, skiing steadily with gravity in my favor, I cover the 5 miles in 1 hour 20 minutes. Of course, being out in the mountains is not about time. It is, for me, about taking it all in. Add the Orbeton Stream trails to your "to do" list!

FIELD NOTES

Flagstaff-Bigelow Region

Flagstaff Lake—Maine's fourth largest at 23 miles long—and the 17 mile Bigelow Range, are the dominant features of this region. Maine Huts and Trails (MHT) operates two full-service lodges in the region, connected by many miles of backcountry groomed ski and snowshoe trail open for day use as well as for overnight guests.

This section of the book describes MHT trails, and snowshoe and ski routes in the Bigelow Preserve.—including a portion of the Appalachian Trail on Little Bigelow, and of the Bigelow Range Trail on Cranberry Peak. This is spectacular country, whether seen from the snowy shores of Flagstaff Lake or the Dead River, Bigelow Range summits, or countless backcountry viewpoints in between.

Maine Huts and Trails:

Flagstaff Lake: East Shore and
Flagstaff Hut   86

Dead River, Grand Falls, and
Grand Falls Hut from
Long Falls Dam Road   90

Dead River, Grand Falls, and
Grand Falls Hut from West Forks   98

Flagstaff Lake South:
Round Barn Site and Bigelow Lodge   104

Little Bigelow Mountain   110

Cranberry Peak   114

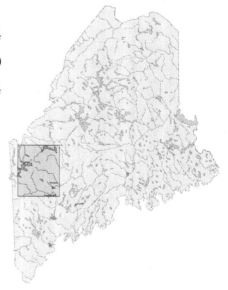

Dead River, Grand Falls - West Forks
✳
Dead River & Grand Falls Hut - LFD
✳

✳Flagstaff Hut & Flagstaff Lake East Shore
✳Flagstaff Lake Round Barn
✳Little Bigelow Mtn.

Cranberry Peak✳
Crommett Trail
Stratton Brook Hut & Oak Knoll   ✳
✳ Poplar Hut & Poplar Stream Falls
Narrow Gauge Pathway

Bonney Point
Hunter Cove
Hatchery Brook

Sugarloaf Outdoor Ct.

Long Falls Dam Road

Rangeley Lakes Trail Ctr.
Rangeley ✳
Bald Mt.✳
Rock & Midway
✳Ponds
✳Piazza Rock
South Bog Trail
✳
Low Aziscohos
✳ Oberton & Hardy Streams
✳ Fly Rod Crosby Trail

Little Jackson Mt.   Blueberry Mt.
Tumbledown Pond & Tumbledown Mt.✳
Byron Road
Center Hill   ✳ ✳Mount Blue
Sandy Rvr   ✳Powderhouse Hill
Intervale✳   Farmington
Bald Mt.   Titcomb Mt✳
Wilton

Flagstaff Lake East Shore and Flagstaff Hut
Maine Huts and Trails
Carrying Place Township

Ski or Snowshoe. No fee for trail use. Lodging/meal cost. (Day Membership is one way of contributing to MHT, but is not required. Contact MHT for details.)

Overview: MHT 2.0 miles (4.0 mile round-trip) ski or snowshoe route, parallel to the East Shore of Flagstaff Lake at the so-called "Mile Beach" area, to Flagstaff Hut of Maine Huts and Trail (MHT). The Hut offers four-season lodging, meals in particular seasons, and day use with drinking water and other amenities. The groomed main ski trail, open to those on snowshoes, is fairly level to gently rolling. Alternate snowshoe trails, not groomed, pass close to the shore and offer views southwest across Flagstaff Lake and beyond toward the Bigelow Range.

Among the four MHT in operation at this writing, Flagstaff Hut offers some of the finest views available in the 120 kilometer (80 mile) network. The day-trip approach route of about 2 miles, with minimal elevation change, makes this a particularly attractive outing.

Trailhead: 22 miles north of North New Portland Village, on Long Falls Dam Road, west side (left). Plowed parking area (sign) with MHT information kiosk.

To reach main MHT trail, head west from parking lot 0.2 mile on connector trail to four-way junction with main trail leading north 1.8 miles to Flagstaff Hut, south 9.3 miles to Poplar Hut.

Straight ahead is a 0.1 mile route to the Shore Trail, a snowshoe trail that passes close to the lakeshore of Mile Beach to reach the Hut in another 1.8 miles.

Maps: Delorme *Maine Atlas* Map #29, 5-B & Map #30, 1-B;
MHT System Map;
Bigelow Preserve Map, Maine Department of Conservation;
USGS: Little Bigelow

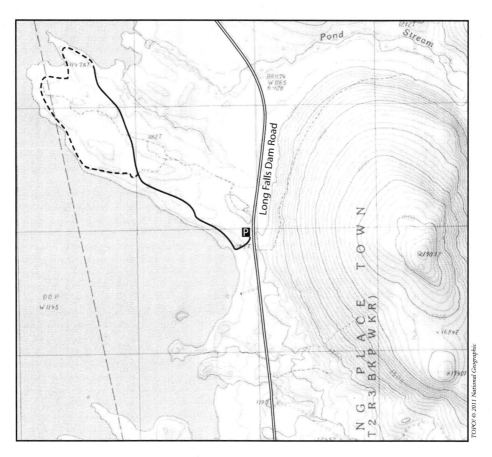

Towns: North New Portland Village has a store with diner; nearest gas in Kingfield or Embden. (Gas up before driving to trailhead.)

Elevation Gain: Negligible

On Trail

The mid-winter sky is as bright as a blue flame as I make my way on snowshoes along the groomed Maine Hut Trail, in the direction of Flagstaff Lake
Hut. The trail winds 2.0 miles one way through a mixed hardwood and softwood
forest, just in from the eastern shore of this great lake, in Carrying Place Township, north of North New Portland.

Rich winter sunlight casts a silver and gold glow on paper birch. Thin tat-
tered strips of white bark flutter in a light breeze. Pine, spruce, and fir rise deep
green against the shimmering backdrop of snow and sky. It is a fine winter day
to be on foot in the Maine woods!

The trail has been tracked and well-groomed for classic or skating-style Nordic skiing, as well as for snowshoeing. Because I plan for some off-trail exploring, I have chosen snowshoes, but the Hut Trail would be a good choice for those looking for a ski outing in a relatively pristine setting. There are no hills of consequence to climb—just stretch after stretch of level to gently rolling trail.

As it is mid-winter, some smaller trees are all but buried in the deep snow. I spy the very top of a young white pine peeking up out of the snow like a seedling, although this future soaring king of the forest was likely a good three feet tall, at least. Around the base of rock maples and birch, hollows have formed from the sun reflecting off the shining trunks. Tracks of deer, snowshoe hare, and fox, cross the trail. Chickadees and Blue Jays work the woods, searching for seeds scattered by winter winds. There is much to be seen in the Maine woods in winter!

On my northward trek, I turn off the main trail when about half way to the Flagstaff Hut, to take the Shore Trail, a side trail that also leads to the Flagstaff Hut, but travels close to the shore line. This trail is *not* groomed for skiing. There are snowshoe tracks from a previous party, and with the combination of the tracks and the trail markings on trees, the way is clear to follow today. A few minutes of hiking bring me to the shore itself, near a lakeside campsite of the Bigelow Preserve. I do not expect to find any signs of the site other than a sign at this time of year, but to my surprise—and appreciation—I discover bowl-shaped designs in the snow where winter campers have tamped down the snow in order to set up tents. This spot offers an extraordinary view westward up the lake. What a site for a night out! I note the location for my canoe trip plans for a future summer.

The view across the lake calls, and I step out onto this great white, unbroken expanse. The great Bigelow Range looms to the southwest. In the bright sunlight, the rocky tops of Avery peak and West Peak shine a shimmering bright white above the gray-green forested slopes rising up from the lake. To the far west I see the heights of the East Kennebago Range. To the north rises Blanchard Mountain, and beyond that, Picked Chicken Hill. The curious name was assigned to this lumpy hill after a logging operation a few generations ago! A great quiet prevails.

I think of the days before the Long Falls Dam was built in 1950. What I look upon today was once the broad valley of the Dead River, with adjacent farming communities of Dead River, Flagstaff, and Bigelow. The valley and these north-country towns were flooded when Long Falls Dam went into operation in 1950. Back then, even on a winter day, the air would have carried the sounds of the people of these villages going to and from one of the local stores, or school, or church, or doing winter work on the farms, harvesting timber, or sawing logs, or at one of the local mills.

I make my way northward on the lake, not far off shore. As it was well into winter, the weather has been cold for quite a stretch, and I expect the ice is safe, but I always bring trekking poles on snow shoe hikes to test the ice. Even in the midst of winter springs on the lake bed can thin the ice in unexpected places. So thick is the ice on this day that it rides up over rock outcrops in the lake, exposing thickness of a foot and a half.

The hike continues! I re-enter the woods to join the Shore Trail again, and follow it to the Flagstaff Hut itself. There I find a large common room warmed by a wood fire. It was lunchtime, and the friendly Hut staff offered a hot chili, with a brownie for dessert, for a very reasonable price. I had worked up an appetite, and decided to save my peanut butter and jelly sandwiches for an afternoon snack later. No contest—I choose the hot meal!

After lunch I accept the crew's offer of a tour of the hut, which offers overnight accommodations in bunk rooms of various sizes such that a family or group could reserve a room for itself, or the solo traveler or small group could pay for individual bunks instead of whole rooms. There are showers heated by solar panels and the toilets are indoors, composting type. Drinking water is available. A reading room complements the set-up. Not a bad destination for a winter overnight snowshoe or ski trip—or, as I was doing—for a good day outing in winter.

On the return trip I step out once again onto the lake. From the hut I could have taken the Maine Hut Trail to head most directly back to the parking area, and my truck. But the view across the white expanse is too good to pass up. As it is now afternoon, the sun has moved southwestward across the sky and the shaded northern slopes of the Bigelow Range now lie in a velvet dark green darkness. I trek to a rock outcrop and sit for a while, taking in this remarkable scene. This vast white panorama has the feel of high country in the Rocky Mountains, but I am here in the Western Mountains of Maine!

Finally it is time to go. I check the topographic map I have with me, locate my position, then head towards shore and into the woods to pick up the Shore Trail. *Voila!* I come onto the Trail only a hundred yards from the trailhead and parking area, to end a great winter day in the Maine woods. We have world-class winter outing opportunities in the Western Maine lake and mountain country. Explore the shores of Flagstaff!

Dead River, Grand Falls, Grand Falls Hut
from Long Falls Dam Rd.
Maine Huts and Trails

T3 R4 BKP WKR
(Township 3, Range 4—Bingham Kennebec Purchase west of Kennebec River)

Ski or Snowshoe. No fee for day use of trails. Lodging/meal cost. Optional "Day Membership" available. (Day Membership is one way of contributing to MHT, but is not required. Contact MHT for details.)

Overview: MHT 6.8 miles one-way (13.6 miles round-trip) backcountry snowshoe hike or ski, on groomed ski trail, from Long Falls Dam Road to Grand Falls on the lower Dead River.

Continue north past Grand Falls 1.2 miles, one way, to Grand Falls Hut of Maine Huts and Trails, for a total outing of 8.0 miles one-way (16.0 miles round-trip from Long Falls Dam Road).

Mostly level to rolling terrain, with some short steep hills either side of the Tom and Kate Chappell Footbridge. Much of the route is riverside over the Dead River intervale. Fine views to the southwest (over the shoulder on the way in) of the Bigelow Range.

The country is remote and wildly beautiful. The Falls are striking at 40' high and 100' across, with natural ice sculptures formed from freezing spray. At various points along the groomed trail there are blue-blazed parallel trails, ungroomed, suitable for snowshoeing. These run along the top of the riverbank, and offer fine views up and down the river. At Grand Falls, and between the Falls and the Hut, there are more snowshoe trail options. Check the MHT system map for details.

Grand Falls Hut is a full-service lodge providing overnight accommodations, meals, and hot showers. Day visitors are welcome to use the great room and toilets, and to resupply drinking water, at no fee. Contact MHT for details on services, rates, and schedule of operation.

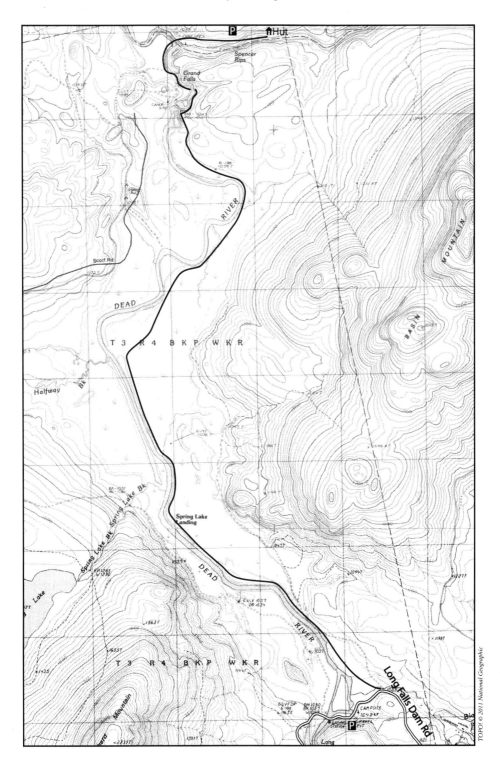

Trailhead: Long Falls Dam Road, at intersection with (unplowed) Dead River Road, on the right, 26.2 miles north of North New Portland. The Maine Huts and Trails main trail crosses the Long Falls Dam Road at this point (signs). This point is 3.2 miles north of Flagstaff Hut via the MHT Trail System.

Dead River Road is 0.2 miles south of Big Eddy on the Long Falls Dam Road. Park at Big Eddy where plows usually clear ample room.

The entrance to the Dead River Road is used to park trail grooming machinery, and for emergency access. Keep this area clear. Please do not block the Dead River Road, and do not park on the Long Falls Dam Road. Snowplows may operate any time of day or night, both during storms, and on clear days following. Log trucks use the road 24 hours a day.

The groomed trail to Grand Falls and Grand Falls Hut follows the Dead River Road for 100', crosses Black Brook over a bridge, then turns left into the woods. All junctions are signed.

Nearest Town: North New Portland Village (store with diner; no gas). Nearest gas: Kingfield, Embden. Gas up before driving to trailhead.

Maps: Delorme Maine Atlas Map #29, 5-A,B;
Maine Huts and Trails System Map;
USGS: Little Bigelow, Basin Mountain

Elevation gain: Cumulative gain over the route estimated at 100'. Be prepared for series of short "roller-coaster" ascents/descents in vicinity of Chappell Bridge.

On Trail

Grand Falls on the Dead River below Flagstaff Lake and Long Falls Dam is worth a visit any time of year—but is especially spectacular in winter. The spray from these 40' waterfalls freezes as it settles on the great ledge outcrops that run along the top of the falls and jut out from its face and base. The results: striking ice sculptures—sculptures that change in the course of the winter, through the thaw-freeze cycle, in response to the rise and fall of the river level, and from the snow loads driven in by winter storms.

Catch the angle of the sun just right and see a rare winter rainbow! The deep thunder-roar of the tumbling water, pitching over the steep drop, set against the quiet backdrop of remote country, offers pure awe. And to come upon the falls while traveling across this wild country on foot …!

One mid-winter day, with the thermometer on my backpack reading 18 degrees, I step into my cross-country skis at the Dead River Road junction with Long Falls Dam Road. With two clear, bright days in the forecast, my plan is to ski 6.8 miles to the Falls, continue 1.2 miles farther to the Grand Falls Hut to spend the night, and then ski the 8.0 miles back to my truck the following day.

A strong northwest wind rocks the conifers lining the trail in the first few hundred feet, raising a pretty good roar. Wind chill? Easily zero degrees! That wind has raced over Flagstaff Lake, then channeled down the road. I am directly in the wind's way. I put on most of my layers of outer wear—even the down jacket I save for emergency use. I am a bit bulky for skiing, but know I will warm quickly once underway.

The trail follows the unplowed Dead River Road for the first 0.1 mile, crossing Black Brook immediately, then takes a northward turn towards the Dead River itself at Dead River Road Crossing #1 (sign). From this point, the trail parallels the river all the way to Grand Falls, with the water usually 50–100 feet to the north, sometimes well within sight, with occasional long views up stream or down. The route has been groomed for both classic and skate technique skiing by Maine Huts and Trails.

For the first mile and a half the trail passes over nearly level terrain through a mixed forest of red spruce, white cedar, hemlock, balsam fir, and occasional high white pine. It swings southward for a short stretch to meet the Dead River Road at Crossing #2, but then immediately swings back to the north.

Returning to its parallel course with the river, the trail emerges from the mixed growth, to drop slightly to low ground bordering an extensive marshland fed by run-off from Pierce Pond Mountain and the adjacent ridge to the south. The marshland was well frozen on this winter day. The terrain is virtually level. The trail crosses a number of bridges over unnamed streams that run from the marsh to the river. These bridges are the width of a groomed ski trail, and with the good snow cover on this day I was able to ski right across.

I am using my waxable classic skis, in anticipation of some off-trail skiing at some point, but the trail is in such good condition that I went to the skating technique. The down jacket goes into the pack, as I have become quite comfortable and the wind has dropped.

Spying blue blazes on the north side of the trail, I opt for some exploring on this alternate route, breaking trail in one-foot-deep snow. The country is so open that I am within eyesight of the parallel main ski trail as I approach the river. I expect an ice-covered river at this point, well-below the turbulence at Big Eddy, but am surprised to find open water. That is not my only surprise. When I reach the crest of the bank, I startle a Red-crested Merganser—which in turn startles me! This great bird takes off over the blue-black water, follows the river westward, and flies out of sight. Mergansers are common on north woods waters in summer, but this was my first winter sighting. They do remain in an area so long as there is open water—otherwise they winter near coastal waters that rarely freeze.

The side trail rejoins the main trail, and I ski on, crossing the great marshland that borders the river for a good five miles at least. This is one of the larger such marshes in this part of Maine, and the level terrain offers great cross-country skiing. To the southwest the high peaks of the Bigelow Range, over 4000' elevation, dominate the horizon, the low winter sun hovering just above Avery Peak. To the east, about two miles off, Basin Mountain caps the ridge at the edge of Pierce Pond Township. Stony Brook Mountain lies to the northeast, only 1410' high, but conspicuous above the lowland.

Closer in, tracks of deer and hare cross the trail. As is common in marsh country, willows, alders, and an occasional solitary cedar or pine, punctuate the grassy lowlands. In one hardwood patch the bark has been scraped about head high—sign of moose? Sure enough, nearby I spied their big cloven tracks plunged into the snow. Much to see on this trail both in the long view, and the short view!

The trail leaves the lowland to enter a section of small hillocks, a sign that I was nearing the Chappell Footbridge that crosses the Dead River above Grand Falls. This bridge is named for trail benefactors Tom and Kate Chappell. I stop here to listen. There—the roar of Grand Falls, out of sight around a bend in the river. Short, steep pitches call for herring bone technique on the ascent, and a bit of side stepping on the way down. Care should be used here to stay in control of the skis, especially when bearing a backpack. The bridge is snow-covered and well-packed, enabling me to ski across. Upstream, west of the bridge are the remains of an old logging dam. Above this is a take-out point for summer-season canoeists who are portaging the falls—which are un-runnable and must be portaged.

On the north side of the Chappell Bridge, the ski trail crosses a snowmobile route that leads downstream (right) 100 yards to a short blue-blazed hiking trail (The "Falls Trail", which may/may not be signed, but blue blazes should be readily seen) to an overlook of Grand Falls. This is the shortest and easiest way to reach the Falls. The overlook is on a rocky promontory that juts out pulpit-like above the falls. Quite a sight—and sound!

Grand Falls is dramatic. In the midst of this great, virtually silent, forest, rises a deep roar—so loud that I have had to raise my voice to be heard. Ice build-up on the rocks forms shapes as intriguing as cloud formations on a summer day. Spray thrown up by water tumbling through the apex of the horseshoe-shaped falls had frozen an overarching curtain of ice, even as behind that curtain water thunders its way down to splash on great boulders below. I have this remarkable display to myself—and linger here. A Black-capped Chick-a-dee, calls its name. A Blue Jay calls. I do have company.

Then, this! A deer enters the water about 50 yards above the falls! It swims to mid-stream, reverses direction, swims back to the bank where it entered the water, then disappears into thick fir growth. I have been hiking for decades, and this is my first sighting of a deer swimming in winter. Spend many days in the out of doors, and who knows what will appear!

Those on snowshoes may continue on the blue-blazed Falls Trail which I had taken to the Falls overlook. Beyond the overlook, the trail climbs over the promontory ridge, drops sharply into a ravine, climbs again and drops once more, crosses a bog brook on a log bridge, then rejoins the Maine Huts Trail route. Ice sometimes takes out this log bridge, which would necessitate backtracking to the Falls to pick up the main MHT trail.

Please note: This route is a short-cut by distance, but is rough, usually untracked, and may take longer than returning by the main MHT trail. For those on skis the Falls Trail north past the overlook would be difficult, although a skier could remove skis and hike up and down the steep pitches. I have done this, wading through knee-deep snow, scrambling up and over the pitches—and I have also had to go around when I discovered that a section of the log bridge had washed away.

A better option for skiers at the Grand Falls overlook is to retrace one's steps to the snowmobile trail, then follow that 150' to the main MHT Trail, above the Chappell Bridge. Follow the Maine Huts Trail as its circumvents the high ground near the falls. There are some steep sections on this route, but the trail is wide and groomed for skiing.

The Maine Huts Trail briefly becomes multiuse, coinciding with a portage trail for the Northern Forest Canoe Trail, which in winter doubles as a snowmobile trail, part of ITS 86/89. The multiuse feature enables the crossing of Spencer Stream over a bridge, after which snowmobiles and foot traffic go in separate ways. Be alert for snowmobile traffic. Proceed in single file.

For the area between the Chappell Bridge, and the Spencer Stream Bridge, read the trail signs closely and refer to the MHT map. I have found the routes to be well marked, but have encountered trekkers who were confused about the way because they were not consulting a map.

The Maine Huts Trail turns east after the Spencer Stream crossing. The snowmobile route turns north. Two snowmobilers pass by, just before I take that eastward turn. We exchange waves. The route climbs to reach the crest of the bluff above the river. I pass the junction for the Fisherman's Trail which drops down to the river, parallels it, passes Spencer Rips on the Dead River. This side trail returns to the main trail near the Grand Falls Hut. This is a narrower trail than the main trail, more suitable for snowshoes than for skis. I am a bit weary now, and have no need to break trail at this point in the day. There is enough of a workout for me on this last up and down groomed section until I arrive at the Hut.

Grand Falls Hut is the third Hut to be built in the Maine Huts and Trails system, and the most remote. I am drawn immediately to its location high above the Dead River, with a view back towards the Bigelow Range to the West. As the river rumbles on a hundred yards or so below and just out of sight, I head inside to register, clean up, enjoy the Great Room with a wood fire roaring, and wait to be called for supper. Solar power heats hot water for the showers—a luxury that contrasts with my years of winter tent-camping. There are plenty of baked goods to replace the calories I burned on the ski in today, and I go to work on some oatmeal chocolate chip cookies.

I have a room to myself as there is ample bed space on this mid-week night. Before I finally turn in, I step outside into the sharply cold night to take in the stars. I spy Orion, dependable winter constellation, listen to the distant rush of the river, then head for bed.

The next morning the outside temperature reads 1 degree above zero. After a pancake breakfast I head back the way I skied in, again moving quickly at first to warm up. The hilly terrain on the way back toward Grand Falls, and beyond to the Chappell footbridge, helps me to generate heat. When I reach the fairly flat, nearly 6 mile section, I move smoothly and get into a good rhythm. What a gift it is to be in such pristine country. At one point I stop, remain still, and scan the nearby marsh. I do this from time to time on all my outings. Sometimes I will see a fox, or hear the crash of a moose moving off. Or maybe I do not see wildlife, but by stopping I do see wing marks on the snow where a hawk or an owl has landed, perhaps in pursuit of the field mice that travel in passages just under the snow.

In good time, but all too soon for a day of such striking beauty, and for a place of such solitude, I reach the end of the trail at the Long Falls Dam trailhead. I drive off for North New Portland for a hot chocolate and an over-sized muffin, then head for home.

Whether for a day trip or an overnight adventure, Grand Falls is a "mustsee." Pack for the remoteness, remembering the self-rescue gear, clothing and food. Travel by snow shoes or by skis, but do plan for a winter visit.

FIELD NOTES

Dead River and Grand Falls Hut
from West Forks
West Forks Plantation, Lower Enchanted Township, and T3R5 BKP WKR

Ski or Snowshoe. No fee for day use of trails. Lodging/meal cost. Optional "Day Membership" available. (Day Membership is one way of contributing to MHT, but is not required. Contact MHT for details.)

Overview: Longest approach route in the Maine Huts and Trails System, to the most remote Hut: 14.4 miles one way from West Forks Trailhead to Grand Falls Hut (28.8 miles round-trip). Groomed trail open for skis and snowshoes.

The trail parallels the Lower Dead River for much of the distance, generally keeping to the bluff above the north side of the river. Along the route, the trail drops steeply multiple times to cross tributary streams, before regaining the high ground. Skiers should be prepared for these drops and climbs. This may include removing skis to walk steep terrain when the trail is icy.

This long route passes through very remote and road-less territory. Travelers are advised to be well-conditioned—and well-equipped with both standard gear and clothing, and emergency gear for self- rescue.

The Dead River in winter is wild and strikingly beautiful—with open water even on the coldest days of winter because of swift current and steady drop. The riverside forest has its own beauty—mixed hardwood-softwood growth of maple, birches, ash, and beech; and fir, spruce, pine, cedar, and hemlock.

Trailhead: West Forks trailhead is on the left (west) side of U.S. Highway 201, north of Bingham, Caratunk, and The Forks. The Trailhead is approximately 2.0 miles north of the Kennebec River Bridge at West Forks. A signed driveway leads to a plowed parking area where there is a trail kiosk.

Maps: Delorme *Maine Atlas* Map #40, 2-E; #30, 1-A; #29, 5-A;
Maine Huts and Trails System Map;
USGS: Pierce Pond

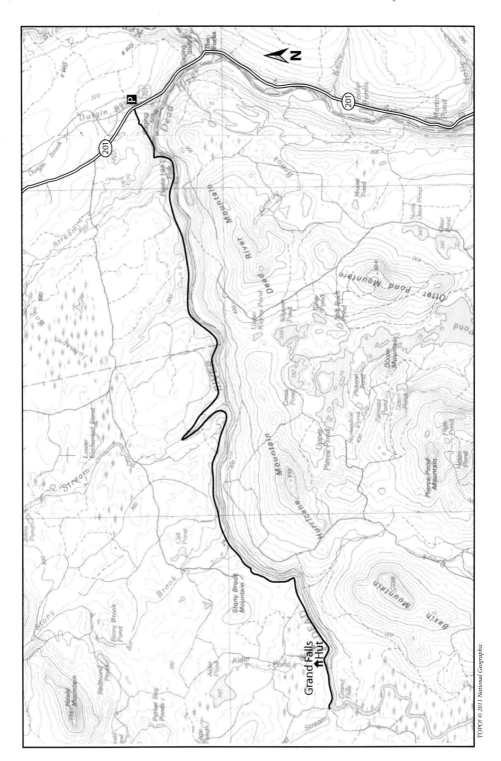

Nearest Towns: Bingham, The Forks

Elevation Gain: 1000′ cumulative over the entire route, from a series of drops/
  climbs as the trail route crosses tributary streams.

On Trail

O n a sharply clear, eye-squint bright morning, temperature in single digits,
I step into my steel-edged cross-country skis at the West Fork Trailhead—
destination Grand Falls Hut. We are a party of three. My plan is to overnight at
the hut, ski the next day to the Flagstaff Hut, then complete the outing by skiing
on the following day to the Airport Trailhead in Carrabassett Valley. My companions will do the same for the first two days, then overnight at Poplar Hut, followed by another overnight, at Stratton Brook Hut—traveling the entire length
of the MHT trail system, north to south.

The first order of business is the 14.4 mile ski trek from West Forks to Grand
Falls. We have equipped ourselves carefully. I carry a 0-degree down sleeping
bag, and a bivy bag, have warm layers packed, and bring extra trail food—along
with standard gear such as headlamp, spare mitts, and anything I might need in
case of a mishap. The route ahead I know to be strikingly beautiful, but it passes
through some of the most remote country in this book, where there is no dependable cell phone service.

Self-rescue preparation—always essential—is all the more paramount here.

A week or so of dry weather had rendered the trail slickly-snowpacked.
The MHT website updates conditions regularly, and advised steel edges on this
route—and I am pleased for the information, and to comply. The night before a
passing front dropped a dusting of 1″ powder, providing a bit of cover. All things
considered, the conditions look good.

The trail tops a knoll just west of the trailhead, then drops sharply into a
draw to cross the first of many bridges over tributary streams to the Dead River.
This is snowplow-technique territory for me, as the trail rounds a number of
curves in the descent, with limited sight distance. I am getting the feel of skiing
with a pack on my back, and those steel edges underneath. This is not let-em-
run terrain. A tumble here could end the trip early! I am having fun as it is!

The sky is cloudless. Early sun throws long shadows over the fresh snowfall,
lights up white and yellow birch, shines on the coppery leaves of beech, and the
deep green of fir. Mighty nice.

Another short climb, then a long descent to the next bridge, at Salmon
Stream. This will be the order and rhythm of the day, as the trail nears the north
bank of the Dead River. Ascend the bluff above the river, ski a short stretch over
level terrain, descend, climb again. The first view of the river impresses—icy

mist rises above purple-blue waters rushing past snow and ice-covered boulders. In protected coves near the shore, ice cover reaches out toward the main current, but not far, as the swift run of the Dead barrels toward the confluence with the Kennebec River, 5 miles downstream.

I foresee a long downhill stretch, let my skis run a bit, decide that I am going faster than I like when I encounter more curves. Solution? I do a controlled fall—slowing as I might, picking out a soft landing spot at the edge of the trail, and sliding to a stop. No harm done. I take a moment getting up, simply to look upward at that clear blue sky, framed by a canopy of maples, birch, fir.

More bridges, one over a small stream draining a narrow pond, then the bridge over the more substantial Gulf Stream. Through the trees, on my left, to the south, across the river rises Dead River Mountain. More up and down, and I arrive at the mid-point, Enchanted Stream. A picnic site of sorts exists here, just short of the bridge. My companions dust off rocks and logs for seats. I sit on the bridge deck. We break out lunch, which for me includes hot tea. In 3.5 hours we have covered over 7 miles—right on plan.

The trial climbs sharply out of Enchanted Stream. I carry my skis rather than herring-bone up the hill. More than once on the trail I take my skis off to walk down a steep pitch. Parties should be prepared to do this. So remote is this trail that it is not advisable to take chances. The goal is to reach the destination, not to ski every foot of trail regardless of conditions.

When the trail tops out of the Enchanted Stream Valley, fine views open up of the string of Black Nubble, just south of Dead River Mountain, Hurricane Mountain to the southwest, and, of course, the swift Dead River with its continuous roar. From this point on the trail runs more closely to the river, at one point dropping to its very edge.

More up and down, and more bridges, though the elevation changes are less sharp than earlier on the trail. The winter sun, low on the southwestern sky, now throws shadows back at me, and approaching an alpenglow, as I reach the Grand Falls Hut, 7 hours after departing from West Forks. I am weary, but it is a good weary. The hut sits on a bluff back from the river, with a view of Basin Mountain. The river, out of sight, sings a steady rumbling rush.

A hot shower, solar powered; a hot meal—hut crew-prepared; good conversation by the wood stove of places we have been, times we have had, and then time for bed. I slide into my sleeping bag in one of the bunkrooms, and am quickly asleep. In the middle of the night I awake, step outside. The air is frigid, fresh, tingling on my face and hands. Overhead the night sky is full of stars. Basin Mountain looms as a dark mass in the distance. The river sings below. Quite a moment.

The next day I ski to Flagstaff Hut, with a stop at Grand Falls.

That route begins with some of the up and down of the West Forks route, but soon moderates. A half-mile beyond the Chappell Bridge the trail runs along level intervale, and I break into a skate technique from time to time on my way to Long Falls Dam Road. There is climbing yet beyond the Road, on the way to the lakeshore. These two days offer a fine combination of rolling and level ski terrain.

Make your way from West Forks, or travel from Flagstaff Hut or Long Falls Dam Road. This is a place apart. See for yourself!

FIELD NOTES

Flagstaff Lake South, Round Barn Area, and Bigelow Lodge
Dead River Township

Ski or snowshoe. No fee. (Note: Bigelow Lodge is not an overnight facility, and is open for day use only on selected days. See article for details.)

Overview: Bigelow Preserve. One way 4.5 miles (9.0 miles round-trip) on groomed multiuse snowmobile trail (ITS Connector 115), with some ascents and descents, to the Safford Brook Trailhead, site of a summer parking area, and access by short driveways to the Round Barn site, and to Bigelow Lodge. The route is over the unplowed East Flagstaff Road from just past the Little Bigelow Trailhead, westward to the Safford Brook/Round Barn/Bigelow Lodge area.

During occasional winter seasons when the road is plowed for Preserve administrative use, the snowmobile trail parallels the road, at some points immediately adjacent and at other points out of sight. The snowmobile trail rejoins the road by the Bigelow Lodge-Round Barn vicinity.

The route is wooded with limited views until reaching the lakeshore near Round Barn where the views are outstanding. When the ice conditions on Flagstaff Lake are safe for travel, the ski or snowshoe trip can continue onto the lake, where more fine views await.

Round Barn is a summer tenting and carry-in boat launch area, on the site of a round-shaped barn that stood here in the days when the Dead River Valley was home to many farms. Although the barn burned in 1952, the spot continues to be referred to locally as "Round Barn". A beach area off the short campsite loop provides the views. This a good spot from which to ski or snowshoe onto the lake—ice conditions permitting.

Bigelow Lodge is accessed by a 0.1 mile access road, north of the Safford Brook Trailhead, by the near end of the summer parking area. This access road is a groomed snowmobile trail, and the route should be obvious. Pass a steel gate (open), a side trail on the right leading to the lake, and then an equipment shed, before reaching the Lodge which sits in a large clearing.

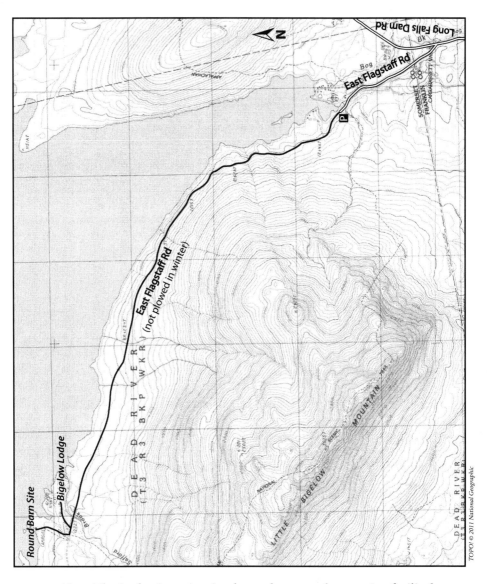

Note: The Lodge is maintained as a *day use only warming facility* by Maine Bureau of Public Lands on 10 winter weekends, beginning with the first weekend in January after the New Year. It is also open Monday-Friday during the week of the Presidents Day holiday in February. To confirm when the Lodge is open in a particular winter season: MBPL : 207-778-8231 (Western Regional Office); 207-287-3821 (Headquarters, Augusta).

The building was constructed at a time when the area was considered for a massive alpine ski area. The lodge reverted to its current use when the voters of Maine passed a ballot initiative in 1976 for the State to purchase the property and create the Bigelow Preserve.

While at the Lodge, have a look at the photographs on the walls from the days before Flagstaff Lake formed behind Long Falls Dam. Three communities occupied the valley—Flagstaff, Dead River Plantation, and Bigelow Plantation.

This is a magnificent area for an outing on cross-country skis or snowshoes. When considering whether to continue the outing by skiing out onto the lake, or to proceed farther along the snowmobile trail, be aware that there remains a 4.5 mile ski back to the parking area from Round Barn. Also, if you are thinking of returning to the parking area via the lake, be advised that the road in (E. Flagstaff Road) sits high above the lake, a steep quarter-mile back, and that the woods between the lake and the road are thick, and the snow untracked. This route would not be a short-cut!

Trailhead: East Flagstaff Road, a left turn (west) 17.4 miles north of North New Portland Village on the Long Falls Dam Road. The road sign may be missing. Watch for a row of mailboxes on the east side of the Long Falls Dam Road at this junction; and a small brown "Bigelow Preserve" sign about 100′ up the road and visible from Long Falls Dam Road.

Follow the East Flagstaff Road past the Maine Huts and Trails crossing, the Bog Brook Road (right), and the Carriage Road (left). The Carriage Road is not maintained for public winter vehicular travel. Continue past the Appalachian Trail crossing (Little Bigelow Trailhead) to a parking area on the left. Here the plowed portion of the road ends. The route continues west into the Bigelow Preserve as a multi-use—cross-country ski, snowshoe, snowmobile—trail for 4.5 miles to Round Barn.

Nearest town: North New Portland (store and diner; no gas). Nearest gas in Kingfield or Embden. (Recommend gas up before driving to this area.)

Maps: Delorme *Maine Atlas* Map #29, 5-C;
Bigelow Preserve Map, Maine Bureau of Public Lands;
"The Valley Below" map of Flagstaff Lake, Maine High Peaks and Flagstaff Area Business Association;
USGS: Little Bigelow

Elevation Gain: 100′

On Trail

Before me, where I stand on skis—lakeside and just off the groomed snowmobile trail—stretches the great white expanse of snow-covered Flagstaff Lake. I have the lake all to myself. The snow lies unbroken, pristine—not a single track of skis, snowshoes, or a snowmobile.

On this bright and clear winter morning the mountains and hills that rim the north and eastern shores of the lake stand in sharp relief: Flagstaff Mountain, Picked Chicken Hill (You know that there must be a good story behind that name!), Blanchard Mountain, Pierce Pond Mountain, and Round Top. Far to the north a snow squall billows, gauze-gray, across the skyline, scatters a white dusting in the vicinity of Spring Lake, and heads in the direction of Grand Falls.

Behind me rises the summit of Bigelow Mountain, Avery Peak, one of Maine's great high peaks at over 4000 feet in elevation. Its bare summit glistens in the full light of the morning sun in a cloudless sky. Behind Avery Peak, named for Myron Avery of Maine, one of the founders of the 2180 mile Appalachian Trail, rises its companion summit, West Peak. The rest of the great Bigelow Range trails westward a good ten miles, out of sight from my lakeside vantage point, to a gap near the village of Stratton. This range is one of the most spectacular mountain *massifs* east of the Rocky Mountains—and it is within a few minutes drive of most of Franklin County.

I reached this spot by skiing on the East Flagstaff Road, well-groomed as ITS Connector Snowmobile Trail 115. The trail is wide, and I had good opportunity to skate-ski on straight-a-ways, herring-bone the hills, and enjoy a well-earned run on the down hills. The snowmobile traffic is light, but I ski as if along a highway—keeping to the left. When I come here with a group, we travel single file, so as not to be strung out across the trail when a snowmobile approaches. This truly is a fine route for skiing, with a good mix of level terrain and skiable hills.

Back to the lake! With the lake to myself, and a light snow cover, I ski westward on snow-covered ice along the south shore, heading past the Round Barn camping area, around a small island just off-shore. Exploring a few coves, I discover that there have been other travelers—non-human—on the lake. Deer and coyote tracks emerge from the woods, head onto the lake, and disappear in wind-driven, packed snow. A great silence prevails, save for the rush of the wind through the spruce, fir, cedar, and pine along the shore. It is as fine a winter day as I have ever seen in Maine!

Far to the northwest, Hurricane Island, distinguished by towering pines, rises in the narrows of the lake like a ship at sea. It is 4.5 miles away—too far to add to my distance for today. I have paddled there many times in summer on a day trip, or to camp for the night.

I retrace my ski route, then, spying the roofline of a building rising on a bluff overlooking the south shore, I head inland for my intended lunch spot, Bigelow Lodge. Managed by the Maine Bureau of Parks and Lands, and located within the 30,000 acre Bigelow Preserve, Bigelow Lodge is a two-story building open to skiers, snowshoers, and snowmobilers, for winter day use on a select schedule. From January to mid-March, it is open Saturdays 10:00 a.m. to 4 p.m., and on Sundays 9:00 a.m. to 3:00 p.m. It is also open during the Maine public school vacation week in February, 10:00 a.m. to 4:00 p.m. (Note: Call the Maine Bureau of Public Lands before your trip to confirm the schedule for the current season.)

A friendly caretaker has a fire going in the great stone fireplace, and has coffee, tea, hot chocolate, and drinking water available. To replace a few of those calories burned on winter outings, there is an assortment of cookies and doughnuts out on a counter! Sit by the fire, or sit in the sunroom that looks northward towards the lake. Life is good.

The lodge is a true gem—a great rest spot on a winter outing. It is fortunate that the Bureau of Parks and Lands maintains this for public use. A special feature of the lodge is a wall display of old photographs of Flagstaff Village and the surrounding Dead River Valley region that was flooded when Long Falls Dam formed Flagstaff Lake in 1950. That display has recently been refurbished, and should not be missed.

On this day I choose to travel both ways on the road, which gives me time to explore a sizeable part of the lake west of Bigelow Lodge, that I might not have had time for otherwise. After my time on the lake, by returning on the groomed route over the East Flagstaff Road, I have a clear route back to where my truck is parked.

On another trip I ski with a friend out onto the lake as the red-orange sun drops in the west toward the height-of-land hills between Flagstaff and Rangeley Lakes. We turn to look in the opposite direction, eastward, over the lake. The great orb of a full moon, the color of a pale yellow rose, lifts into view in the gap between Round Top Mountain and Bates Ridge. For a moment both the sun and the full moon hang at opposite ends of Flagstaff Lake. The sun slips from sight into a red-orange sky. The moon, sky to itself now, rises higher, and brighter. This is a jaw-dropping moment.

What will you discover on your trip here?

Little Bigelow Mountain
Dead River Township

Snowshoe. No fee.

Overview: Bigelow Preserve. Appalachian Trail. 3.0 miles one-way (6.0 miles round-trip) to 3040′ peak at the east end of the Bigelow Range. Fine views south to Carrabassett Valley, and westward towards Sugarloaf. Exceptional viewpoint for Avery Peak. More views over southeast end of Flagstaff Lake, and eastward towards Poplar Mountain and the valley of Poplar Stream.

High meadows on route to the summit afford intermediate destinations with good views in the event that snow conditions make for slow hiking, or if a party wishes to have a hike shorter than the 6 mile round-trip. The summit itself is a long cliff-edge that extends westward, making it possible to extend a hike for additional views. The western end of the long summit area is 4.4 miles from the trailhead (8.8 miles round-trip).

Little Bigelow has become a popular snowshoe day hike as one of the more manageable winter ascents in the Bigelow Range, as most other peaks require long approaches and ascend more steeply to much higher elevations.

Note: The Appalachian Trail (southbound) intersects with the Safford Brook Trail at Safford Notch, 6.3 miles from the trailhead. The 2.5 miles Safford Brook Trail descends to the Round Barn area, from which it is 4.5 miles back to the Little Bigelow Trailhead by the East Flagstaff Road. This long route of 13.3 miles is not recommended, as trail-breaking will likely be necessary beyond Little Bigelow summit ridge and snow in Safford Notch may be quite deep.

Trailhead: East Flagstaff Road, a left turn (west) 17.4 miles north of North New Portland Village on the Long Falls Dam Road. The road sign may be missing. Watch for a row of mailboxes on the east side of the Long Falls Dam Road at this junction; and a small brown "Bigelow Preserve" sign about 100′ up the road and visible from Long Falls Dam Road.

Follow the East Flagstaff Road past the Maine Huts and Trails crossing, the Bog Brook Road (right), and the Carriage Road (left). The

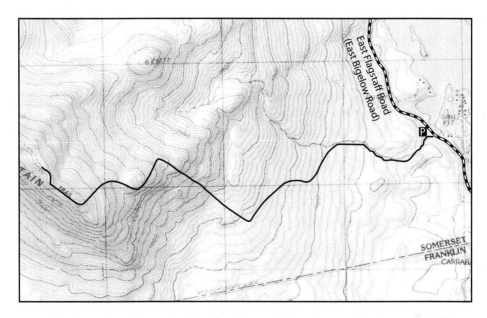

Carriage Road is not maintained for public winter vehicular travel. The Little Bigelow Trailhead is on the left side of the road, at the Appalachian Trail crossing. Watch for a sign and white paint blazes on trees.

Parking is in a plowed area on the right, across the road from the trailhead.

Nearest town: North New Portland (store and diner; no gas). Nearest gas in Kingfield or Embden. (Recommend gas up before driving to this area.)

Maps: Delorme *Maine Atlas* Map #29, 5-C;
Bigelow Preserve Map, Maine Bureau of Public Lands;
"The Valley Below" map of Flagstaff Lake, Maine High Peaks and Flagstaff Area Business Association.;
USGS: Little Bigelow.

Elevation Gain: 1970'

Maps: Delorme *Maine Atlas* Map #30, 2-E;
Maine Appalachian Trail Map #5, Kennebec River to Maine Highway 27;
Maine Huts and Trails System Map;
USGS: Little Bigelow

On Trail

A hiking friend and I set out on one of the last days of March to hike Little Bigelow before spring thaws soften the deep snowpack. We find the trail well-tramped down at the trailhead, and briefly consider hiking without snowshoes, but think better of it. If the day warms enough, we may sink in the snow—and if those who hiked ahead of us turn around short of where we wish to, we would have a hard go of things. We wear our snowshoes. These provide more stability in conditions like those we face, even if not absolutely necessary just yet.

It is a glorious day, with full sun. A Blue Jay protests our presence. Chick-a-dees fly nearby, fly off. Tracks of hare cross the trail. This is transition hardwood-softwood forest—bare maple, white birch, yellow birch, and beech; pointed fir and spruce. Trees shine in the early brightness. Beech provides the most color—coppery-gold parchment leaves flutter in a light breeze, hanging on until the new green growth of the spring season unfolds.

The trail rises gradually at first, crosses an unplowed woods road, and parallels Bog Brook briefly as it climbs the east end of the Bigelow Range. In just under an hour, at 1.3 miles, we reach the 0.1 mile side trail that leads to the Little Bigelow Lean-to, an Adirondack-style shelter. I have camped here in summer, and on both overnight and day hikes have enjoyed a bracing dip into the "bath-tubs" in the upper reaches of Bog Brook below the lean-to. This is not a day for dips in a brook—and we pass by the side trail, continue upwards.

Ascending steadily, the trail reaches the first of a series of open ledges and small meadows. The first views are of the glacier-scoured ponds to the east of the range. At higher points we have views into the southeast cove of Flagstaff Lake where Bog Brook enters the lake, and east and northeast towards Stewart Mountain and Roundtop Mountain. There is a glimpse of the Long Falls Road. Otherwise, the north woods run to the horizon, largely unbroken.

Farther along, more ledge and meadows, well-buried in the deep snow, offer more views, and the view-shed opens south and west to take in the Bigelow Range, Sugarloaf and Burnt Mountains, and the Carrabassett River and Poplar Stream Valleys. Striking a view it is always, and particularly so on this bright winter day.

We pass other hikers, who have hiked to one side of a clearing to have lunch and take in the view. This is the snowshoe equivalent of spring skiing—a sharply-bright day, temperatures rising into the 40s, long views, lunch in a sun-warmed spot. Life is good. Soon we stop at a farther high point, pull out swatches of closed cell foam for seats on the snow, and do our own kicking-back, have our lunch.

There will be days of wind and snowstorm, overcast and fog—but this is not one of them!

We descend as I so often do—reluctantly! But we are grateful for a fine hike on a pristine day. On the way down we snowshoe-ski a bit on the warmed snow-pack, glad now that we kept our snowshoes. By the time we reach the trailhead, the day has the feel of a fine maple sap-running day. I am off for home to tend my sap buckets. I will be boiling for syrup before the day is over.

Early winter, mid-winter, late winter, early spring—put Little Bigelow on the snowshoe hike list!

Cranberry Peak
Coplin and Wyman Plantations

Snowshoe. No fee.

Overview: Bigelow Range. Bigelow Range Trail. 2.5 miles one-way (5.0 mile round-trip) snowshoe hike ascends the steep southwestern end of the Bigelow Range to outlooks at Cranberry Ledges, and beyond to the 3213′ open summit of Cranberry Peak. The ledges offer views and a turn-around point for a shorter hike. Outstanding views up the Bigelow Range of the Horns of Bigelow and West Peak, with occasional views of Avery Peak, partly hidden by West Peak. Extensive views over Flagstaff Lake, northward to border mountains with Quebec. More views towards Sugar-loaf, the Crocker Mountains, and the High Peaks region in general.

Trailhead: Currie Street, Stratton Village, just north of the Eustis/Coplin Town Line, off Maine Highway 27. One street north of Appalachian Street. Watch for a brown sign for the Bigelow Range Trail, with a hiker logo. The street is usually plowed to accommodate residences. Trailhead is 0.3 miles beyond the last residence driveway, up a hill and beyond to an open area. *Please do not block this road.* If there are multiple vehicles in the party, consider consolidating passengers and leaving extra vehicles in Stratton Village. If there is no room to park, inquire of nearby businesses or walk from town.

Nearest Town: Stratton Village in the Town of Eustis.

Elevation Gain: 2300′

On Trail

Cranberry Peak in the Bigelow Range, near Stratton, in Northern Franklin County, offers an outstanding winter hiking destination. The round-trip of a little over 5 miles offers fine views in all directions from an intermediate look-out point at the western end of the Range, and from the bare summit.

On the early winter day that I choose for my snowshoe hike, winter is trying to make up its mind whether to make a complete entrance, or continue a pattern of snowing then melting, snowing, melting. I begin with winter hiking boots, but I am packing both snowshoes and flexible boot crampons.

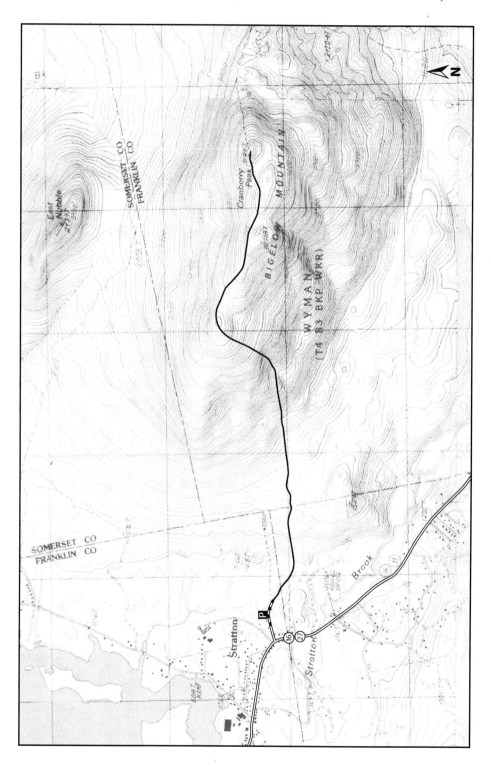

When I start from the Currie Street parking area at the southwest side of the mountain, I enjoy October-like conditions, with low-angle sun playing on the deep green fir, spruce, hemlock, and pine, and filtering through the bare hardwoods to brighten the leaf cover on the forest floor. This section enjoys southern exposure, and recent snows have largely melted.

But when the trail swings around to the north side, shaded from the sun, I will be in a land of ice and snow! This side of the mountain will not know the rays of the sun for months to come. Fortunately, I have those flexible boot crampons to pull over the soles of my winter boots.

The blue-blazed trail climbs steadily through a mixed hardwood and softwood forest, heading east at first, then more northerly until it reaches the curiously named Panberry Creek, a play on "Cranberry Peak." Here the trail makes a sharp right turn to climb towards the west end of the ridge. As I move higher in elevation I encounter the first patches of snow. There will be more!

An hour into the hike I reach the foot of Cranberry Ledges, and Arnold's Well, a spring located well down in a crevice. On summer hikes I have seen ice in the spring; on this winter day ice again covers the surface of the spring. Keeping silence, I hear the drip-drip of melt water as the sun, low as it is, beams through the trees to warm the opening in the forest where the spring lay.

Just above this point and just to the right of the trail are high ledges that afford views down the valley of the Carrabassett, and across to Sugarloaf Mountain—which, incidentally, at 4327' is the highest mountain in Maine outside of Baxter and Hamlin Peaks on Mount Katahdin. This is a good lunch spot, but the hour is early. I aim for Cranberry Peak itself for my mid-day break.

To avoid a rough scramble over the irregular ledges that mark the ridge top, the trail turns north and drops down from the high ground, before heading east again, paralleling the ridge. Here I enter a wholly different season—snow and ice completely covers the sun-sheltered trail. The trail is mighty slippery.

After a few yards of balancing acts, I stop to attach crampons to my boots. I have a sturdy type that has the type of sharp points found on mountaineering crampons, but held together by a tough but flexible rubber link so that they may be used on typical hiking boots. A tightening strap holds them snugly. I have my trekking poles, to which I have attached snow baskets for winter travel. So equipped, I make my way along the trail, scrambling up and over the boulders so common to the Bigelow Range, and continue to progress toward Cranberry Peak.

After one half-hour of hiking from the vicinity of Arnold's Well and Cranberry Ledges, I come to a point where the trail makes a 45-degree angle turn to the right, and makes a beeline for the summit. The route leaves the woods and the low scrub around the summit, to emerge on the summit ledges. The views are outstanding! Northeast, along the Bigelow Range, rise the Horns of Bigelow, and beyond these, West Peak, which may partially hide Avery Peak beyond, depending upon one's vantage point. To the south rises Sugarloaf and Burnt Mountains. Flagstaff Lake, snow covered, shows its crooked expanse to the north of the Bigelow Range. Straight north rise the mountains along the boundary with Quebec.

Cranberry Peak is the most accessible of the Bigelow Range Peaks in winter—lower in elevation than its high-rising neighbors farther along the Range, yet offering a 360 degree view. The location of the trailhead, just off Maine Highway 27, is convenient. On the mountain, the route over snow and ice to the summit offers an authentic winter ascent.

Obtain a copy of the map "The Valley Below" from the High Peaks Visitors Information Center in Carrabassett Valley, on Highway 27, near the Airport—or contact Maine High Peaks <www.mainehighpeaks.com> Flagstaff Area Business Association <www.eustismaine.org>. This map depicts Flagstaff Lake and the former towns of Flagstaff, Dead River, and Bigelow, which were flooded when the Long Falls Dam went into operation in 1950, creating the lake.

I come to the Bigelow Range often. Hike Cranberry to see why!

Carrabassett Valley-Sugarloaf Region

Major features of this region are the valley of the Carrabassett River, the great *massif* of Sugarloaf Mountain, highest mountain range in Maine after the summits of Mount Katahdin, the Maine Huts and Trails System access to foothills of the Bigelow Range, and stream-side trails.

Maine Huts and Trails maintains two full service huts here: the Stratton Brook Hut sits atop 1880' Oak Knoll, and Poplar Hut, a 15–20 minute hike from two sets of Poplar Stream waterfalls.

The Sugarloaf Outdoor Center (SOC) is a major, four-season recreation center offering 90 kilometers of groomed Nordic trails—the largest Nordic Center in Maine. There is an extensive network of marked snowshoe trails.

Sugarloaf Outdoor Center   120

Stratton Brook Hut and Oak Knoll   126

Poplar Stream and Poplar Hut   134

South Poplar Stream Falls   140

Narrow Gauge Pathway   144

Crommett Trail   150

Dead River, Grand Falls - West Forks
Dead River & Grand Falls Hut - LFD

Flagstaff Hut & Flagstaff Lake East Shore
Flagstaff Lake Round Barn
Little Bigelow Mtn.

Cranberry Peak
Crommett Trail
Stratton Brook Hut & Oak Knoll
Poplar Hut & Poplar Stream Falls
Narrow Gauge Pathway

Bonney Point
Hunter Cove
Hatchery Brook

Sugarloaf Outdoor Ct.

Long Falls Dam Road

Rangeley Lakes Trail Ctr.
Rangeley
Bald Mt.
Rock & Midway
Ponds
South Bog Trail
Piazza Rock
Low Aziscohos
Oberton & Hardy Streams
Fly Rod Crosby Trail

Little Jackson Mt.
Blueberry Mt.
Tumbledown Pond & Tumbledown Mt.
Byron Road
Center Hill
Mount Blue
Sandy Rvr
Intervale
Powderhouse Hill
Farmington
Titcomb Mt.
Bald Mt.
Wilton

27 · 16 · 16 · 16 · 16 · 27 · 16 · 142 · 16 · 17 · 4 · 27 · 142 · 4 · 17 · 156 · 2 · 27 · 142 · 156 · 2 · 4

Sugarloaf Outdoor Center
Carrabassett Valley

Ski or snowshoe. Fee. Food. Rentals. Lessons.

Overview: The Sugarloaf Outdoor Center is a major center for cross-country skiing and snowshoeing, with 90 kilometers of ski trails groomed for both classic and skate skiing, and an extensive network of marked snowshoe trails. (There is also an outdoor ice rink with an artificial ice surface, and skate rentals are available.) Outings here may circle in close proximity to the lodge, or extend well up onto a shoulder of Burnt Mountain for a back-country experience of many miles.

Both the ski and the snowshoe trail systems offer choices from level and gently rolling terrain, to steady ascents and long-running descents. Trails are well-marked, and ski trails are marked as Easier, More Difficult, and Most Difficult.

The trail system connects with the Sugarloaf alpine ski area, making it possible for parties staying in on-mountain accommodations to access the Outdoor Center without driving.

Ski or snowshoe for an hour, or for the day. I have enjoyed remarkable wildlife viewing and animal track discoveries here. Steadily ascending trails in the direction of Burnt Mountain afford fine long views from high look-out points. Trails in the immediate area of the lodge look directly out to Sugarloaf—one of the more dramatic views in the region.

The Center usually has snow early in the season, and the snow tends to remain late in the season. I have enjoyed skiing here in early December and in April as well.

The lodge hosts the ticket counter, equipment shop and rental service, lesson headquarters, a snack bar, a great room, and toilets. Trail conditions, rates, and other information: 207-237-6830 or <www.sugarloaf.com>.

Trailhead: One mile south of the Sugarloaf Access Road, on Maine Highway 27 (sign). Drive 0.6 miles to the parking area. Lodge is on the far side of the outdoor ice rink. Entire trail system may be accessed from the lodge.

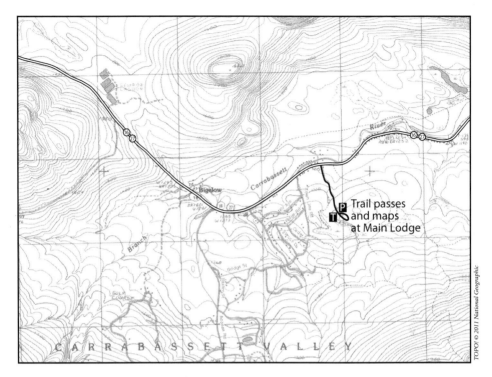

Trail passes and maps at Main Lodge

TOPO! © 2011 National Geographic

Maps: Delorme *Maine Atlas* Map #29, C,D-4;
   Sugarloaf Outdoor Center Trail Map;
   USGS: Sugarloaf Mountain

Nearest Town: Carrabassett Valley. Services located along Highway 27, clustering near the Sugarloaf Access Road, and in the vicinity of the Sugarloaf Airport.

On Trail

With 90 kilometers of groomed trails—that is over 55 *miles*—the Sugarloaf Outdoor Center in Carrabassett Valley provides Nordic ski access to a wide range of Maine forest and mountain terrain in the High Peaks region. To the west, visible from time-to-time through breaks in the forest cover, rises the great mountain mass of Sugarloaf, Maine's second highest mountain range at an elevation of 4237 feet. Nordic skiers make their way literally and figuratively, in the shadow of Sugarloaf and its nearby peak, the 3595-foot Burnt Mountain.

I have skied on the Center trail system for over 20 years, and make it my destination when I want to put in a good 4–5 hours on trail, be able to climb high for long views, and enjoy long downhill runs on the return. But the Center is also a good choice for those who are learning the Nordic technique—or simply want a quiet outing over gentle ground. Easier trails, fairly level or gradually rising and descending, pass by Moose Bog and Pretty Bog, or wind through a classic foothill forest of fir, white birch, rock maple, beech, and the occasional white pine.

Most of these easier trails, color-coded in green on the trail map, and on signage, are arranged in loops that provide close access to the main Lodge, with its gathering room and Bull Moose Café. More challenging routes ascend or cross the lower slopes of Burnt Mountain. Their blue or black color coding identifies these as More Difficult or Most Difficult, respectively, making route planning a straightforward process. The Main Lodge has trail maps, and these maps provide a good many suggested loops based upon the level of difficulty a skier chooses.

One mid-winter day, when the Sugarloaf area had enjoyed a fresh 2″ snowfall the night before, I head for the Center with two destinations in mind. One was Redington Pond, a 64-acre pond at the eastern extreme of the trail system. (Note that this is not Franklin County's *other* Redington Pond, which is located in Redington Township, northeast of the Saddleback Range.) Another destination is a 2000′ elevation shoulder of Burnt Mountain, the highest point on the trail system, and a good 600′ climb from the Lodge.

Expecting to be well away from the Lodge for my outing I carry a day pack with lunch, water, hot tea, spare mitts and spare neck warmer, along with my usual just-in-case gear: headlamp, extra long-sleeve wicking t-shirt, lip balm, duct tape, small multi-purpose tool, note pad, and camera. These items weigh very little—and can mean the difference between having the capacity to make a repair, or change into drier gear—or face a long chilly trek back. To be sure, I rarely have need of these, but over the years they have come in handy either for me or for another skier along the way—so I carry them as standard gear.

To warm up I start on the green (easier) loop around Moose Bog. I am one of the first people on trail that morning, and enjoy setting out on unbroken trail after that fresh snowfall. I had not skied a hundred feet when I encounter my ski trail version of "Oh-My-Gosh Corner", with a striking view of Sugarloaf as I cross the earthen dam at the outlet of Moose Bog. Two loops around the bog warm me up and provide some gentle stretching. Now I am off to Redington Pond.

The route to Redington Pond is listed as one of the easier trails, coded green, and is one of a number of suggested loops designated on the SOC trail system map. This loop covers 11 kilometers, just under 7 miles. I chose my own, more indirect route to the pond, slabbing my way to a point above the pond by taking a number of blue-coded (more difficult) trials, thereby to explore the trail system.

Such a day! Fresh snow, bright rich light from the low-lying winter sun, and a profound quiet. The muffled crunch and squeak of skis on snow, and the light puffing of my own breathing, are the only sounds on this winter morning. I will see other skiers on trail this day, but with my early start I have the trail to myself this far.

I approach Redington Pond from above, crossing the outlet stream over a ski trail bridge, reaching a narrow, ungroomed side-trail in about 100 yards. This side trail is fairly obvious, but has no sign. The pond itself is just barely visible through the trees. Ski tracks, half-covered from the new snowfall indicate that others had gone before me, though not yet on this day. In 50 yards I reach the shore.

Wow! Redington Pond lies in full sun, the snow cover unbroken. A picnic table sits at pond edge, its surface free of snow. I enjoy a food break—my standard peanut butter and jelly sandwich on homemade bread, washed down with hot tea. My face warms in the ever-higher lifting sun. Life is good.

Refueled, I set out to ski the perimeter of the pond, breaking trail. I checked the ice, of course. After weeks of freezing temperatures, the pond ice is solid beneath the snow. Off I go, a kid in a candy store, sliding my skis through pristine snow on a day turned bright and clear.

I pass a beaver lodge, occupants surely enjoying a long winter's nap, with occasional forays out to resupply from the food supply of gnawed hardwood branches and saplings felled in the weeks leading up to winter. Near the far shore I discover coyote tracks, distinguished by their determined straight line, and a 4–5 foot span from leading to trailing paw prints.

As I look out to scan the pond for the direction of the track—another discovery! On the northern horizon, high above the forested pond-side, rises the Bigelow Range. Avery and West Peak, both over 4000' high, their snow-covered rocky summit ridges bright white in the sun. West of these summits rises South Horn, with a shoulder of North Horn barely visible beyond. Quite a view, and quite a perspective. This expansive view had been behind me, until I turned to look back across the pond. For a moment I have a strong sense of place. Here I am, a solitary figure on skis, on a high Maine pond, those high peaks trailing across the edge of the northern sky—not a building, not one other person, in sight.

More discovery! Another set of tracks, web prints on a "half-pipe" trail, as though the creature had pulled a sagging belly over the snow. This is a beaver track. I have seen them before, but they are a rare find in winter. Following the track for a hundred yards, I come to the mound of another snow-covered beaver lodge. Here the tracks end at two holes in the snow, each about about 6″ in diameter. The tracks look very fresh—certainly put down after the fresh snowfall of the night before. Quite a find!

I complete my perimeter ski of Redington Pond, and head back onto the trail system for my next destination of the day, the highest point on the trail system, a shoulder of Burnt Mountain. Route 50, black-coded as "Most Difficult" is the route to the high ground. Fortunately I am well into the ski season and have built up some conditioning—the trail is steady-steep.

Up, up I go, sometimes stepping, sometimes skating, and often using the herring-bone technique to gain elevation. As I puff along, I notice the forest growth to change from mixed softwood-hardwood to a predominant spruce and fir forest, typical of higher elevations. Suddenly a ruffed grouse bursts out of a trail-side mound of snow, scattering fresh powder—and startling me! My heart pounds! Grouse are known for that—no warning, just an explosion of snow, and a bird shoots across the trail, and out of sight.

Mainly I was sorry to have disturbed that creature's rest! Grouse hunker down in the snow for warmth as their way of managing the Maine winter. I continue on, mindful of how there is a great cycle of life in these mountains, life always going forward here—that of the coyote, the beaver, the grouse, and all else.

Finally I top out at the high point of the trail. The spot is marked by a junction with a snowshoe trail from the Main Lodge. This blue-blazed trail provides access to a hiking trail by which one could ascend even higher onto the slopes of Burnt Mountain. I pause here, take in my surroundings, the faint smell of fir on the slight wind. I stand, look, listen, catch my breath, have a drink of water, enjoy the sweet crunch of a Macintosh apple.

Now the fun—or more fun—begins. I turn my skis downhill and away I go, down, down, down—all that climbing rewarded with a long, long, downhill run. On steep pitches I use a modified snowplow; otherwise I let the skis run. This is Nordic ski "candy"!

The winding trail swings north opening a view to South Horn on the Bigelow Range. The perfect cone peak rises a speckled white and green against a bright blue sky. I continue my downward run, reaching the lower trail system, and after one of the most enjoyable runs of this or any winter season, I reach the Main Lodge.

There I make one more discovery—of a human kind. Dozens of school-age children have come to the Trail Center for their own outing. Some are on skis, others skate on the rink. I am glad to see kids here, where they may draw close to the world of the forest and the mountains in winter, and thereby learn many a fine life-lesson, make their own discoveries, enjoy life-long sports.

My own outing, including the stop at Redington Pond, has lasted a bit over four hours. I am weary, but find it hard to leave after such a fine day. As it is, I have covered only a small portion of the SOC terrain—and that is why I return here, year after year. I head for home, and will be back.

FIELD NOTES

Oak Knoll and Stratton Brook Hut
Maine Huts and Trails
Carrabassett Valley

Ski or snowshoe. No fee for trail use. Lodging/meals cost. Optional "Day Membership" available. (Day Membership is one way of contributing to MHT, but is not required. Contact MHT for details.)

Overview: 2.9 miles one-way (5.8 miles round trip) ski or snowshoe route to 1880′ elevation ridge-top hut, located in a clearing bordered by a stand of Red Oak. This is the highest elevation of all huts in the MHT system at this writing. Outstanding views northward of the Bigelow Range, including the High Peaks of West Peak and Avery Peak; and south to Sugarloaf and Burnt Mountains. An alternate route, the Oak Knoll snowshoe trail, offers outlook points to the northwest and west, including the East Kennebago Range, and the 4000′ Crocker peaks, North and South.

Variety of day and overnight use itineraries possible in the area, including up and back ski or snowshoe hikes, snowshoe ascent by one route, and descent by the other; and access to connecting trails of the MHT System.

The name of the hut derives from its *overlook* of Stratton Brook and Stratton Brook Ponds, located 1000′ of elevation below the hut, and 2.0 miles distant.

The 2.9 mile groomed ski and snowshoe trail begins on the level terrain of the former Narrow Gauge Railway bed; then climbs steadily, and in the final 0.9 mile, steeply, to reach the hut via the Newton's Revenge Trail. Oak Knoll Trail departs Newton's Revenge 0.3 miles from the Narrow Gauge Pathway to ascend steadily to a high plateau, traverse around the western slope of the knoll, then climbs to a superb northwest lookout point before ending at the hut.

Stratton Brook Hut is a full service lodge offering overnight accommodations, meals, and hot showers. Contact MHT for rates, services by season, trail conditions, and gear recommendations. No charge for use of the trail system. Day visitors may purchase hot lunch in certain seasons at specified hours of the day, and may resupply drinking water.

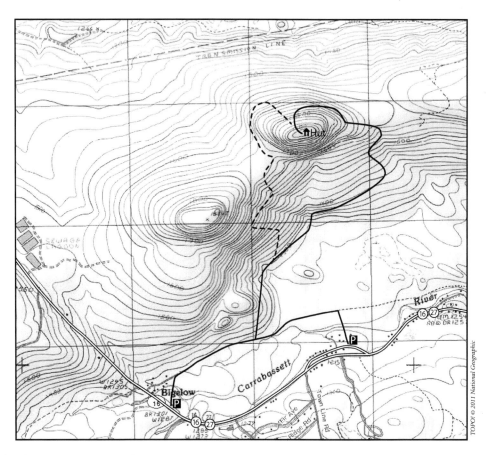

Elevation Gain: 600′

Trailhead: Stratton Brook Hut Trailhead, with plowed parking, is 0.1 mile
north of the Sugarloaf Access Road, off Maine Highway 27 (sign). There
is a trail kiosk.

Nearest Town: Carrabassett Valley

Maps: Delorme *Maine Atlas* Map #29, 4-C;
Maine Huts and Trails System Map;
USGS: Sugarloaf Mountain

On Trail

Once unknown to all but a few locals, the ridge which is now the site of the
Stratton Brook Hut of Maine Huts and Trails—so-called "Oak Knoll"—has
become one of the more popular on-foot winter destinations in the High Peaks

region. The uphill trek by snowshoes or skis from Maine Highway 27 affords fine views of Sugarloaf and Burnt Mountain to the south as the 2.9 miles trail winds its way upward toward the Hut. In the last mile of the ascent, the great west-to-east sweep of the Bigelow Range commands the view. Cranberry Peak, South Horn, West Peak, Avery Peak, and Little Bigelow rise impressively out of the unbroken forest of the Bigelow Preserve, each with a distinctive configuration. This is a remarkable spot!

Lest there be any misunderstanding, the route to the ridge top and to Stratton Brook Hut is an ascent—a climb! Yes—heading *up*, to a Hut named for a brook! The name for the hut, highest in the Maine Huts System at 1880 feet, and fourth of the Huts to be constructed, derives from its fine view of Stratton Brook, 500 feet of elevation below. The Brook is distinguished by a broad serpentine pond, where the flowage pauses in stillwater before rushing northwestward to skirt the western end of the Bigelow Range, and flow into Flagstaff Lake.

I have skied up to the hut many times, made the ascent on snowshoes, and also hiked this route in the summer season. The trip is a fine choice for a day outing, and, of course, it is possible to make the Hut a base for further day trips by staying overnight. MHT continues to add to its trail system, with both long-distance routes, and short trails in the vicinity of each hut.

The main route to the Hut from the Stratton Brook Hut Trailhead is the Newton's Revenge Trail, reached from the Narrow Gauge Pathway. An alternative for snowshoes only is the Oak Knoll Trail, which leaves Newton's Revenge 0.6 mile north of the Narrow Gauge junction. Oak Knoll Trail ascends the ridge from the northwest, meeting Newton's Revenge Trail near the Hut. This snowshoe route (available for mountain biking in summer) offers extensive views towards the northwest peaks of Franklin County, taking in the high peaks of North and South Crocker, the East Kennebago Range, and beyond.

Trailhead for the Stratton Brook Hut is 0.1 mile north of the Sugarloaf Access Road, off Maine Highway 27 (sign). There is a trail information kiosk here, with a map display. I carry my own copy of the Maine Huts and Trails (MHT) System map. These (free) maps are widely available at Franklin County information points, stores and motels, and from <www.mainehuts.org>.

Know where you are in the Maine woods! A map is standard equipment for well-prepared hikers. Diamond shaped markers indicate the main trails, and there are mileage signs at trail junctions.

I make my most recent trip on snowshoes on a clear, brisk winter day when the temperature at trailhead was 10 degrees Fahrenheit—perfect conditions. The trail is groomed for skate-skiing and classic-track skiing, as well as for snowshoe travelers. I head out on trail from the north end of the parking lot, take a sharp left turn after 0.1 mile, then cross a bridge spanning a tributary to the Carrabassett River. The dark blue-black water courses its way through ice that has marched out from the shore in the course of the winter. Another 0.2 miles of easy travel, and I reach the Narrow Gauge Pathway, where the route turns right (sign). Visible to the far left of this junction are a few buildings at what was

once Bigelow Station. This location was the northern terminus of the railroad line which connected the timber-rich north country with Farmington, 40 miles to the south. What was once a working railway route is now a fine four-season recreation route for non-motorized travel—and one of my favorite places to ski, snowshoe, hike, and bike.

The Narrow Gauge former railbed extends 6.0 miles to the village center of Carrabassett Valley, near the Town Office, running parallel to the Carrabassett River which is visible for much of that distance. I have enjoyed many a fine winter day skiing the Pathway itself—sometimes for a one-way ski by spotting vehicles, or as a round-trip. The Pathway serves as a MHT route to its Poplar Hut and points beyond—and is also part of the Sugarloaf Outdoor Center trail system. The gentle grade of the route makes it ideal for skate or classic skiing. Skate and glide, kick and glide—the terrain here can be as good as it ever gets anywhere for cross-country skiing.

The woods are pristine and still. The tracks of hare, fox, and squirrel mark otherwise unbroken snow trailside. Before the day is over I will see wild turkey tracks—but not the quirky birds themselves. Two Blue Jays cross overhead, alight on separate branches of a white birch, have a look at me, and remain uncharacteristically quiet. No "Thief! Thief!" scream today. Perhaps it is too cold,— or too breathing-taking? A red squirrel, regular coniferous forest dweller, nibbles a pine cone, perks up as I near, fakes right, darts left, scampers up a tree and out of sight.

After 15–20 minutes on snowshoes I reach the trail junction for the Newton's Revenge Trail to ascend the remaining 2.2 miles and 500' of elevation, to the ridge-top site of Stratton Brook Hut. The curious name for the trail is linked to Isaac Newton, 1643–1717, a physicist and mathematician considered to the greatest scientist of his time. There is nothing in Newton's biography about skiing or snowshoeing, but he is credited with the scientific theory of gravity. As I worked my way upward to the highest point in the Maine Huts System, I admit that I did, from time to time, have a heightened awareness of gravity!

On fairly level to gently rising terrain, I pass an old log yard, then across the southern base of the ridge. The ridge-top itself is visible, but the Hut has been carefully sited to offer fine views, but to fit in so well with the surrounding forest, of red oak, maple, and fir, that it is generally not visible until you come upon it at the very top. Soon I see to my right a stand of cedar rise in what would be a three-season damp area, well-snow covered and frozen in winter. To the left old twitch trails head up the slope, among beech young trees that have prospered in the light-filled forest following wood harvests. They are the last of the hardwoods to let go of their parchment-like leaves that glow in the rich winter sunlight. I pass a trail marker indicating 2.0 miles remaining to the Hut, and in 0.1 mile beyond a snowshoe (and biking) route, flagged with blue tape, heads up one of these twitch trails. That will be my route on the way down. On the way up I continue, on a steady grade, on Newton's Revenge.

A prominent glacial erratic boulder rests trailside at the bottom of a short pitch, at about the half-way point of the route. When I top this, the trail levels out a bit. I enjoy a westward view of Sugarloaf and Burnt Mountains through the trees. To the south runs the valley of the Carrabassett River. Along this trail section rise white ash with their furrowed bark, interspersed with rock maple, and occasional yellow birch. More boulders line the slopes, some snow-blanketed, others bare and rough-gray from exposure to the winter sun.

The trail begins its steepest ascent after I reach a trail junction 0.9 miles below the top. Newton's Revenge climbs left in a serpentine route, passing large pine and hemlock, swinging back and forth, west to east, with alternating views of Sugarloaf and the Bigelow Range.

The other trail at the afore-mentioned junction heads south 3.0 miles along a shoulder of the ridge, descending moderately to join the Narrow Gauge Pathway 0.9 miles west of the Airport Trailhead spur trail. The trail continues past the Airport spur to the MHT Poplar Hut. The stretch of trail between Newton's Revenge and the narrow gauge junction route is referred to locally as the Crommett Trail.

The Crommett designation derives from a viewpoint with picnic table 1.1 miles down the trail, honoring the late Dick Crommett of the Carrabassett Valley Outdoor Association—an advocate for outdoor recreation in the Western Maine Mountains. At its southern end this trail is known to some people as the Narrow Gauge Bypass, but I rarely hear that reference. To avoid confusion, check the map.

This trail opens up a number of possibilities for skiers and snowshoers, serving as an alternate route to Poplar Hut, and an alternate route—though a far longer one—back to the trailhead on Route 27. Consult the map, and check with the folks at MHT if considering this long route for a day trip.

I often ski from the Airport Trailhead to Stratton Brook Hut via the Narrow Gauge and Newton's Revenge—then return by the Crommett Trail and that last 0.9 section of the Narrow Gauge. That near-loop is level to ascending on the way in, and mostly a long downhill run—just under 5 miles—on the way out. (Note: See the separate "Crommett Trail" entry in this book for details.)

Let's go! From the "Crommett Trail" junction, the trail swings left and begins a steady climb. My snowshoes have built-in crampons. These provide good grip on the slope. I have trekking poles as well, with snow baskets. When I have climbed this section on skis I have alternated between herring bone ascent, and skating. Take your time. Enjoy the surroundings. The trail is wide, well-groomed, and well-marked. When descending on skis, the reward for the hike up is that gravity can then become your friend. Do ski in control on the way down, alert to those who are hiking or skiing upwards towards you. In icy conditions I have removed my skis for short stretches of the downhill, to avoid injury, and to protect the base of my skis.

But I am still ascending. The heights of the ridge fascinate me with peculiar rock outcrops, the proximity of high country firs with towering red oaks—and of course the view of the Bigelow Range. One more turn and I reach the Hut—two wings joined by a porch, firewood stacked outside, and the warm smell of the kitchen within. Day hikers are welcome with no charge. Hot soup is available for purchase in season, along with baked goods. I have packed my own lunch this day, but do not pass up the generously-sized home-made apple squares that beckon in the dining area.

Caretaker for this day, Scott, welcomes me. He is from Georgia, and has hiked the high peaks of the Southern Appalachians in Georgia, North Carolina, Tennessee, and Virginia, as have I, and we share mountain stories. We also share our appreciation for this setting with its overlook of the spectacular Bigelow Range.

Warmed, fed, and appreciative of good conversation, I pack up for my snowshoe hike down. I choose the Oak Knoll Trail. This route begins with a short, less-than-5-minute, walk on a side trail to a viewpoint overlooking Stratton Brook and Pond, far below. The view is striking—not a human-made structure in sight. From the watercourse far, far below, my eye runs up the slopes of the Bigelow Range, first through a forest largely of bare hardwoods, then to the fir and spruce of the high ground, finally to the distinctive shapes of the many peaks—anvil-like Cranberry Peak, the near perfect cone of South Horn, the high rising West Peak, the bare summit of Avery Peak. Quite a sight.

I make my way down, my tracks the first on this day. My descent begins in north-side shade, but soon I swing around to the west to welcome the full light of the sun, now riding just above the summit of Sugarloaf. Down, down, I go, following a route set on old twitch trails. There are more beech trees glowing trailside, the mass of Sugarloaf and Burnt Mountain straight ahead. I regain Newton's Revenge and the Narrow Gauge, reaching my vehicle at the trailhead in just under 90 minutes—about the same time I took to make my way to the to the top, for a total of 3 hours on trail. When I have skied to the Hut and back, all the way on Newton's Revenge, I have covered the round-trip in about 2 hours. This does not count time at the Hut—and you will likely want to spend some time there.

FIELD NOTES

Poplar Stream and Poplar Hut
Maine Huts and Trails
Carrabassett Valley

Ski or Snowshoe. No fee for trail use. Lodging/meal cost. Optional "Day
Membership" available. (Day Membership is one way of contributing to
MHT, but is not required. Contact MHT for details.)

Overview: Ski or snowshoe to this full-service lodge located in a clearing on
the north slope of Little Poplar Mountain, about 15 minutes from two
major waterfalls—one on Poplar Stream, the other on South Poplar
Stream. Airport Trailhead to Poplar Hut is 3.2 miles one-way (6.4 miles
round-trip) over groomed trail. Route is generally a steady ascent, with a
few level stretches and a quick drop to the cross the Carriage Road. The
reverse route offers a long downhill run.

The route is forested throughout its length, passing through a hardwood-softwood mix of maple, beech, yellow birch, white birch and
ash—and fir, spruce, hemlock, cedar and pine. At its upper end, there are
views through the trees of Little Bigelow Mountain.

*Note: The Gauge Road Trailhead closed on Fall 2014, and the 0.7 mile
spur between that trailhead and the MHT trail between Stratton Brook Hut
and Poplar Hut is no longer maintained. The Airport Trailhead is now the
closest to Poplar Hut.*

Many visitors combine a hike or ski to the Hut with a hike to one
or both Poplar Stream area waterfalls. Because the falls are reached by
snowshoe trails—not groomed ski trails—I describe a snowshoe hike
directly to the falls in the next chapter *Poplar Stream Falls*, via Larry's
Trail.

However, the distance to either falls from the main MHT groomed
ski trail is not far—0.1 to South Falls and 0.3 to the Main Falls. When
the trail is well-packed I have removed skis and hiked in my boots. In
deep snow this would be difficult. Hut staff can advise skiers about a falls
hike.

Another trip using the Hut as a base, would be 1.8 miles one-way (3.6
miles round-trip) north of the Hut, in the direction of Flagstaff Hut, to

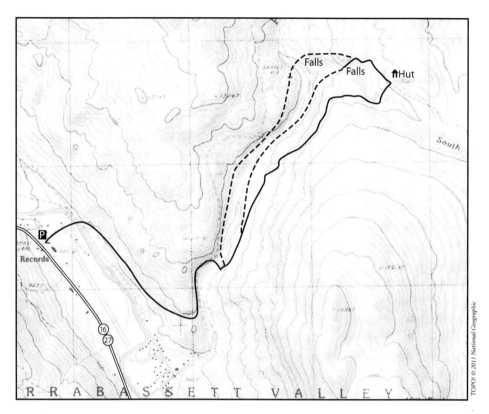

a small pond and bridged stream-crossing. Here there is an end view of Little Bigelow Mountain.

Poplar Hut, first hut in the MHT System is a full service, fee-charging, lodge offering overnight accommodations, meals, and hot showers. Day use at no charge, with drinking water available, and hot lunch in season at scheduled hours. Contact MHT for rates, schedules, and services. Those who use the trail system for day use might consider a donation towards trail maintenance, or a Day Membership.

Quiet destination offering fine opportunity to explore Maine woods in winter, and to observe signs of wintering mammals and birds. Forested surroundings provides protection from high winds on blustery days. The two waterfalls form natural ice sculptures that change as the winter season progresses.

Trailhead: Airport Trailhead, Maine Highway 27, which is 0.1 mile north of Sugarloaf Airport, on airport side of the highway. Driveway (sign) is immediately south of a new indoor recreation complex. Plowed parking area with trail kiosk.

Nearest Town: Carrabassett Valley

Maps: Delorme *Maine Atlas* Map #29, 5-C;
    Maine Huts and Trails System Map;
    USGS: Poplar Mountain

Elevation Gain: 450′

On Trail:

The ice-sculptures formed by the tumbling waters and the spray thrown into the cold winter air are fascinating, changing from year to year and even during a particular winter season. The opening of the Poplar Hut in the Maine Huts and Trails System has drawn attention to these falls, made all the more accessible by a network of trails available for skiing and snowshoeing, and in summer, hiking and mountain biking.

The trails pass through a mixed hardwood-softwood forest: rock maple, ash, white birch, yellow birch, and beech; along with fir, spruce, white pine. At farther points along the route watch for cedar, particularly near water, and great hemlock with the hint of red to the bark. The Poplar area is a fine one for learning to differentiate among the trees of Maine's Western Mountain Region, and to be observant for the signs of the mammals and birds that make this forest their home. Do carry identification charts or books for trees, birds, and mammals! I have accompanied groups of school children along this route. When they have been given an orientation about what to look for, they become excited at discovering signs of wildlife. The thoughtful teachers of some children's groups I have hiked with assigned 5th graders to sit in the woods, remaining quiet, for 15 minutes. In their rock or log sitting places, they sketch their observations and write notes in a journal. Experienced persons of the out of doors—hikers, hunters, those who fish—know this technique well. To sit, quietly observant, is not just for kids!

It is a gusty day, cold and clear, when I ski from the Airport Trailhead, heading for Poplar Hut. Wind-whipped snow swirls across the open field beyond the airport runway. In the distance the Bigelow Range—West Peak and Avery Peak, and Little Bigelow—have a snow-globe appearance. This is a good day for a Poplar ski. The valley of Poplar Stream and the trail-lining forest provide good shelter from the wind.

Other skiers are out this day. I pass a snowshoe party just returning. The snow is packed powder and conditions are excellent.

I cross a bridge over the Carrabassett River to reach the main trail connecting Stratton Brook Hut with Poplar Hut and points beyond. There is a 5-way intersection here, where snowmobile trails and the MHT trails diverge. Prominent signage indicates the way. Off I go, wind briefly at my back now, until I get a bit farther into the woods.

The Main Hut trail rises gradually at first, skirts the southern end of a low ridge, then drops steeply to cross the Carriage Road. When the snow is fast I remove my skis to walk down this pitch. I will remove them to cross the road anyway, and I have no desire to attempt a quick "hockey-stop" at the bottom of a fast hill—so off they come. Those on snowshoes may walk the pitch. Just in from the road crossing, Warren's Trail, a snow shoe route (signed) diverges to the left before a foot bridge over Poplar Stream.

Warren's Trail leads north 1.6 miles along the west bank of Poplar Stream, at first stream-side, later above and occasionally out-of-sight of the stream, until reaching the Main Falls. From the Falls, snowshoe hikers may continue on a marked snowshoe trail to the high falls on South Poplar Stream, returning downstream via Larry's Trail, or proceed to the Hut and return via the MHT main route towards the Airport Trailhead.

My destination is the Hut itself. I am out for a 3 hour ski, combining views of Poplar Stream, the exercise of the ascent to the Hut, and an intended sweet, long downhill run on the return. At the bridge crossing I pause for a look at the stream, deeply covered by unbroken snow, and silent. No wind here. Shadow-throwing sun pours through breaks in the trees. It is a good day!

I ski on level terrain, stream on the left—and notice a break in the stream snow-cover. Current has kept open a 10′ long gap at mid-stream. Blue-black water rushes on, exposing a 3′ cut into the ice and snow over the stream. A cold day in mid-winter—yes—but water is a powerful force, and on it runs. There is a caution here—a stream may be snow covered, but current runs silently just below the snow, posing a danger to those who might think of skiing or snowshoeing over the stream.

The discontinued spur trail to the now-closed Gauge Road Trailhead comes in on the right, 0.1 mile after the bridge crossing. From here I ski a steady uphill route for 1.4 miles, until the trail swings around a shoulder of Little Poplar Mountain, descends to cross South Poplar Stream over a bridge, then climbs 0.1 mile to the Hut. The uphill work warms me. I alternate between track-skiing and herring bone technique. Life is good.

At the Hut I stop for a break in the Great Room before a woodstove fire—have some hot tea, talk with the crew, and also talk with guests who are first-time visitors, whose home is in Pennsylvania. They have skied down from Flagstaff Hut, will spend the night at Poplar, then ski back to Flagstaff for another night there. The crew is working on supper, which reminds me of supper at home—I pack up and head for home.

The long downhill is a Nordic skier's reward for the uphill work. It is a sweet run over good snow. The ascent, from trailhead to Hut, with stops to look at Poplar Stream, inspect the tracks of deer, fox, and hare, and do some tree identification, took me an hour and a half. With the downhill advantage I reach my truck at the Airport Trailhead in 45 minutes.

Of course, this is not a race or a time trial. On other days I have poked around, skied north of the hut, made my way to the falls—whatever moves me that day. Enjoy this Maine woods ski!

FIELD NOTES

South Poplar Stream Falls

Carrabassett Valley

Snowshoe. No fee.

Overview: South Poplar Stream Falls drop 30′ into a pool near the base of the north slope of Little Poplar Mountain. The 2.9 miles (5.8 mile round trip) begin on groomed MHT ski-snowshoe trail, then diverge on Larry's Trail, a snowshoe route, for the final 1.0 mile. The falls are a true beauty—ice-sculptures on the face, waters tumbling behind the curtains of ice. Force of the water keeps a broad pool open at the base of the falls throughout the winter.

Larry's Trail, marked with blue paint blazes and blue MHT diamonds, follows an old stream-side road from its junction with the Stratton Brook Hut-Poplar Main Trail, to the falls. There is little elevation gain. Beyond the falls, the trail climbs steeply out of the small gorge carved by South Poplar Stream, passing a side trail leading left 0.2 mile to the Main Falls on Poplar Stream.

The Main Falls are not so high as those on Poplar Stream, but are longer and wider—certainly worth a visit. On some trips I have made this a lunch spot. Beyond the falls, and over a bridge Warren's Trail descends along the west bank of Poplar Stream to join the main route between Poplar and Stratton Brook Huts, near the Carriage Road.

Snowshoe hikers may ascend one route, and descend the other—or combine a hike to one or both sets of falls with a visit to Poplar Hut. The Hut itself is 0.6 miles above South Poplar Stream Falls. All intersections are well-signed. For information about Poplar Hut, and the groomed ski-snowshoe trail approach, see the previous chapter, *Poplar Stream and Poplar Hut*. Because the falls are reached by snowshoe trails, and not groomed ski trail, I provide the two separate chapters.

The route is forested throughout its length, passing through a hardwood-softwood mix of maple, beech, yellow birch, white birch and ash—and fir, spruce, hemlock, cedar and pine. Look for the towering hemlock and cedar trees that rise on either side of the falls, and above them.

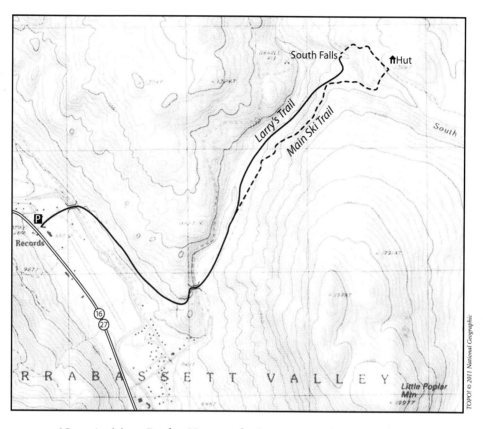

Note: A visit to Poplar Hut may be incorporated into a trip to Poplar Stream Falls. See the previous entry for Poplar Hut.

Note: The Gauge Road Trailhead closed on Fall 2014, and the 0.7 mile spur between that trailhead and the MHT trail between Stratton Brook Hut and Poplar Hut is no longer maintained. The Airport Trailhead is now the closest to Poplar Hut.

Trailhead: Airport Trailhead, Maine Highway 27, which is 0.1 mile north of Sugarloaf Airport, on airport side of the highway. Driveway (sign) is immediately south of a new indoor recreation complex. Plowed parking area with trail kiosk.

Nearest Town: Carrabassett Valley

Maps: Delorme *Maine Atlas* Map #29, 5-C;
Maine Huts and Trails System Map;
USGS: Poplar Mountain

Elevation Gain: 450′

On Trail:

Enjoying the long view up Carrabassett Valley toward the Bigelow Range, I snowshoe my way from the Airport Trailhead to cross the Carrabassett River on the multi-use bridge. The rushing water has carved an ice gorge at mid-stream—the ice and snow equivalent of a road-cut, exposing layers of ice, topped by as much as 3′ of snow.

An angled right turn, and I am on the MHT main route between Stratton Brook Hut and Poplar Hut. The first section of trail, fairly level, passes through forest of 4–6″ diameter fir, birch, and maple and curves around the far end of a long ridge separating the valley of the Carrabassett River and Huston Brook from the valley of Poplar Stream. There are some ups and downs before the trail comes to the top of a steep descent to the Carriage Road.

Here the trail crosses the road, passes the junction with Warren's Trail, a snowshoe route up the west bank of Poplar Stream to Poplar Stream Falls, then crosses Poplar Stream over a footbridge. Beyond the bridge, 0.4 miles, Larry's Trail diverges to the left (sign). This is my choice for the day—destination South Poplar Stream Falls. The falls are 1.0 mile from this point.

I find the trail to be straight-forward, fairly level, following what was once an old road, now grown-in on the sides, but offering a readily traveled footpath. Others have gone before. The trail is well-tracked. This is good—as when I poke the snow beside the snowshoe track ahead, my trekking poles sink 2′!

The level route continues, crossing a few small side streams. There are log bridges, but these are mostly buried, and would be difficult on snowshoes anyway. I test the deep snow on the crossings before snowshoeing across. Poplar Stream is but a few feet to my left. I stay away from that, as its swift current could undermine the ice and snow cover there.

A footbridge, wide enough for snowshoes, spans South Poplar Stream. A ravine opens to my right. Through the trees I see the ice front of the falls. In summer the falls announce themselves with a loud roar early in season, a steady hiss in the drier months. Today—silence.

The trail winds its way to the base of the falls—a great curtain of ice that cold and water have formed in the course of the winter. Sun breaking through the trees brightens the ice face. Quite a sight. Silent from a distance, the falls are very much alive. Water tumbles from behind the ice curtain into a pool, the only break in an otherwise great stillness.

I linger here for a time.

The trail climbs steeply out of the gorge—so steeply that I remove the snowshoes. There are rock steps leading up the slope, but in most snow years these will be well-buried. It is easier to kick steps into the snow with my boots, than to rely on the built-in snowshoe crampons for a grip at such a sharp angle. After 50′

of ascent, if that, I am on top, where the trail to the Main Falls on Poplar Stream (sign) leads 0.2 miles west, and the Main MHT groomed trail lies 0.1 mile ahead over snowshoe trail.

Choices, choices. On some days I turn to the Main Falls, then descend by Warren's Trail along the west bank of Poplar Stream—back to the Carriage Road There are other choices! One could snowshoe to South Poplar Stream Falls as I have, then turn around and head back by the same route. This would keep most of the route on fairly level terrain.

Most days I continue straight for 0.1 mile to an intersection with the main trail between Poplar Hut and Flagstaff Hut, turn right, and head to Poplar Hut for a break in the Great Room. The distance from the South Falls to the Hut is 0.6 miles. I do like to stop at the Hut for a chat with crew about trail conditions, any new developments in the MHT System, and for general trail information swapping over a cup of hot tea.

For the descent, more choices: The groomed, main MHT trail south is the quickest, with its packed surface. Reverse direction, head back to the South Falls, and, after descending into the gorge, travel over level snowshoe trail—perhaps already packed by the hike in—to the Carriage Road. Or hike to the Main Falls on Poplar Stream over snowshoe trail, to descend by Warren's Trail to the Carriage Road.

Mix it up! Explore all the routes, a different one each trip!

Narrow Gauge Pathway

Carrabassett Valley

Ski or snowshoe. No fee.

Overview: Town of Carrabassett Valley governs this trail, which is also part of the Maine Huts and Trails System, and may be accessed from Sugarloaf Outdoor Center. 5.0 miles one way (10 miles round-trip) on groomed, level to gently ascending/descending (depending upon direction of travel) pathway, route of the former Narrow Gauge Railway, parallel to the Carrabassett River. Upper end: views toward Avery and West Peak in the Bigelow Range. In vicinity of Airport Trailhead: broad views of the Bigelow Range. In winter, the tumbling waters of the Carrabassett River form ice sculptures, or carve away at the ice to expose ice strata.

This is a popular route. Along with other skiers and snowshoers, expect to see runners, "fat-bike" riders, and people walking dogs. No motorized vehicles.

This is a rare groomed trail where dogs are permitted. Please note that for deer yard protection and trekker safety, dogs are not permitted elsewhere in the MHT trail system or at the huts. *Note*: No dogs permitted on MHT trails that intersect with the Narrow Gauge Pathway, including Newton's Revenge and the so-called Crommett Trail.

Trailheads: Airport Trailhead, 0.1 mile north of Sugarloaf Airport—plowed, trail kiosk, overnight parking.

Campbell Field Trailhead, across highway from Sugarloaf Outdoor Center, on the right—plowed, trail kiosk, day parking only.

Stratton Brook Hut Trailhead, 0.1 mile north of Sugarloaf Access Road—plowed, trail kiosk, overnight parking.

All trailheads are off Maine Highway 27 in Carrabassett Valley. Consult an MHT map.

Maps: Delorme *Maine Atlas* Map #29, 4,5-C;
Maine Huts and Trails System Map;
USGS: Sugarloaf Mountain, Poplar Mountain

Nearest Town: Carrabassett Valley

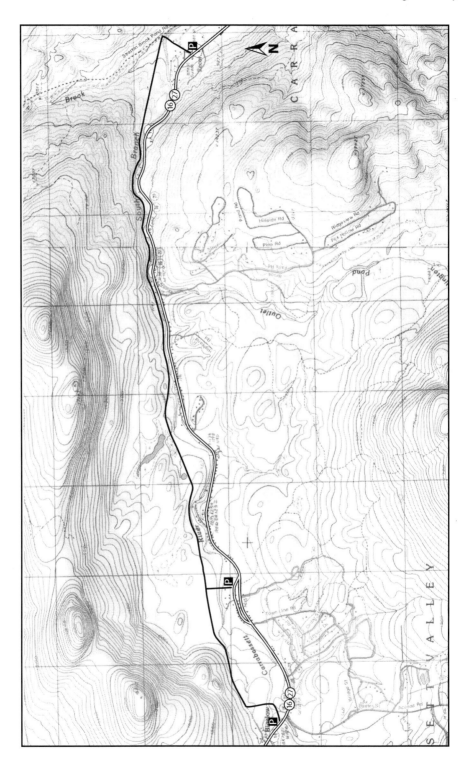

Elevation Gain: Under 100′

On Trail

The temperature stands in single digits as I snap into my Nordic skis and head north out of Carrabassett Valley on the Narrow Gauge Pathway. My destination—or turn-around point actually—is Campbell Field, about five miles away. My plan is to work the uphill grade on the Narrow Gauge to generate some warmth, then enjoy the long downward run back to my starting place.

What a day it is! The sky—cloudless, a sharp, deep blue. The high peaks of the Bigelow Range—Avery Peak and West Peak, snow-covered, rise on the distant horizon. Trailside, Huston Brook rumbles and gurgles its way on its downstream run to join the Carrabassett River a few hundred yards to the south. The air is still; the sound of my breathing and the creak and swish of skis on snow, the book mumblings, the only sounds.

I enter the Narrow Gauge Pathway from the Airport Trailhead of Maine Huts and Trails. A 0.3 mile spur trail leads from the parking area north to a bridge over the Carrabassett River. The bridge is shared by those on foot, and snowmobilers. At the far side of the bridge the foot trails and snowmobile routes separate. For skiers and those on snowshoes, a left turn leads to the Narrow Gauge. (A diagonal right turn, well-signed, leads towards Poplar Stream and Poplar Hut, on the MHT Trail.)

No doubt about which route is the Narrow Gauge—a prominent sign marks the way, where the groomed "Gauge" crosses Huston Brook by a bridge. The trail runs up the valley of the Carrabassett River, to the right of the river. A rarity in the Maine woods—I look out on an utterly straight trail running before me through the forest as far as I can see. The route, after all, is a railroad bed.

I ski through a classic Western Maine Mountains mid-elevation forest: spruce, fir, pine, and cedar and hemlock, for conifers. That makes for five of Maine's six coniferous trees—only the tamarack is missing in this stretch. While on a summer hike on the Gauge, I took the short connector trail between the Gauge and the Crommett Trail, and walked through a stand of tamarack. They are here too! And who knows, because the tamarack is the only coniferous tree to shed its needles, I may well have passed one on my ski trek and not realized it. As for the deciduous trees—they are here, too: bare sugar maples, paper birch, beech, and white ash.

It is cold early on. I work into a skate rhythm and in 15 minutes I have generated enough heat to dispel the tingling cold in my hands. Time for a clothing adjustment. Off comes the neck gaiter. I lower the zipper on my outer shell.

Up, up I go, in the gradual ascent of the old railroad bed, passing a ledge cut where rock had been blasted away to fit the railroad bed between the sharp hillside and the river. Icicles hang from the rock face, which lay in full sun—a

nice ice show for passers-by. Years ago this was the route for log-bearing trains to haul timber southward to Maine mills, meet the nation and the world's need for lumber.

A woman passes me on skis, the silence so prevailing that I do not hear her approach from behind me—only her "Hello!" in greeting as she skates by. She becomes a speck on the trail far ahead, then skis out of sight. She would return in a half-hour or so—the only other person I see this day.

It looks like ice sculpture time on the nearby Carrabassett River. Swift current courses through the ice pack, exposing foot-thick layers of ice perched on river boulders. In places water flows over existing ice, freezing here and there in peculiar hues of sage-green and yellow-blue.

An hour and a half of steady skiing brings me to a long wooden bridge that spans a broad bog. Here the trail is well away from the river, which is out of sight. But that was not always the case. Once the main river channel flowed here; the bog is the remnant. Tracks of snowshoe hare, red fox, and of deer cross the bog. In the woods beyond—who knows, perhaps a fisher, a pine martin, or a bobcat watches me ski past.

Above the bridge the Narrow Gauge levels out from the steady ascent it has held over the first 3 miles, and passes to the left of another, smaller bog. Side trails, some designated as mountain bike routes, show snowshoe use. The trail passes an old camp, paint a faded red, bearing the sign "Riverside 1900" over the front door. Imagine staying in that camp, fishing the Carrabassett, or hunting the ridge above the Narrow Gauge decades ago. A stack of firewood on the porch speaks that someone still finds this old camp to be a cherished place of retreat.

I pass the Campbell Field side trail, with only 0.5 miles to the junction of the Narrow Gauge with Newton's Revenge—the route to Stratton Brook Hut. The Gauge continues straight and level, and I make good time to that junction. Here I stop for some water, and a sandwich of peanut butter and strawberry preserves that my wife and I put up last summer. I chase all that with hot tea.

At the junction there is a good view of Avery Peak and West Peak on the Bigelow Range. The lowering sun throws a rich glow onto the bare, snowy summits.

A chill, and I know it is time to turn around. On other days I have continued to ski up Newton's Revenge to the Hut, or on a snowshoe hike have snowshoed up the groomed main trail to the Hut, and descended on the Oak Knoll snowshoe route. On yet other outings I have made a turn on the upper reaches of Newton's Revenge to the so-called Crommett Trail, a more direct route between Stratton Brook Hut and Poplar Hut, which brings me to within 0.9 miles of my Airport Trailhead starting point. I do ski another half mile or so up Newton's Revenge for vantage points on Sugarloaf, then turn around for the long downhill run back on the Narrow Gauge.

I am certainly happy with this outing—a 10 mile round trip. The long gradual downhill is a Nordic skier's joy—miles and miles of descent. At times I step into the classic tracks and just let the skis run, run, run—down, down past ledges, the muffled roar of the river, the play of the last rays of the sun on snow and bare bark of the hardwoods. Gravity is so much in my favor that my toes begin to chill. I return to the skate technique to warm myself a bit, then alternate, skate, glide, all the way back to the beginning of the Narrow Gauge, and on to the Airport Trailhead.

Warm up on the way up. Enjoy the gentle downhill grade on the way back down. Take in the serenity either way. The Narrow Gauge Pathway offers skiers—and snowshoers—a fine winter outing in the shadows of the High Peaks.

Crommett Trail

Carrabasset Valley

Ski or snowshoe. No fee.

Overview: "Crommett Trail" is the unofficial name for a 3.0 section of the Maine Huts and Trails System between Stratton Brook Hut and Poplar Hut. The name derives from the Crommett Overlook, a viewpoint along the way that offers a face-on view of Sugarloaf and Burnt Mountains.

Although it functions as an alternate connector between the two huts above, the Crommett Trail is a fine route in its own right, with long runs, a classic Sugarloaf view, and less foot traffic than is found on the Narrow Gauge.

The overlook has a picnic table with an attached metal plaque honoring the late Dick Crommett, an advocate for outdoor pursuits in this remarkable mountain country, and a member of the Carrabassett Valley Outdoor Association.

The lower end of the trail connects to the Narrow Gauge Pathway 0.9 miles above the junction of the Narrow Gauge with the spur to the Airport Trailhead. This lower section of the Crommet Trail has at times been known as the Narrow Gauge Bypass, but is rarely referred to as such. The upper end begins at an MHT trail junction (sign) 0.7 miles below Stratton Brook Hut on the MHT Newton's Revenge Trail.

The Crommett Trail enables MHT travelers to go between Stratton Brook and Poplar Huts by a more direct route than taking the Narrow Gauge Pathway for most of the way. For day outings the Crommett Trail opens many route options. Start at the Airport Trailhead, ski or snowshoe up the Narrow Gauge Pathway to Newton's Revenge Trail, then turn on the Crommett Trail to return to the Pathway only 0.5 mile from the Airport connecting trail. Or travel this route in reverse. Add in a trip to Stratton Brook Hut. Or start at the Stratton Brook Hut Trailhead, or Campbell Field Trailhead. Obtain a MHT System Map. Look for the "Crommett's Overlook" on the map to identify this route.

In the direction eastward between Newton's Revenge Junction and the Narrow Gauge Pathway the route is mostly a steady descent, with some

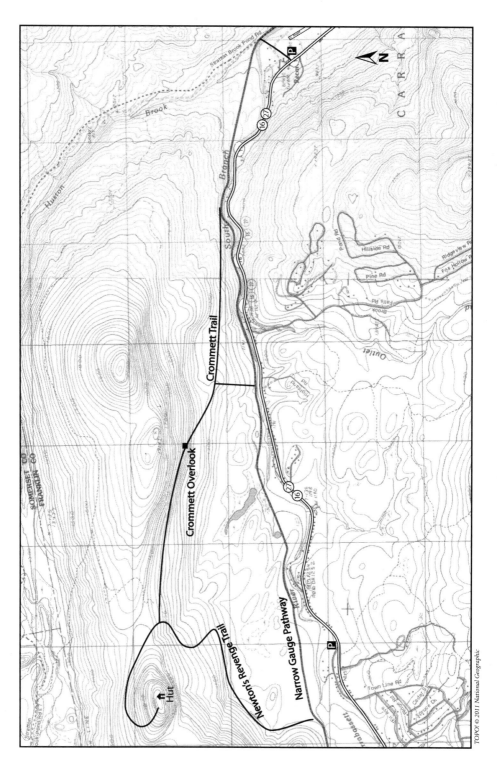

level portions, and a quarter-mile of ascent. When approaching from the lower end, heading west, up towards Stratton Brook Hut, accordingly, the route is mostly a steady ascent, steepest at the lower end, becoming more gradual near the upper end, at Newton's Revenge Junction.

Trailhead: This is an interior trail, with upper end at a trail junction with Newton's Revenge, 2.0 miles from the Stratton Brook Hut Trailhead on Maine Highway 27, 0.1 mile north of the Sugarloaf Access Road. From the Campbell Field Trailhead, distance is 2.1 miles.

The lower end is at a junction (sign) with the Narrow Gauge Pathway, 0.9 miles "upstream" from the five-way intersection at the multiuse trail bridge over the Carrabassett River, 0.3 miles from the Carrabassett Valley Airport and the MHT Airport parking area. MHT parking areas are plowed.

Maps: Delorme *Maine Atlas* #29, 4-C (not shown on map, but contours and nearby features are);
Maine Huts and Trails System Map; USGS: Sugarloaf Mountain, Poplar Mountain

Nearest Town: Carrabassett Valley

Elevation (Gain): Estimated 300–400′ loss from upper to lower point, with a 100′ gain near the half-way point.

On Trail

I am on skis, and on Newton's Revenge Trail, named, I expect, for Isaac Newton, responsible for the Theory of Gravity. After a 600′ elevation gain from the Narrow Gauge Pathway to the Stratton Brook Hut, I am mindful of gravity. But now comes the payback—or continues the payback, as I have already enjoyed the swift, curving 0.9 mile downhill run from the Hut to this trail junction.

My options at the junction are to retrace my route down Newton's Revenge to the Narrow Gauge Pathway, or to take Maine Huts and Trails newer, and more direct, route towards the Airport Trailhead, and beyond towards Poplar Hut. This direct route is known locally as the Crommett Trail. I ski it often, enjoying the bit wilder feel of this trail over the Narrow Gauge (though the Gauge remains one of my favorite ski-snowshoe-jog-bike routes).

So off I go, or rather down I go, as the trail begins with a long steady descent, slabbing the south slope of the east-west ridge that divides the Carrabassett River drainage from that of Huston Brook. This is groomed trail, and I enjoy a good downhill run. The forest to my left is mostly hardwoods, fairly open from a timber harvest of recent years. Down the lower slope to my right fir, spruce, and a few cedar mix with the maples, beech, ash, and yellow birch.

I start in the groomed classic tracks, but in a short while I step out of them onto the wider part of the trail groomed for skate-skiing—this to check my speed. Back and forth I go, from skate to in-track gliding, occasionally kick-and-glide as the trail levels out, descends, even has a short rise or two.

This is "fun" skiing. Sun plays on the tree canopy. The woods are still, with no wind. Life is good. Swish!

In 15 minutes I reach the Crommett Overlook, with its "Oh-my-gosh" view, framed by white birch, of Sugarloaf, across the valley of the Carrabassett. I take a water and food break here, my first since leaving Stratton Brook Hut. Far below, I see a portion of the Narrow Gauge Pathway, a long, narrow open break in the trees. A snow-covered picnic table occupies the overlook. I brush off snow to expose a metal plaque honoring the late Dick Crommett. Otherwise, following skiers or snowshoes would be unlikely to see it. Wherever there is a trail in the Maine woods, someone or some-ones, had the vision for it, and took the time to mark it, clear it. Others maintain it. We hike, or ski, benefitting from the efforts of those before us.

Sustained with my nutrition stop, and the view, I continue on the steady descent for another 0.5 mile to a junction (signed) with a short connector trail that drops 0.4 mile to the Narrow Gauge Pathway. At the Gauge end of this connector there is a sign "Camel Humps" for an area popular with mountain bikers. On some trips, when I have started at the Stratton Brook Hut Trailhead or at Campbell Field, I have taken this connector, then skied "upriver" to my starting point.

Some woods lore! This connector passes through a stand of Tamarack, also known as Larch or Hackmatack. This is a deciduous conifer—a needle-bearing tree that drops the needles in fall.

Back to skiing the main MHT Trail, I ascend out of the draw of the just-mentioned junction, and gain about 100' of elevation over 0.5 miles. The trail crests, enters an area of glacial erratic boulders either side of the route, then descends smartly over the final 1.0 mile to its junction with the Narrow Gauge Pathway. This stretch offers a fast run!

Today, I bear left at the junction for the Airport Trailhead spur trail, 0.9 miles distant. On days that I have started at the Stratton Brook Hut Trailhead, or Campbell Field, I turn right to return to my vehicle.

The Crommett route has become the preferred for traveling from Stratton Brook Hut towards Poplar Hut and points north of Poplar Hut. It also extends the options for those on a day outing. Combined with the Narrow Gauge Pathway, Newton's Revenge, and the connector in the vicinity of the Camel's Humps, there are at least a half-dozen different day outings possible.

It is a fine addition to the MHT System.

Weld-Tumbledown Region

Weld has been a popular hiking destination for decades. Multiple peaks between 2000' and just under 4000' elevation ring a valley of remarkable beauty where Webb Lake is the centerpiece. The striking views awaiting summer hikers are there in the winter for the growing number of those who travel by snowshoes or cross-country skis.

Some trailheads are readily accessible in winter, such as Bald Mountain, Blueberry Mountain, and the Center Hill snowshoe and ski terrain managed by Mount Blue State Park. Others such as Tumbledown, Little Jackson, and Mount Blue, become remote destinations in winter when the approach roads are not maintained.

The State Park winter trail system of tracked ski trails and marked snowshoe routes provides fine access into remote country, where one may come across a bobcat track, or crest a hill to discover a see-forever view of the Tumbledown Range, bright in mid-day sun.

Mount Blue State Park:

Ski Trails: Center Hill and
Hedgehog Hill   156

Snowshoe Trails: Center Hill   162

Mt. Blue Road to Mt. Blue Trailhead 166

Mount Blue   170

Bald Mountain   174

Tumbledown Pond and Parker Ridge 178

Little Jackson   184

Blueberry Mountain   192

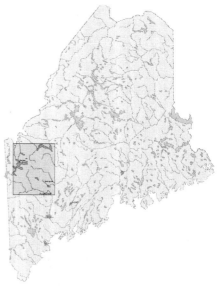

Dead River, Grand Falls - West Forks
Dead River & Grand Falls Hut - LFD

❋Flagstaff Hut & Flagstaff Lake East Shore
❋Flagstaff Lake Round Barn
❋Little Bigelow Mtn.

Cranberry Peak❋
Crommett Trail
Stratton Brook Hut & Oak Knoll
❋Poplar Hut & Poplar Stream Falls
Narrow Gauge Pathway

Bonney Point
Hunter Cove
Hatchery Brook

Sugarloaf Outdoor Ct.

Rangeley Lakes Trail Ctr.
Rangeley ❋

Long Falls Dam Road

Bald Mt.❋
Rock & Midway
❋Ponds
South Bog Trail
❋Piazza Rock
Low Aziscohos

❋Oberton & Hardy Streams
❋Fly Rod Crosby Trail

Little Jackson Mt.
Blueberry Mt.

Tumbledown Pond & Tumbledown Mt.❋

Byron Road

❋ ❋Mount Blue
Center Hill

Sandy Rvr ❋Powderhouse Hill
Intervale❋ *Farmington*
Titcomb Mt❋

Bald Mt.

Wilton

Center Hill Ski Trails
Mount Blue State Park
Weld

Ski. Fee at self-pay station.

Overview: 15 mile system of 6 ski trails groomed single track for classic skiing only (not wide enough for skate-skiing). Information on trail conditions, 24 hours a day at 585-2261.

Mostly forested routes, with periodic fine lookout points towards Mount Blue, the Weld Valley, Byron Notch, and the Tumbledown-Jackson Range. Distances range from the 1.5 mile Fox Trail Loop to the 10.0 mile Maple Trail Loop. Other routes are the Birch, a loop which connects to the Maple Trail; and the Central, Moose, and Pine Trails in the vicinity of Parlin Brook, with good views towards Blueberry Mountain and the Jacksons.

Ski through fine conifer and deciduous stands in an area that was a thriving farming region in the 1800s—and where some farms were active into the mid-1900s. Old stone walls in the woods mark the edges of fields or pasture long since returned to forest growth. Discontinued roads that once connected outlying farms are incorporated into the trail system. Fairly well protected from wind, and therefore a good choice on a blustery day.

Highest point in the system is Hedgehog Hill, 1402', reached from a spur off the Maple Trail. Outstanding views over the entire Weld Valley—up Byron Notch toward Dolly Mountain, Tumbledown Cliffs, peaks of the Tumbledown-Jackson Range, Bald Mountain and Saddleback Wind, Webb Lake—one of the best views in the Western Mountains of Maine.

Fee area. Self-pay station at the Trailhead.

Trailhead: Mount Blue State Park Headquarters parking lot, Center Hill Road (sign). From the four corners in Weld Village, turn right off Maine Highway 156 on to Center Hill Road. Headquarters is at a white farmhouse across the road from an open view over Weld Valley and Webb Lake.

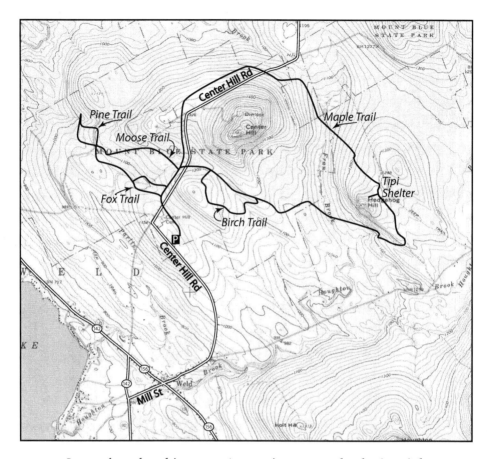

Large plowed parking area. A warming yurt and a skating rink are on the near side of the parking area. Trailhead, kiosk, and self-pay on far side (east). Vault toilet. Fee varies with state of residence.

Nearest Town: Weld

Maps: Delorme *Maine Atlas* Map #19, 2,3-C;
Mount Blue State Park and Tumbledown Public Lands Guide and Map, Maine Bureau of Public Lands, <www.maine.gov/dacf/parks>;
Mount Blue State Park Cross Country Ski Trails Map, at Trailhead kiosk

Elevation Gain: Varies with trail choice, 50′ to 200′.

On Trail

A skiing buddy and I step onto the Trail System at mid-morning on a bright winter day, not a cloud in the sky. Our plan is to ski the 10-mile Maple Trail, which offers long, mostly gradual, ascents and descents through a variety of forest stands in the valley of Fran Brook, between Center Hill and Mount Blue. Along the way, we will take a spur trail to the summit of Hedgehog Hill, only 1402′ in elevation, but providing a commanding view of the Weld Valley.

A variety of ski bottom surfaces.

We begin on the Central Trail, the main access route to all other trails. Skiing through predominantly fir and pine, we descend, cross a snowmobile trail, descend farther to cross Center Hill Road—removing our skis to prevent damage from the sand spread on the road. On the other side of the road, the trail divides.

The Moose Trail, a 1.0 mile loop, diverges to the left. Two other trails, Fox Trail, 0.5 miles; and Pine Trail, 1.0 mile, may be reached from the Moose Trail. I have skied all of these on other days. The terrain is fairly level, with moderate descent and ascent for the crossing of Parlin Brook.

To reach our major route for the day, the Maple Trail, we turn right at this junction and ski parallel to the Center Hill Road for about 0.4 miles to reach the next trail junction. There is a quick descent to cross a tributary to Parlin Brook. We ski this drop, but on other days, when conditions are icy I have walked partway down. No point in risking breaking a ski—or an ankle. But the groomed track is in excellent condition today—so away we go.

The next trail junction is for the Birch Trail (right) and Maple Trail (straight ahead). *However, the Maple Trail may be skied by going in either direction.* My preferred route is counter-clockwise, beginning with the Birch Trail. The ascents seem to be shorter and more gradual in this direction, and the descents provide good long runs. I have met skiers going in either direction. We turn right on the Birch Trail, cross Center Hill Road again, cross a snowmobile trail, head up an incline, bear left at a Y-intersection—and we enter a different world.

The road well behind us, we ski along a low, fir and pine forested ridge, south of Center Hill, in utter quiet. There is no wind this day. Heavy recent snowfalls have covered the forest floor to a depth of 3–4′. Tracks appear—deer, red squirrel, fox, snowshoe hare, white-footed mice. We cross the Park snowshoe trail that leads to the top of Center Hill, arrive at the Maple Trail-Birch Trail Junction, and bear a diagonal left for the Maple Trail.

Here begins a long descent to the valley of Fran Brook. I have been striding a fair amount to this point. Now I double-pole and let the skis run. Swish … Through the soundless forest, pristine snow cover … low winter sun throwing tree-shadows across the trail …. It is quite a time.

We ski past one of many "pasture pine", a great Eastern white pine, 60′ high, crotched, with long, thick limbs reaching as far out as 20′. This terrain was once pasture. When abandoned as farm land, seed from wind-blown pine cones took root here. With wide open space in all directions, the pasture pines developed their far-reaching branch systems. This then rendered them poor choices for lumber, and crotched pines were all the poorer for practical use. So it is that deep in today's forest, sometimes towering among neighbor trees, these old and imperfect trees endure. Had they been perfect they long ago would have fallen under the axe or saw.

The forest changes as we travel on—from fir and pine, to beech and maple, then to white birch and maple, then to a mix of white ash, sugar maple, yellow and white birch. Good route for tree study! Mount Blue rises to the east, framed by the trail opening in the forest, the summit tower sharply visible. We ski across Fran Brook over a bridge. Before us looms the south cliff face of Hedge Hog Hill. The spur trail we seek is on the north side. The trail turns right to skirt the east slope of the Hill over level ground, then makes a near 180-degree turn left at an intersection with an old, unplowed road, to ascend to the spur trail.

At the well-marked spur trail junction stands a tipi, offering a location out of the wind for those who wish to take a break here. This is a substantial tipi, 14' diameter. Inside, a wooden bench provides a place to sit. There is firewood for those who wish to make a small warming fire. Tipi fires should be well-kindled and kept small. Wet wood will smoke, and a hot fire will be too hot for gatherers to remain inside—and pose a danger to the tipi itself.

The day is cold, but not uncomfortably so, as there is no wind. We do not need a windbreak or a fire. My friend and I ski up the 0.2 mile spur to a point where the trail steepens, at the base of the summit ledges. We remove our skis. Our daypacks with us, we clamber up the forested slope, following a path worn into the snow by previous visitors.

The view is stunning. I look northwest to Byron Notch, the angular cliffs of Tumbledown Mountain, and the snowy open summit of Little Jackson Mountain. Straight west lies the long white expanse of Webb Lake, and beyond that the ridge of Spruce Mountain. Below, just beyond the base of the cliffs of Hedge Hog lies the valley of Fran Brook, which we have largely circled to arrive here. To the right rises the dome of Center Hill, with its own high ledges and valley-facing cliffs. The sun blazes brightly in a blue-flame sky.

Caution: Stay well back from the cliff edge. Snow cornice may reach over the edge.

We pause here for lunch and hot tea, digging out a picnic table placed here during the summer season. Spare pairs of mitts serve as insulation from the cold, as we sit at the table, and take in that view. This Hedge Hog view is one of the finest in the Western Maine Mountains.

Although we had pulled on additional layers to retain heat, it is not long before we feel the cold. It is time to generate some warmth. We hike down the hill, return to our skis, head past the tipi to the Maple Trail, and turn left. The next stretch of trail is a long, steady descent—much pole and glide, pole and glide. We cross the upper reach of Fran Brook, ascend to cross the snowmobile trail and the Center Hill Road, and turn left to cover a long series of up and down terrain as we ski in the direction of Park Headquarters.

The day is far from done. There are yet discoveries to be made. I look out toward Blueberry Mountain, and as I do, I see through a low gap a distant snow-covered summit, far to the north. It is Saddleback Mountain in Rangeley. Only the very summit is exposed—but this shines a bright white in the afternoon sun. Had I not looked up exactly when I did, I would have missed it. There is more— a bobcat track crosses the trail. And this—an abandoned apple orchard is thick with trees that have sprung up from decades of apple drops rotting and releasing their seeds. A break in the stillness—a pileated woodpecker rattles away.

We reach the Center Trail, where we began the Maple Trail Loop, and now are truly near the end of our outing. Ever-lowering sun greets us full-on as we ascend the remaining half-mile to the Trailhead, and one more long view over the Weld Valley.

Nothing fancy here. Much beauty in simplicity. Stunning views, quiet woods, animal tracks aplenty. This is one of my favorite places.

Center Hill Snowshoe Trails
Mount Blue State Park
Weld

Snowshoe. Fee at self-pay station. Rentals (self-pay) at trailhead warming yurt. Note: No drinking water.

Overview: Two signed and marked ungroomed snowshoe trails. Both are 1.5 miles one-way (3.0 miles round trip). One leads north to Center Hill where there are excellent views west to Byron Notch and the Tumble-down-Jackson Range, and from the Center Hill Ledges, of Mount Blue and the south-lying low peaks that form the height of land between Weld Valley and the Wilson Stream drainage—Chandler Hill, Houghton Ledges, and Holt Hill. The second snowshoe trail heads west from the trailhead to lookout point by great glacial erratic boulder. Views include Blueberry Mountain and Big Jackson Mountain.

The Park map describes both routes as "strenuous" and recommends allowing 3 hours for the 3 mile round-trip. The strenuous label derives from the up and down terrain, and the possibility that trekkers may be breaking trail in deep snow. Because winter conditions may vary widely on any snowshoe trail—snow scant or deep, icy, crusted, or slush—it is prudent to allow ample time.

Trailhead: Mount Blue State Park Headquarters parking lot, Center Hill Road (sign). From the four corners in Weld Village, turn right off Maine Highway 156 on to Center Hill Road. Headquarters is at a white farmhouse across the road from an open view over Weld Valley and Webb Lake.

Large plowed parking area. A stove-warmed yurt and a skating rink are adjacent to the parking area. Trailhead is at a kiosk on the far side (east). Vault toilet. Be advised that here is no lodge, no sales of food, clothing, or gear, and no drinking water available. Bring a trail lunch and water for the day. All this said, Mount Blue State Park is a true gem, compelling for its simple beauty. Come here to trek the high forest of this quiet, remote, pristine valley.

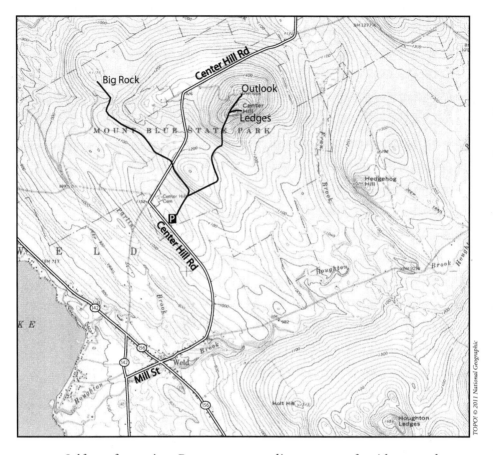

Self-pay fee station. Rates vary according to state of residence and age. Limited number of snowshoes (and ice skates) available for rent in the yurt.

Nearest Town: Weld

Maps: Delorme *Maine Atlas* Map #19, 2,3-C;
Mount Blue State Park and Tumbledown Public Lands Guide and Map, Maine Bureau of Public Lands <www.aine.gov/dacf/parks> Mount Blue State Park Ski and Snowshoe Trails Map, available at Trailhead kiosk.

Elevation Gain: Center Hill Trail, 600´; Big Rock Trail, 100´

On Trail

After many a trip to the Park to ski on cross-country trails, I decided to give the snowshoe terrain a try—and am I glad that I did! On two separate trips a week apart, I hike the Rock Lookout Trail and the Center Hill Trail. I recommend both for their routes through fine forest stands, and for excellent views of Webb Lake, the Tumbledown Range, Byron Notch, and beyond.

The two trails begin as one to the right of the kiosk, immediately cross a snowmobile trail, and head into the woods through a stand of high white pines. Flagging tape marks the route: green for Rock Lookout, pink for Center Hill. In a few moments I come to a stone wall—a reminder that where I now stand was once cleared farm, as early settlers sought the high ground for sunlight and drainage, and thereby extend the number of frost-free days in this high valley.

The trail crosses the wall and descends into a sheltered draw. This is prime deer wintering area, and deer tracks crisscross the trail. The cedar and fir in this draw between two low ridges provide shelter from the wind, and limit the amount of snow on the forest floor. In a few places deer have pawed the snow cover to graze on moss that thrives in the moist low-light conditions found here in summer.

Ten minutes of walking bring me to the junction for the Rock Lookout Trail, which bears left, northward, continuing through the draw, with many more deer sign—tracks, pellets, and feeding spots. Trailside, young white pine, two or three feet high, poke through the snow—with the nearest mature pine on a ridge top a good 200 yards away. Such is the power of the prevailing winds to toss seed-bearing cones far into the woods!

The trail rises gradually, crosses the graveled Center Hill Road, then heads northerly through a mixed hardwood and softwood forest towards the Rock Lookout. Watch for silver-gray beech trees with coppery leaves still clinging at mid-winter. Along the way rise a stand of white ash, with deep, diamond shaped furrows, a tree that offers the makings for canoe thwarts and baseball bats. This is a place of great quiet, and simple beauty. I stop to listen to the silence of the Maine woods—quite a treat in a noisy world! Near a thick growth of fir snowshoe hare tracks run in all directions—this is a good place to study tracks. Finally I reach the rock lookout itself, with a fine view of the Tumbledown Cliffs, and Little Jackson and Big Jackson Mountains. The rock juts out over a great ravine that falls away a good forty feet. I make this my lunch spot, before I retrace my steps, over the now well-tracked trail, back to the trailhead and parking area.

One week later I return to the Park for a snowshoe hike on the Center Hill Trail. Where the green-flagged Rock Lookout Trail bears left, this pink-flagged route goes straight ahead, easterly, crossing a series of low ridges. I enjoy quite a display of Maine trees along the way—grey and white birch, rock maple, black ash, and beech, along with white pine, black spruce, fir, and hemlock.

At one point a massive crotched white pine rises by the trail, towering over all other nearby trees. These solitary old timers are usually "pasture pine", born of a day when the wind flung a seed-bearing cone into an abandoned pasture.

Abundant daylight, room to grow, and grow they did—tall and wide. Proliferation of branches rendered them poor choices for timber, and often these were crotched. This imperfection spared them from the axe.

Farther on I come to a great red oak, a good four feet across at the base, one last curled, brown leaf clinging to an upper branch. Beyond these, a curiosity—a stand of a dozen red pine, more commonly found in the sandy soil of big lakes, but here, on a hillside. This is a great trail for tree identification.

Thirty minutes of hiking bring me to an overlook where Mount Blue commands the eastern skyline, Little Blue adjacent, northward. To the left of the view rise the gray ledges of Center Hill, my destination. The trail swings left and climbs steadily, passing snow-mounded glacial erratics, great boulders left as glaciers, carving out the present-day landscape, retreated some 10,000 years ago. My trekking poles provide stability as I ascend the steady slope.

A trail junction offers the choice of ascending directly to the ledges, or heading towards the snow covered Center Hill picnic area. I choose the ledges and am rewarded with a 180-degree view from Mount Blue to Webb Lake to the Tumbledown Range. The Center Hill Ledges are a stop on the 0.4 mile Nature Trail Loop. I am familiar with that loop from many an outing with our children. I hike the loop, passing more outlooks towards Mount Blue, some with snow-buried wooden benches. The loop trail ends at the Center Hill Picnic Area, which is snow-covered, as the access road is not plowed. I trek 100 yards down the road to the point where the Center Hill Snowshoe Trail enters on the left. Remember that turn I made to reach the Ledges? If I had stayed on the main trail, this is the point I would have reached.

With occasional stops to enjoy views, examine animal tracks, and check out tree specimens along the way, each hike was a three-hour round trip—precisely what Park personnel indicate. The Rock Lookout hike is the less strenuous of the two, but I certainly recommend both. If new to snowshoeing, Park visitors could forgo hiking the full length of these trails and simply enjoy a shorter snowshoe outing. We are fortunate to have this fine Maine State Park in our Franklin County backyard! Enjoy!

Mt. Blue Road to Mt. Blue Trailhead
Mount Blue State Park
Weld

Ski or snowshoe. No fee.

Overview: 2.0 mile (4.0 mile round-trip) ski or snowshoe route, to base of Mount Blue, where there is a picnic shelter at the edge of a field, offering views towards the Weld Valley. The route is over unplowed park road, and doubles as a snowmobile trail. Combination of steady ascents and descents, providing for some long runs.

Note that this road route is *not* part of the snowshoe and cross-country trail system of the Park, and does not appear on maps for Park winter trails. It may readily be found on the maps listed below.

The route is not groomed for skiing. However, snowmobile use, and frequent travel by those on snowshoes or skis, usually provides for a packed surface.

The 1.6 mile hiking trail up Mount Blue leaves from the parking area at the end of the road near the picnic shelter. There is a prominent trail sign here for that hiking trail. Those who wish to hike Mount Blue may ski the 2.0 miles to the base of the mountain, then switch to snowshoes for the steep hike to the summit—or travel on snowshoes the entire way. (See the entry in this book for the ascent of Mount Blue.)

Trailhead: Center Hill Road junction with Mt. Blue Road, where Center Hill Road makes a 90 degree left turn, approximately 2.0 miles past Park Headquarters. Parking is very limited here, as there is a private home at this corner, and the short plowed part of the Mt. Blue Road has room for only one or two vehicles.

Please do not park in a way that blocks the road or the driveway to the private residence. I have observed some skiers park back on the Center Hill Road a few hundred feet, close to the snow banks. Use good judgment, by parking well away from turns, driveways, and narrow stretches of the road.

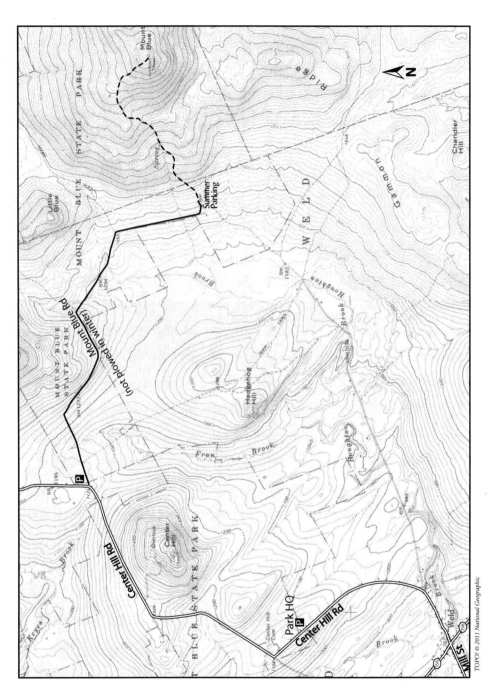

It is possible to park at Park Headquarters and ski on snowmobile trail to this point. That would add another 2 miles one way, and involves some ascending and descending, but is worth considering. If there are multiple vehicles in a party, an option is to park all vehicles but one at the Park Headquarters parking area, and shuttle to the trailhead. This would require the parking of only one vehicle near the trailhead.

Nearest Town: Weld

Maps: Delorme *Maine Atlas* Map #19, 2,3-C;
Mount Blue State Park and Tumbledown Public Lands Guide and Map, Maine Bureau of Public Lands. <www.parksandlands.com>

Elevation Gain: 200′

On Trail

When our family first moved to the Western Mountains region, we often skied the snow-covered Mt. Blue Road from the Center Hill Road to the Mt. Blue Trailhead. The distance over the unplowed road is about 2.0 miles one-way. Although the road gains elevation over this distance, there are ascents and descents along the way, which offer variety to an outing.

I climb over the snowbank berm that marks the entrance to the unplowed Mt. Blue Road, step into my skis, and I am off. The way is packed from the travel of others on skis or snowshoes, and I am quickly into a classic stride. The Mt. Blue Road lies in an easterly direction at first, and is fairly level. In about 200 yards snowmobile trail ITS 89 enters on the right. This trail is groomed frequently, which can make for a good skiing surface. Ski single file and be prepared to step aside when snowmobiles are on the trail.

On my most recent trip I meet four snowmobile parties. I wave when they pass, and they wave back. Two of the parties were new to the area, and stopped to ask questions about the Park. I usually stop to talk whenever a snowmobile party is stopped. We exchange trail information, and it is always of interest to me to meet new people and learn what has brought them to the Maine Woods.

The level stretch eventually becomes a downhill run, making a right turn as the road slabs the west side of Little Blue. Farther on the road climbs to an ITS 89 junction west of the saddle between Little Blue and Mount Blue. ITS 89 swings left. The Mount Blue Road now heads in a southerly direction, which it maintains over a long, gradual climb before ending at the parking lot for the hiking trail to the summit of Mount Blue. To the right (south) of the parking area stands a picnic shelter and a vault toilet. These are situated on the clearing of an old farm site, with a few surviving apple trees scattered in the open area below the shelter. There are views through the trees towards the high ground above Weld Village.

I stop for lunch at the shelter, as bright sun pours in from the southwest. Although I could turn around and ski back to where I started, and have enjoyed a fine outing, I instead exchange my skis for snowshoes, and set out on the Mount Blue hiking trail. My plan is to hike until a predetermined turn-around time. I have climbed the mountain in snow previously, a number of times. This day is so bright and clear, that I decided to bring my snowshoes just in case I could make good time on the ski in, and I did.

The hiking trail to Mount Blue passes a sign listing the distance to the top as 1.6 miles. That may not seem a far distance—after all, I have already skied 2 miles—but the trail is unrelentingly steep. In snowshoes the going is slow. I move along with steady progress. The sky is clear overhead. The tops of high maples sway a bit in the wind, but where I am at ground level, the woods block that wind, and I feel little of it. It is a cold day, with temperatures in the single numbers, but I am warmed by my exertion and am wearing wicking layers to prevent a chill.

In deep snow it takes nearly an hour to reach the site of the Fire Warden's cabin, long abandoned, where it sits on a side trail above a stream. The stream itself is buried in deep snow.

As I continue upward, I am mindful of the daily hike to the fire tower by those who lived in the cabin. They worked themselves into good shape fairly quickly in the course of the fire watch season.

Mount Blue
Mount Blue State Park
Weld

Snowshoe; or Ski *and* Snowshoe. No fee.

Overview: 1.6 mile (3.2 miles round-trip) steady and steep ascent to 3140′ summit of Mount Blue, the most prominent peak in Southern Franklin County. Add 2.0 miles (4 miles round trip) for Mount Blue Road (unplowed) approach—total of 7.2 miles.

Note that the Mount Blue hiking trail is *not* part of the State Park snowshoe trail system, and therefore does not appear on the snowshoe trail map. Summer hiking maps depict the trail.

This former fire tower peak has a new tower that houses emergency communication facilities, but is designed in the shape of a traditional fire tower. The profile of a square cabin atop a four-legged steel tower is visible for many miles. The tower may be climbed to its half-way point where there is an observation platform. There is no access to the false cabin atop the tower. Icy conditions may render the tower dangerous to climb.

This is a snowshoe hike. When ice or slick crust are present, crampons may be helpful, or even essential. The built-in crampons on some snowshoes may not be effective for steep, slippery sections of the trail. I carry boot crampons on all mountain snowshoe hikes.

The summit holds a clearing, rimmed by scrub fir, which limit long views from ground level. Hence the tower. There are four outlook points offering fine views to the North, East, West, and South. The West-facing point is 20 yards to the right of the hiking trail, just below the summit. The South view is from the base of the tower. For views to the East and North, there are side trails of 50–100′ from the summit clearing. Snow depth may determine how apparent these side trails are.

The West view is a favorite spot. On a clear day I have looked out at Mount Washington in the Presidential Range of New Hampshire. It is the highest peak in the Northeast USA, 6288′. The mountain-ringed Weld Valley, Webb Lake at the center, lies in the foreground.

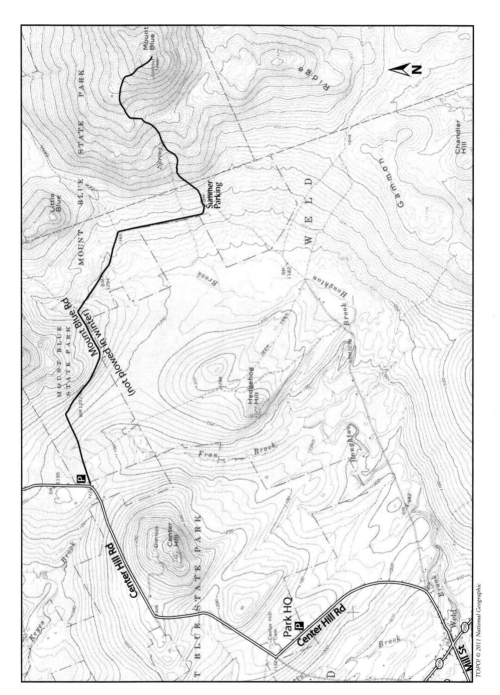

Trailhead: End of 2.0 mile unplowed Mt. Blue Road, which may be traveled on skis or snowshoes to reach the start of the hiking trail at the north end of the unplowed parking lot.

Trail kiosk and a separate "Mt. Blue Trail 1.6 Miles" sign.

For a description of the Mt. Blue Road approach, see the separate entry in this book, *Mount Blue Road*.

Nearest Town: Weld

Maps: Maps: Delorme *Maine Atlas* Map #19, C-2,3;
Mount Blue State Park and Tumbledown Public Lands Guide and Map,
Maine Bureau of Public Lands, <www.maine.gov.dacf/parks>.

Elevation Gain: 1800′

On Trail

The hiking trail to Mount Blue passes a sign listing the distance to the top as 1.6 miles. That may not seem a far distance—after all, I have already skied two miles—but the trail is unrelentingly steep. The first 100 feet seem easy enough—virtually level.

Then the route begins its ascent. Stone work has been placed in the trail to reduce erosion—but all of that work lies out of sight under 3′ of snow at this time of year. Blue paint blazes mark the way. I observe that the blazes seem low on the trees—then remember that I am standing 3′ above ground. Blazes that were head-high in summer, are waist high in winter.

On a steep trail I seek a steady pace, however slow, in order that I am not continually starting and stopping. Steady progress is more important than speed. It is particularly important to limit perspiring—which is all but impossible with the exertion, but can be approached, if not achieved, by a "steady and slow" rhythm.

I observe the day. The sky, visible through leafless deciduous trees, is clear. The tops of high maples sway in a wind whipping in from the northwest, but where I am at ground level, the woods block that wind, and I feel little of it. The day is cold, with temperatures in the single numbers, but I am warmed by my exertion. My wicking clothing layers do their job, and prevent a chill.

In deep snow it takes an hour to reach the site of the derelict Fire Warden's cabin, long abandoned, where it sits on a side trail to the left of the main trail, and above a stream. The stream is well-buried in deep snow today. It is common to find mountain streams running even on the coldest days. But today? Not a sight, not a sound.

As I continue upward, I am mindful of the daily hike to the fire tower by those who lived in the cabin. They worked themselves into good shape fairly quickly in the course of the fire watch season.

The trail ascends to a shoulder to the northwest of the summit cone. There are views towards Little Blue and the Saddleback Range beyond—and northeast towards Mount Abraham. In summer the thick canopy hides most of the view here, but this is predominantly a hardwood shoulder, and with the leaves gone, I enjoy these rare views.

To ascend to the summit, the trail angles right from this shoulder, and resumes its steepness, and winds its way upward. Occasionally I am in "four-point" mode—using both hands and both feet to ascend steep pitches. The forest here is mostly fir, characteristic of high elevations. High winds have dropped a few blowdowns across the trail. Trail maintenance season begins with summer. I crawl under some, over others, and squeeze my way through thick fir to get around others yet.

At a point 100 feet below the summit, a short side trail leads to a viewpoint at the top of a west-facing cliff face. This is worth a stop, whether or not the plan is to climb the tower. This is a niche location that, despite its westward view, may afford some protection from prevailing northwest winds. I have a look over Webb Lake, toward west-lying Spruce Mountain, then in the direction of the Mahoosuc Range.

Above me, through the trees, rises the summit tower. I return to the main trail, and enter the summit clearing in what seems only a minute or two. I am intrigued with the mountains far to the southeast, and take them to be the Camden Hills. More to the south rise the Kennebec Highlands, not particularly high, but striking from this vantage point because they stand in relief above the Sandy River Valley.

I make the rounds of viewpoints, including the tower. Then reluctantly—seems as though I am always reluctant to leave a summit—I head down, mindful that I have not only the mountain to descend, but also the two mile ski back to my vehicle. On the way down, I have the benefit of the trail I broke coming up. Between that factor, and gravity, I make good time.

An important consideration for Mount Blue—and truly any winter mountain hike—is to have extra clothing, food and water, and self-rescue gear. My pack holds an emergency bivouac bag, headlamp with spare batteries, signal whistle, compass, map, knife, fire starter, and repair kit for both snowshoes and skis.

Mount Blue offers a well-earned vantage point over a major portion of Western Maine. Get into condition for a mountain ascent, and make the climb!

Bald Mountain – Weld

Washington Township

Snowshoe. No fee.

Overview : 1.3 mile one way (2.6 mile round trip) snowshoe hike, steady and occasionally steep ascent over blue-blazed trail. Striking views over the Weld Valley, Webb Lake, and the Tumbledown-Jackson Range to the north: to Mount Washington and the Presidential Range in New Hampshire beyond the Mahossuc Range to the west; and to Wilson Lake to the south and prominent Mount Blue to the northeast.

Snowshoes with crampons advised, with boot crampons also recommended in case of icy conditions on summit ledges. Passes through mostly hardwood forest in the first 0 .7 miles, then enters fir and spruce growth to reach steep ledge.

Upper reaches of trail, marked by rock cairns and occasional blue paint blazes (often covered by snow) are over ledges that give the mountain its name.

Trailhead: Left (west) side of Maine Highway 156, north of Wilton, south of Weld. Prominent sign. Parking along road, which is usually plowed wide enough for vehicles to park well off the highway. This point is 0.1 mile south of the Washington/Perkins Township line.

Nearest Towns: Weld, Wilton

Maps: Delorme *Maine Atlas* Map #19, 3-D;
USGS: Mount Blue

Elevation Gain: 1400′

On Trail

On a mid-winter day not long after a succession of heavy snowstorms, I had a yearning to climb a mountain. I had much to do during the first part of the day, but knew that I would have the afternoon open—so I pack my daypack, put my snowshoeing clothes in another bag, and put all this with my snowshoes in my truck. Destination in mind—Bald Mountain, north of Wilton, south of

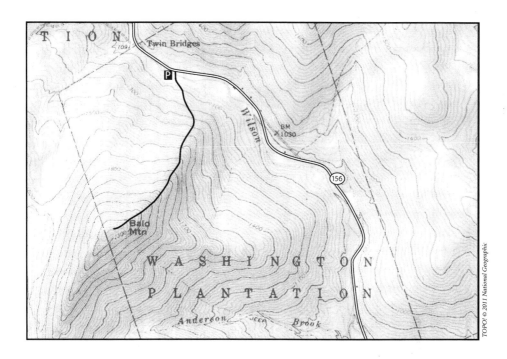

Weld, in Washington Township, just west of Maine Highway 156. This 2386′ mountain, with its open ledges on the top, is a popular choice for spring, summer, and fall hikes. I enjoy it as a winter hike of choice.

Rising at the south end of the Webb Lake Valley, Bald Mountain, and its sister peak, Saddleback (referred to on some maps as Saddleback Wind, but rarely so by local people) offer a 360-degree view that ranges from New Hampshire's White Mountains to the west, Tumbledown Range to the north, Saddleback Range and the Spaulding-Sugarloaf Ridge to the northeast, and to the southeast a long view over gentle country to the Camden Hills. In the center of the northward view sits Webb Lake. For a hike that usually takes a bit over one hour, these views are exceptional.

In 50′ from the trailhead the trail crosses Wilson Stream. Snow covers the rocks which in summer make for a rock-hop crossing, and extends over ice that has formed close to shore. I test with my snowshoe poles, seeking firm landing places as I prepare to cross. Do use care, as a step into water here would end the hike at the very beginning.

On the far side of the stream the trail begins a steady, straight-line ascent that continues for nearly 1.0 mile to a steep section of ledge and the first sweeping views. On the way I tramp over trail well-broken by other hikers. Bald is a popular destination year-round, and it is more common to meet other hikers here than not. Today will be an exception, as I am the only one on the mountain, but the tracks are fresh enough that someone may have been here earlier in the day—or to catch the light of the moon on the previous evening.

After passing through young hardwoods—maple, white birch, and beech—regenerating after a harvest here 15 years ago, I reach a section of boulders. I scramble up one pitch in the trail, pass into softwoods—fir and spruce, and reach the base of the summit ledges that give the mountain its name.

Choices. The main route climbs steep, high angle rock to a rounded section of ledge. There are signs in the vicinity for an alternate route, to the left, which works its way up a small draw, and offers a few trees for hand grips. Depth of snow, and presence or absence of ice, may determine which route is optimal on a given day. I opt for the more straight-ahead route, but discover that the snow on the rounded ledge above covers ice formed by the thaw-freeze cycle on ledge above that.

My snowshoes have built-in crampons. Will that suffice? Do I need to remove my snowshoes and put on the boot crampons I carry in my pack? It is a high step to gain a grip on the ledge. Using my poles for stability, and deliberate in my snowshoe placement, I complete the step, and move up and over the ledge.

This is a different world up here—something like stepping through a trap door to come out on a rooftop. Mount Blue is visible to the northeast.

Below sits Hills Pond. If I move toward the south I will gain a view towards Wilton and Wilson Lake. I continue the climb towards the summit, however, as high clouds have developed and I hope for a full Weld Valley view over Webb Lake from the very top before the clouds lower.

In summer cairns and blue paint blazes on rock mark the way over the ledges and up to the summit. In winter, save for a few opportune spots where the wind has blown snow away from a blaze, only the cairns mark the route. I have been here many times and have learned to follow the cairns. Although the way to the top seems simple enough, there are deep clefts between sections of ledge, and these must be avoided. The trail seems circuitous in places, but is the quickest—and safest—way.

As I climb a steep spine of ledge I gain enough elevation and sufficient northward angle that I soon have a fairly good chunk of that valley view. The Tumbledown-Jackson Range rides the northern skyline. Mount Blue becomes all the more distinct.

Short of the summit, which is the highest rounded section of ledge, the trail skirts a small depression, which looks like a 20' stretch of meadow and therefore a shortcut. Ignoring my own advice I step off the cairn-marked route, and hike for the meadow—only to sink up to my knees in the unsettled snow. Shorter in distance maybe, but not in time. I wade my way back to ledge, climb for a final 30' and I am on top.

Webb Lake lies in the center of the valley, its panhandle south end forming the outlet to the Webb River. Although cloud cover now obscures the sun, the ceiling rides just above the peaks that circle the valley. An intriguing perspective—the individual peaks stand out in relief more starkly than is the case on bright sunny days. The great forest that rides up the mountainsides is a mix of mottled grays among the lower elevation hardwoods, and the dark black-ish greens of spruce and fir above. White caps of snow top Little Jackson and Blueberry mountains—and Saddleback Wind Mountain off Bald to the immediate west.

I pull out a foam pad for a seat, take in the views, drink some tea, have something to eat, do some journaling. Not bad for a cloudy day. The air is still. There is no sound. Utter quiet. Time stands still.

Indeed, as far as I look out over the Weld Valley, nothing moves. Oh, I have seen hare track and deer track on my way up, and seen the track and heard the chattering of a red squirrel. But here at the very top—a great stillness. I look at the varying shapes of the mountains, and think of how glacier forces shaped each a bit differently. At times like this I image early homesteaders in this great valley, on a mid-winter day such as this one—hunting, trapping, turning to the root cellar or the dingle for food raised in the previous summer season, parceling out the firewood against a cold winter day.

Fire, warmth … I am cooling off. Time to move. I retrace my route down over the ledges. When I reach the icy ledge where I performed my step-up maneuver, I opt this time for the more tree-lined route. It is still steep and requires deliberateness, but I wish to avoid either a slip, or a catch of the crampons, on the other route. I drop down to the straight-line trail with little difficulty, and make my way back to the stream crossing and my waiting truck.

Again, Bald is one of Western Maine's most popular hikes—year-round. See why!

Tumbledown Pond and Parker Ridge
Weld

Snowshoe. No fee.

Overview: Maine Public Lands. 8.7 mile loop snowshoe hike; first on a 2.8 mile approach from the last plowed point on the West Brook Road to the Brook Trail Trailhead; a 1.5 mile Brook Trail ascent of 1550' to Tumbledown Pond; then a 2.2 mile 1500' descent via the Parker Ridge Trail ridge to the Little Jackson Trail at the upper end of the Morgan Road, 0.8 miles down the Morgan Road, and 1.4 miles back to the last plowed point on the West Brook Road. (If up and back to Tumbledown Pond only, via Brook Rail, round-trip to/from West Brook Road is 8.6 miles.)

Steep and icy pitches may require boot crampons.

Striking beautiful setting. Pristine high mountain pond, and open ridge with long views over the Weld Valley. Byron Notch Road is not maintained in winter, necessitating the 2.8 mile approach noted above.

Readily accessible in summer, the area is remote and seldom visited in winter. Parties should be well-equipped and experienced in back-country travel.

Trailhead: The Brook Trail trailhead on the Byron Notch Road is the starting point for the hike to Tumbledown Pond. To reach this Trailhead in winter involves a 2.8 mile snowshoe approach to the Brook Trail from the last plowed point on the West Brook Road. Our route begins where road plowing ends on the West Brook Road, south of the Tumbledown-Jackson Range. West *Brook* Road departs from the West *Side* Road 1.7 miles west of Weld Corner on Route 142 north of Weld Village.

Be careful not to block the turnaround area on the West Brook Road as it provides access to a mailbox for a private home. This spot could also be used as a base for rescue vehicles and personnel in event of an emergency. Snowplows may work here at any hour of the day or night.

A good rule when parking for any hike is never to block a gate or roadway. Consolidate passengers by leaving unneeded vehicles in Weld Village. There is not much room here for vehicles.

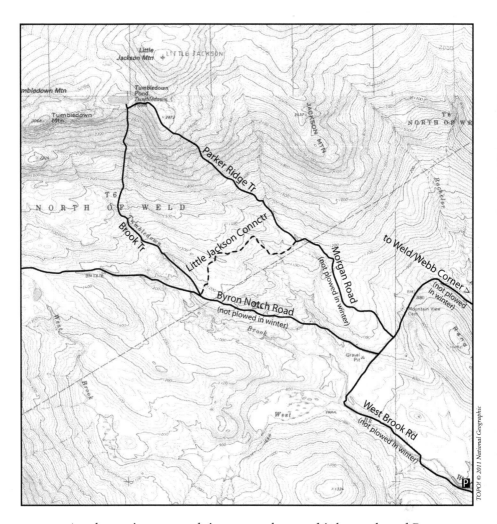

An alternative approach is to snowshoe or ski the unplowed Byron Notch Road 4.0 miles to the Brook Trail trailhead. Byron Notch Road is 0.5 miles west of Weld (aka Webb) Corner on Highway 142. This choice is 1.2 miles longer each way that the West Brook Road route (2.4 miles total).

Maps: Delorme *Maine Atlas* Map #19, 1-C;
Maine Bureau of Public Lands: Tumbledown-Jackson Range and Mount Blue State Park;
USGS: Weld

Nearest town: Weld

Elevation Gain: 1550′

On Trail:

On a clear, cold, April (Yes—April!) morning, I strap on my snowshoes and set out with a hiking companion to climb to Tumbledown Pond near Weld. Tumbledown is one of the most popular summer hikes in all of Maine, but is visited rarely visited in winter. Snow this day is deep—3–4 feet. April is a winter weather month in the Tumbledown-Jackson Range.

The open field at the snowplow turnaround point provides a fine view of the open, snow-covered summit of Little Jackson, and its forested neighbor, Big Jackson. We have picked a good day, with the promise of long views from high ground.

Let's hike! The unplowed section of West Brook Road leads northward over level ground, with the brook to the left, and a broad field of unbroken snow to the right. We pass a cut from a recent logging operation, then begin the ascent to reach the Byron Notch Road. Snowmobile use has packed the trail and we make good time.

Ruffed Grouse tracks cross the trail before us. Just as I stop to inspect the— whoosh! The bird bursts out of a snowbank 10′ ahead, scattering snow, shoots across our line of travel, beats the air towards thicker cover. That surprise raises the heart rate!

In 40 minutes, with occasional striking views toward Tumbledown Cliffs, we reach the Byron Notch Road at a T-junction. The Byron Notch Road is not maintained in winter. Instead, this snow-packed route serves as a snowmobile route connecting Weld with Coos Canyon to the west. The trailhead for the Brook Trail and the Little Jackson Connector lies westward. A second trailhead, for the Parker Ridge Trail to Tumbledown, and to the Little Jackson Trail, lies to the east, at the upper end of the Morgan Road.

Our plan is to hike a loop—ascend to the pond via the Brook Trail, descend to the Morgan Road by way of Parker Ridge. Whether we proceed as planned, or retrace our steps on the Brook Trail, depends upon what kind of time we can make in the deep snowpack, and whether trail markers on the high, open ground of Parker Ridge have been obscured by snow. We head west on the Byron Notch Road, climbing, descending to cross a brook, then climb again. Three snowmo-bilers come by, heading east. We stop to talk. They are from Gray, Maine, which they tell us has a fair amount of bare ground at this point in the year. It will be a few weeks yet before bare ground emerges in the Weld high country.

Shortly past a Maine Bureau of Public Lands sign the road descends to the Brook Trail trailhead, which is on the right before the bridge over Tumbledown Brook. There is a trail kiosk here, with a map of Tumbledown-Jackson trails. From our vehicle on the West Brook Road to this point, we have trekked on snowshoes for 1 hour, 15 minutes.

There are two trails here. The Little Jackson Connector leads northeast 1.1 miles to the Parker Ridge Trail, and to the Little Jackson-Big Jackson trails. For summer hikers, this Brook Trail trailhead is a good spot from which to start and end many hikes into the Tumbledown-Jackson Range, as there is ample off-road parking. The Brook Trail itself, our route to Tumbledown Pond, heads north.

I am struck by the pristine beauty of the trail, stretching before us through the mixed forest of fir, maple, and birch. There is not a single footprint—the snow lies completely unbroken. This well-traveled route in summer has not had a visitor in the weeks since the most recent significant snowfall. Snow crystals catch the sunlight. We stop for a moment to take in the sight—unbroken trail, a bright winter day, beech leaves fluttering in a light breeze. That temperature is in the balmy teens—good for winter hiking, not too warm, not too cold.

We are likely to be the only people on the mountain this day. Other people know we are here, as we have left a copy of our itinerary with responsible people. We have packed gear to handle an emergency: bivouac bags, down jackets, spare wicking long underwear, hats, mitts, hand warmers, extra food, ample water, first aid supplies, signal whistles, compasses, topographic maps, and headlamps with spare batteries.

We have cellphones but know that battery life shortens quickly at cold temperatures, and that reception is unreliable in these mountains. I carry repair items to fix broken snowshoes or trekking poles, and two spare snow baskets for the poles. Note that trekking poles alone, without the snow baskets, are useless in deep snow. If there should be a mishap, we have to be prepared to take care of ourselves. Many hours would pass before a rescue team could reach this remote spot—and that time would be in addition to the time it would take to get word out that help was needed.

A hard freeze has left a sturdy crust on the snowpack. We make good time. The blue-blazed trail has been freshly painted in recent seasons. This is a help, as the well-worn summer footpath is now well snow-buried this day. I do notice that instead of looking up, or at eye level, at the trail blazes, I look *down*. As I stand mid-trail, my head bumps against tree branches that would be three or feet over my head in summer!

Tracks aplenty: snowshoe hare, fox, red squirrel, moose. The light-weight critters are able to scamper lightly over the snow, but the moose tracks take the term "post-holing" to a new depth! I stick a trekking pole deep into a track—3 feet! I am glad that I do not weigh in at 1000 pounds at this snow depth.

The route follows an old logging road, climbing gradually at first, then more steadily. Eventually the road ends and the trail ascends in a series of s-turns, crosses a brook, snow-bridged and soundless. With the hardwoods bare in this season, we enjoy good views to the south and west, behind us. To the south rises the long ridge of Spruce Mountain. To the west we enjoy a side-on look at Tumbledown Cliffs.

The views prompt a lunch break—first of a number of these. When I hike I usually eat about every 90 minutes in order to keep well-fueled and well-hydrated—thereby I eat a series of small meals throughout the day, rather than wait for a mid-day lunch. The calories are burning! It is important to drink water regularly on a winter hike. When the air is cold, there can be less of an inclination to drink water, but dehydration can occur in winter, and can contribute to hypothermia. I watch the time, and eat and drink regularly.

We make our way with ease over the boulder field just below the pond. In summer I pick my way along in this section, careful to identify good footholds. But today, with the snow so deep, we simply trek over the snow-buried boulders on our snowshoes. We scramble a bit up a long reach and there it is—Tumbledown Pond, snow-covered, drifted in small dune-like ridges, embraced in a great winter silence.

The multiple peaks of Tumbledown Mountain rise beyond the pond, and to the west. They are rocky, snow-laden. In their distinctive, bee-hive shape they resemble outcrops from another part of the planet. Above us rise the bare upper slopes of Little Jackson, and below them the Little Jackson cliffs. The Little Jackson summit itself lies beyond our view. Off to the southeast Mount Blue commands the horizon. To the south lie Bald Mountain and Saddleback, forming the southern end of the Webb Lake Valley. What a sight!

A steady wind whips down from the peaks above us and across the pond. We pull on warm layers as we explore the area. Time to move on. We opt for the Parker Ridge Trail, anticipating more fine views from its open ledges, but first we must find the trail. I am familiar with the route, but recall that an arrow pointing to the start of the trail is painted on a rock—and therefore buried from view.

My companion stands at a point where he can see the pond, and I can see him and I walk in a sweep looking for a blue paint blaze on the scrub trees at this elevation. There! I holler to him, and off we go. We immediately pass the junction for the Pond Cutoff Trail, which connects in 0.9 miles with the Little Jackson Trail high on the mountain before the steep section of that trail that leads to the Little Jackson ridge. I am tempted to take the Cutoff Trail, but that would add to our time and distance, and I decide to defer that to another day.

We ascend to the heights of Parker Ridge, and I am reminded of why I chose this route in the first place. The open ledges offer superb views of the Weld Valley, Lake Webb, and the surrounding peaks, and then, beyond to the west we can see the Presidential range in New Hampshire, and the summit of Mount Washington. The ridge itself surrounds us with its own beauty. Great glacial boulders lie along the ridge-top, as though strewn by a giant hand. Stretches of ledge that have heated in the winter sun lie bare, alongside deep snow that has settled in the draws between them. I am reminded of snowy ridges I have ascended above tree-line in the Rocky Mountains of Colorado. This is one of the great viewpoints in the Western Mountains of Maine.

Oh yes, that wind! We move on, to generate heat, and to leave plenty of daylight for our hike down. It would be possible to hike back to Tumbledown Pond, then retrace our route on the Brook Trail, as we have not hiked very far to reach Parker Ridge from the pond. We opt to continue to descend by the Parker Ridge Trail, which was our original plan. The trail is marked by rock cairns, with occasional paint blazes placed on open ledge. At one point we employ our trail-finding technique again, when all blazes and cairns lie buried by snow. My hiking companion stands in view of the last marker, as I do a sweep, keeping him in view. I locate a marker, and off we go.

We reach a steep, icy, downward pitch. I do not like the looks of this. To descend on snowshoes risks pitching forward. Off come the snowshoes. On go our flexible boot crampons. Our snowshoes have built in crampons, but these are no match for the angle of drop and slickness of this icy slope. We make our way down this 30′ stretch, enter the trees, go back to our snowshoes.

Down, down, down, and we reach the intersection with the Little Jackson Connector, which links the Parker Ridge Trail to the trailhead on the Byron Notch Road by the Brook Trail. We continue on the Parker Ridge Trail a quarter mile, cross a stream, then reach the Little Jackson Trail which at this point is an old logging road. We turn right to reach the upper end of the rough Morgan Road, marked by an old sign for the Little Jackson Trail.

We continue down the Morgan Road for 0.8 miles to the Byron Notch Road. The sign for the Morgan Road is missing—only the bare pipe of a signpost remains, standing in the snow. We turn right (west) for 0.2 mile to reach the West Brook Road, and the way back to our vehicle.

Our trek up to Tumbledown Pond and down Parker Ridge Trail, starting and ending on the West Brook Road, took 6 hours. It was as a fine a winter day as I have ever enjoyed in our mountains. For well-prepared and well-equipped hikers, Tumbledown Pond beckons in winter!

Little Jackson
Weld

Snowshoe. No Fee.

Overview: Maine Public Lands, above Morgan Road. 5.2 miles ascent, one-way from Byron Notch Road via the Morgan Road, with additional 1.4 miles from West Brook Road last plowed point, to reach the base of the Morgan Road—totaling 6.6 miles one way from vehicle to summit. The round-trip from West Brook Road totals 13.2 miles—a long snowshoe distance.

Open summit with superb 360-degree views, including the Saddle-back Range, Four Ponds Mountain, West Kennebago and neighboring Northern Franklin peaks of the Kennebago Divide, Webb Valley and Webb Lake.

Steep elevation gain of 2700'—the most of any hike in this book. Final 0.5 mile on exposed ridge, Steep, icy, stretches may require boot crampons.

As is the case for Tumbledown routes, because the Byron Notch Road is not maintained in winter, hikers face the additional hike to reach the trailhead—as indicated above, 1.4 miles. Little Jackson becomes highly remote in winter, visited even less often than Tumbledown. Parties must be well-conditioned, properly-equipped, and experienced.

Trailhead: North end of the Morgan Road, 0.8 miles north of the Byron Notch Road. Two approaches. The first, described here, in *On Trail*, is the last plowed point on the West Brook Road, then over the remaining 1.2 miles of the West Brook Road, to the Byron Notch Road, then east 0.2 miles to the Morgan Road. *Parking note: The snowplow turn-around on the West Brook Road is across a bridge over West Brook at a private residence. Do not block the driveway, mailbox, or turn-around area for delivery vehicles. Be aware that snowplows may operate here at any time of the day or night. If multiple vehicles in a party, combine participants in one vehicle, leaving other(s) in town.*

The second (longer) approach is from the junction of the (unplowed) Byron Notch Road and the West *Side* Road, at a point 0.5 miles west of Weld Corner, Maine Highway 142, north of Weld Village. From this

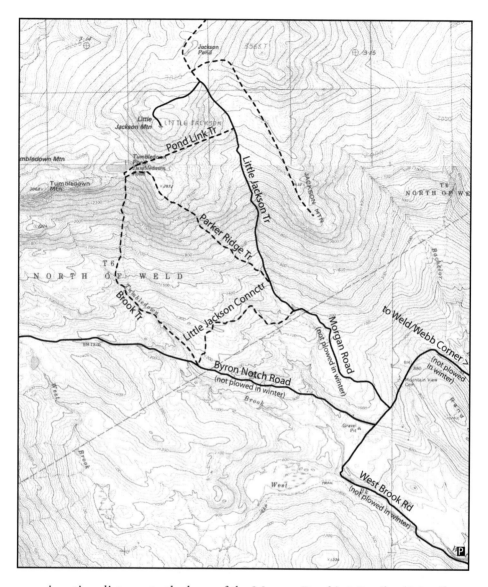

junction distance to the base of the Morgan Road is 2.2 miles (0.8 miles farther than the West Brook Road route (1.6 miles round-trip). Traveling this way would make the total trip to the summit 7.4 miles one-way (14.8 miles round-trip). There may be more room to park here, but the Byron Notch Road itself, though unplowed, must be kept open for rescue vehicles and snowmobile trail grooming equipment.

Parties might cross-country ski on the Byron Notch Road, to the Morgan Road—and even part-way up the Morgan Road, packing snowshoes;

then switch to snowshoes to ascend Little Jackson, stashing skis for the return ski at the end of the outing.

Note: Another Trailhead for Little Jackson is at the Brook Trail Trailhead, 1.6 miles west of the Morgan Road, where the Little Jackson Connector Trail leads 1.1 mile to meet the Little Jackson Trail just north of the Morgan Road terminus. However, the Brook Trail Trailhead is out of the way for winter-hiking Little Jackson—2.8 miles from the West Brook Road last plowed point.

Maps: Delorme *Maine Atlas* Map #19: 1-B,C;
Maine Bureau of Pubic Lands, Tumbledown Unit Map;
USGS: Weld

Elevation Gain: 2700′ from West Brook Road; 2500′ from Morgan Road at Byron Notch Road.

On Trail:

L ittle Jackson is one of my favorite hikes in summer, and a rewarding, yet demanding, snowshoe hike in winter conditions. It offers an above-tree-line ridge walk of a half mile, and long views in all directions. Although it tops out at 3434′ of elevation, the high ledge and rocky top resemble that of bare-summited four thousand footers like Saddleback, Mount Abraham (Abram), and North Brother in Baxter Park. The elevation gain is 2200′ by the Little Jackson Connector and Little Jackson Trails. In winter, hikers start at a lower elevation, adding more miles to the hike, and close to a total of 2700′ of vertical gain. It is a moderately sized mountain with big mountain features.

To the north lies Four Ponds Mountains in the foreground, and the Canada border peaks beyond. In the far west rises the Presidential Range in New Hampshire, topped by 6288′ Mount Washington, highest peak in the Northeastern United States. The Webb Lake valley, ringed by the Weld Mountains, lies to the immediate south. To the east, the forested summit cone of Big Jackson looms large, appearing nearer than its mile and a half distance. North of Big Jackson rises the Saddleback Range. Immediately below Little Jackson to the north, the mountain slope falls away to a great roadless valley, where Jackson Pond sits in a marshy lowland. Immediately westward are the multiple peaks of Tumbledown Mountain, and, from the west-lying edge of the open summit, a glimpse of a slice of Tumbledown Pond.

For a well-prepared party, experienced in winter travel, Little Jackson offers a fine winter outing. Because access roads are not plowed, the distance to be traveled on foot is greater in winter. Byron Notch Road is not maintained between

November 1 and April 30, and West Brook Road is plowed only to about one mile from the Byron Notch Road.

Remoteness becomes an issue. Popular and readily accessible in summer, the Tumbledown-Jackson Range is lightly visited in winter, and it is a long way to secure help if a mishap should occur.

The Little Jackson Trail becomes steep in its upper portion as it approaches the long east-west lying summit ridge. The route over the summit ledges to the peak can be difficult to follow because snow may obscure trail markings. The trail drops into three draws, two of them fairly steep, and requiring some four-point scrambling (hands and feet). Further, the east-west conformation of the Tumbledown-Jackson Range may block strong winter winds that blow in out of the northwest. Once on the summit ridge, the hiker is fully exposed to those winds. In other words, the weather one experiences on the top may be utterly different from the weather found on the way up.

I double check my gear list when I come here in winter to be certain that I have extra clothing, food, and water, repair materials for my equipment, and bivouac items in case of an emergency. Many times I have come here in winter, and on one occasion decided to turn back when soft snow conditions made the going very slow, and I questioned whether our party could make our way back to our vehicle before dark. Winter parties should have a common understanding before a trip starts, that a trip may be shortened in the interest of safety when conditions turn poor or time is short.

Let's go! From the junction of the West Brook Road with the Byron Notch Road, a hiking friend and I turn right on the notch road and travel about one-quarter mile, ascending steadily. At the point where the notch road tops out, the Morgan Road is a 90-degree left turn. The sign for the Morgan Road is missing, but the metal support pole sticks up out of the snow. We follow the unplowed road, covered in unmarked snow, to its end, passing old side roads blocked by berms. The end is a small open area at the top of a short, steep hill, used for parking during summer months. (In summer I suggest parking at one of the turn-offs lower on the Morgan Road, as this parking area is tight with little room to turn around.)

A faded blue and white sign for Little Jackson on the east side of the parking area confirms the route. The blue-blazed trail follows an old logging road through a mixed hardwood-softwood forest. Rock maples predominate. There are both White Birch (also known as Paper Birch) and Yellow Birch. The latter takes on a coppery sheen in the rich light of winter sun. Watch for Beech trees holding their parchment leaves well through the winter. These leaves too, glow in the winter light, which is all the richer at this early morning hour.

In less than a quarter mile, the Parker Ridge Trail and the route to the Little Jackson Connector to the Tumbledown Brook Trailhead diverge to the left, crossing a nearby stream that flows down the valley between Parker Ridge and Big Jackson. At this point the trail has left the private property along the Morgan Road and is now on Maine Public Land. The Little Jackson Trail stays to the right of this stream, steadily moving away from it as the trail gains elevation.

The route on the old road is clear, cutting an 8–10 foot wide swath up the mountainside, without the encroachment of tree growth to be found in upper sections. The snow before us lies unbroken—at least by human tracks—but the tracks of moose and red squirrel remind us that there is life in these woods in mid-winter.

My snowshoes provide good flotation on snow that has settled to a depth about a foot and a half. We make steady progress. I am heating up from the exercise! To limit perspiring, I remove my outer layer, a rain-wind shell.

Recent trail work by the Maine Conservation Corps has rerouted the trail away from the most badly eroded stretches of the old road. The first of these re-routes swings to the left (west), to switchback up the slope. A second, longer than the first, turns right (east), makes a sharp turn northward, then proceeds for a quarter mile to rejoin the route of the old road. The changes are clearly marked with blue paint blazes—most of them on trees at a height of 5'. This placement causes them to be visible even when the snowfall is deep. I do have to adjust to looking *down* for a blaze when the snowpack reaches a depth of 3–4 feet!

We reach the Pond Cutoff Trail junction one hour and 15 minutes from the intersection of the Morgan Road with the Byron Road. This trail leads west 1.1 miles to Tumbledown Pond. Hikers may head this way to the pond, then return to the Morgan Road area via the Parker Ridge Trail. It would also be possible to hike to the summit of Little Jackson, return to this trail junction, then hike to Tumbledown Pond on the Pond Cutoff Trail, before descending via the Parker Ridge Trail. This, however, would make for a long day, and would require an early start by well-conditioned parties.

As we make our way up the stream valley, the old road grows rougher and more narrow, until the route resembles a mountain trail more than an old road. After the crossing of the largest of the streams, where there is a bit of open water, the trail climbs more steeply, now among the fir and spruce common to higher elevation. On another trip when I was trekking through deep, soft snow, the going had become so slow that I made this stream crossing my turnaround point— stopping here to sit on a rock in the sun while enjoying a food break. I take winter hikes with a predetermined turn-around time—the time of day when I must be heading back down the mountain. This time is calculated in order that I may return to my vehicle with at least one hour of daylight remaining.

After a steady climb, the trail emerges from fir and spruce, suddenly, it seems, to open ground in the col between Little Jackson to the west and Big Jackson to the east. There is a good view of Webb Lake to the south. In a few yards, the trail divides: Little Jackson to the left; Big Jackson to the right. Although Big Jackson is higher than Little Jackson, as the mountain names imply, Big Jackson trail is less-frequently hiked because the summit is wooded, and the views limited. I have hiked to the top and located a summit register in a glass jar. The notes therein describe a number of winter ascents.

The Big Jackson route is marked by cairns, and occasional flagging tape, but was not paint blazed on my most recent hike. The first one hundred yards may cause hikers to wonder whether they are on the correct trail, as the route takes a sharp northward turn, and begins a descent on a trail that suddenly widens. But after 50 yards a prominent sign marks another junction, where the Big Jackson trail enters the woods, follows a low ridge to the base of the summit cone, then ascends steadily to the wooded summit. There are occasional views through the trees of the upper reaches of Big Jackson. On the descent there are views of Little Jackson. Parties planning to hike Big Jackson should expect a round-trip of 2 hours minimum. Snow conditions could extend that time.

Back to the ascent of Little Jackson, we move westward, gaining elevation, with the main summit slightly to the southwest. A second, north-lying summit is not the main peak. The trail leading to the open summit of Little Jackson winds its way westward across the ridge, dropping into one draw after another, then climbing out again. The route is marked by cairns, most of them spaced frequently. There are blue blazes painted on the ledge in places, but most of these are snow-covered in winter.

The route over the summit ridge to the peak is neither straight nor intuitive, but it is the optimal route. We avoid the urge to take a shortcut, as a straight line approach leads to short cliff faces, steep pitches, and thickly forested draws where the snow could be shoulder deep. The distance from turn at the col between Little and Big Jackson to the summit is about 0.5 miles. I am glad to have snowshoes with crampons built in, as I scramble out of the draws. In case of ice or hard-pack snow, I have boot crampons in my pack if these may be needed to negotiate a slippery pitch.

When we reach the open top, which is surprisingly flat, with a series of low outcrops, we enjoy long views in every direction. A particularly intriguing view is that of the west and main peaks of Tumbledown Mountain with their curious beehive configurations. It is remarkable that mountains so very close to one another, and shaped by the same retreating glaciers, have such utterly different shapes.

We trek westward from the summit about 100′, losing a bit of our hard-gained elevation, to have a view of the far western edge of Tumbledown Pond, snow covered on this day. The pond appears close, but the Pond Link Trail, which we passed on the ascent, is the optimal route for those who want to include the pond on a Little Jackson hike. A direct line descent from Little Jackson summit to the pond will bring hikers to an impassable cliff, which cannot be seen from the summit. The shortest distance between two points may be a straight line, but that does not mean that the short distance can be covered in the shortest time.

We return to the summit to enjoy our helicopter-view of the Western Mountains of Maine in winter, having pulled on our cold weather gear so as not to become chilled while we are stopped. By the way, where is the high point? It is where a triangular rock sits atop a cairn, beside another cairn with blue blazes on either side. At the base of the triangle-rock cairn, the wind has blown snow clear to reveal a round United States Geological Summit Marker.

Over the years hikers have constructed a stone windbreak about 3' high, just north of the summit. The exposed high ground is wind-blown enough that the snow cover is thin, and we are able to hunker down out of that wind, using the windbreak as shelter. I enjoy hot soup and chunks of cheddar cheese, good fuel for a winter day. This is the good life, on Little Jackson—ample snow, sun, long views, good eats.

On the descent we have the afternoon sun fairly in our faces, which is good. That sun throws railroad tie shadows across the trail. We make good time on the way out, with the benefit of a trail packed by our ascent. When we reach the truck, we enjoy sandwiches we stowed for this moment. We have burned some calories on our winter hike. Time to replenish.

Little Jackson—out of the way, wildly beautiful!

FIELD NOTES

Blueberry Mountain
Weld

Snowshoe. No fee.

Overview: Maine Public Land (summit area). Blueberry Mountain Bible Camp (lower trail). 1.1 miles one-way (2.2 miles round trip) steady ascent, often steep, Blueberry offers some of the region's finest views. Rocky, open summit, elevation 2942′, provides a good look at many of the high peaks of Franklin County: Saddleback, Mount Abram, North and South Crocker, and Sugarloaf.

A good choice for a spring, summer, or fall hike, Blueberry is also a great winter ascent—a good snowshoe workout without the distance and time involved in tackling one of Maine's 4000-footers. One of the lesser known peaks in the Western Mountains of Maine, Blueberry Mountain is a favorite. I make a point of coming here at least once each winter.

The lower half of the trail is on private land of Blueberry Mountain Bible Camp. Whenever I see camp personnel I take time to thank them for providing access to the trail. I have made a small donation to the cost of plowing the road and parking lot, which is not expected, but a consideration. Maine has a long tradition of public access to private forest and mountain land. Hikers have a role in maintaining mutually respectful landowner relationships.

The upper half of the trail, including the summit, is part of Tumbledown Public Lands, managed by the Maine Bureau of Public Lands.

Trailhead: Upper end of 1.8 mile Blueberry Mountain Bible Camp Road, also known as Blueberry Mountain Road, off Maine Highway 142, north of Weld Corner, aka Webb Corner, which is north of Weld Village. The turnoff is 3.8 miles north of the crossroads in downtown Weld, and 1.4 miles north of Weld Corner. If coming from the Rangeley or Phillips area, it is 8.5 miles southwest of the intersection of Maine Highways 27 and 142. Watch for the camp sign, 716 Phillips Road.

Some maps and guidebooks show this road to be gated, but I have not yet found the gate closed. The Bible Camp facilities serve as a year-round residence for the camp director family who leave the gate open. However,

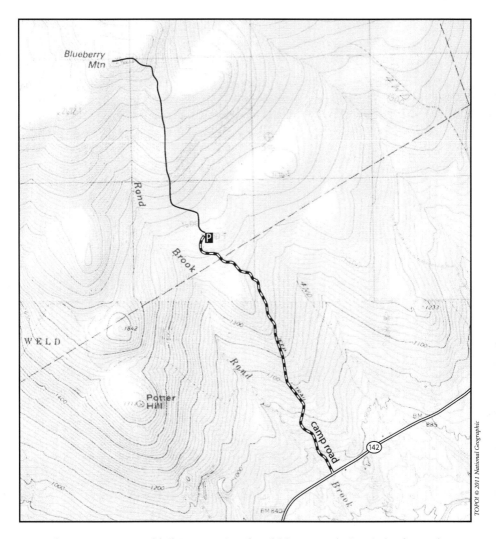

there is a gate, and hiking parties should be prepared to hike from the gate to the trailhead if extraordinary circumstances cause it to be closed.

Drive to the end of the road, choosing the more substantial road at intersections with twitch roads, to arrive at the camp complex and a parking area across from the large brown-painted main lodge. Park in the parking area only, and not next to the lodge or in the area by maintenance sheds.

With a back to the lodge, facing the parking lot, look to the right for a driveway that leads north to an athletic field. Cross the field directly to enter the woods on the other side by a forest road. Look for blue paint blazes on trees. One hundred yards into the woods, the road veers to the left and the Blueberry Mountain Trail diverges to the right to begin a steep ascent.

There may be signage, but if not, look for the blue blazes.

Nearest Towns: Weld, south on Maine Highway 142; Phillips, north on Maine Highway 142.

Maps: Delorme *Maine Atlas* Map #19, 2-C;
Mount Blue State Park and Tumbledown Public Lands Guide and Map, Maine Bureau of Parks and www.maine.gov/dacf/park;
USGS: Madrid, Weld

Elevation Gain: 1300'

On Trail

On a very bright and completely cloudless winter day a hiking companion and I set out from the trailhead in two-foot powder snow that overlays a firm crust. We soon discover that we are the first hikers on the mountain following a few weeks of winter storms. That means breaking trail—more work, but offering a pristine quality to the day. We are well prepared. Each of us has snowshoes with built-in crampons underneath, and we use trekking poles with snow baskets to provide stability. Our daypacks hold plenty of food and water, and extra layers of windproof gear in case we encounter strong winds above the tree line. We are off to an early start—important in winter when the hours of daylight are limited. Our gear includes sunglasses and even headlamps in case an emergency causes us to be out after dark.

As we make our way steadily upward, views open through the leafless maple, yellow birch, and gray birch. We have a good look at Mount Blue and Center Hill to the southeast. Southward lies the white expanse of Webb Lake. So clear is the view this bright winter day that we see at the southern extreme of the lake the beginning of the now-snow-covered Webb River angling its way to its distant meeting with the Androscoggin River in Dixfield.

The wind breezes through the forest where spruce and fir predominate, the higher we hike. A few Black-capped Chickadees flit from tree to nearby tree, and an occasional Blue Jay bothers at us with a noisy cry of "Thief!" Above soars a raven, sending its throaty "Caw!" echoing in the mountain stillness. The sky over our heads is such a deep shade of blue-purple. Such a day!

The trail ascends steeply for the first half of its length, then levels out over a short shoulder of the mountain, before ascending again, leveling again, and so on—like a series of great stair steps. As I prepare to ascend one particular steep pitch, I pull up short at an unexpected sight. A snowball, about the size of a soccer ball, lies in the snow in front of me.

How did that get here? I look around for snowshoe tracks from some other party—none! Is there another route up the mountain that I have never heard of, and other hikers rolling snowballs down the mountain? But the hillside above is pure unbroken snow—except for a narrow chute that extends from the snowball up the slope to its source. And that source is the base of a small fir poking out of the snow at the top of the pitch.

I piece together the story. A clump of fresh snow on a fir bough warms in the mid-day sun, lets go and … "plop". Gravity takes over. The clump tumbles down the hill, gathers snow as it rolls, and becomes that snowball—which stopped rolling at the base of the hill, surely only a few moments before I show up. How about that. "If a snowball forms on its own in the forest, and there is no one around to hear it, does it make a sound?" (Or something along those lines.)

More discoveries. As we reach the last of the level areas on the step-like route, moose tracks abound. A large depression in the snow indicates that a moose had rested here, legs folded beneath it. A rare sight. While we did not see the moose, it was quite a thrill to imagine this as a place where moose seek shelter, day or night. Indeed, although the northwest winter wind has whipped about us for much of the hike, this very spot is well-sheltered by the configuration of the mountain, and by a thick stand of fir.

In its final stretch the trail climbs steeply to break out of the trees onto summit ledge amidst low scrub. Views northeast to Saddleback and Mount Abraham open up. On to the summit! We keep to the high ground, head west, and in 50 yards, reach the summit marker, a large cairn jutting out of the snow.

The view is virtually unbroken. To the east, a crow-fly mile distant, looms Big Jackson, with rocky Parker Ridge in the foreground. To the far west the Presidential Range in the White Mountains of New Hampshire, topped by the summit cone of Mount Washington, commands the horizon. To the north a series of summits spread beyond Rangeley—the angular peak of West Kennebago, and its neighbor mountains that drain to the Kennebago, Cupsuptic, or Magalloway Rivers. Beyond these rise peaks along the international border with Canada. To the northeast runs the Saddleback Range and the great Appalachian Trail Route toward Sugarloaf and beyond. Southward spreads the Weld Valley. Quite a sight for a 1.1 mile hike!

The short view, right at our feet, offers its own rewards. The wind has sculpted the snow into delicate ridges—like sandstone patterns in the desert Southwest. There are swirls, wing-like designs, miniature white contour maps, all manner of wind sculptures. The rock of Zion Canyon and Arches National Parks come to mind, except that these are snow sculptures at my feet. Unlike their sandstone counterparts two thousand miles distant, these will change shape in the next sweeping wind.

We linger on top having lunch, water, and hot tea—and take in that 360-degree view. Although we quickly donned extra clothing layers when we reached the top, we feel a chill coming on. Time to move. We shoulder our packs, make one last circle turn to take in the broad view—a sight all the more rich in color in the light of the lowering afternoon sun.

With benefit of a now-broken trail, we make good time on the way down. On an occasional snowy pitch I lean back just a bit on my snowshoes, use my trekking poles as ski poles, and enjoy a few feet of snowshoe-skiing, slipping through the light powder. Fun!

Franklin County has some of the finest snowshoe terrain to be found in the Eastern United States. Strap on your snowshoes and head out!

FIELD NOTES

Farmington-Foothills Region

The Foothills Region of Southern Franklin County has been a center for cross-country skiing for decades. Many local ski athletes have proceeded to compete or coach at the university or national team level.

A major reason is the Titcomb Mountain Ski Area in West Farmington, with 16 kilometers of groomed cross-country trails, beginner to expert, including 2.3k lighted trails for night skiing. The trail system is also available for snowshoeing. Other ski and snowshoe opportunities are available in nearby Powder House Hill Trails and along the Sandy River.

Visitors may be pleased to know that it is possible to have a workout, or relaxing outing, at the start or end of a travel day or business day—and not have to leave town.

Titcomb Mountain Trails   200

Powderhouse Hill Trails   204

Sandy River Intervale   208

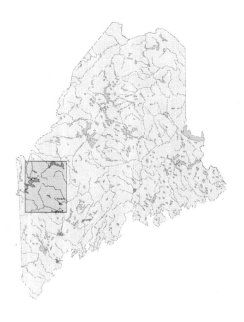

Dead River, Grand Falls - West Forks
✳
Dead River & Grand Falls Hut - LFD
✳

✳Flagstaff Hut & Flagstaff Lake East Shore
✳Flagstaff Lake Round Barn
✳Little Bigelow Mtn.
Cranberry Peak✳
Crommett Trail
Stratton Brook Hut & Oak Knoll ✳ ✳Poplar Hut & Poplar Stream Falls
Narrow Gauge Pathway
Sugarloaf Outdoor Ct.
Long Falls Dam Road
Rangeley Lakes Trail Ctr.
Rangeley ✳
Bald Mt.✳ Rock & Midway
✳Ponds
South Bog Trail ✳Piazza Rock
Low Aziscohos ✳
✳Oberton & Hardy Streams
✳Fly Rod Crosby Trail
Little Jackson Mt. Blueberry Mt.
Tumbledown Pond & Tumbledown Mt.✳
Byron Road
✳ ✳Mount Blue
Center Hill
Sandy Rvr ✳Powderhouse Hill
Intervale✳ *Farmington*
Titcomb Mt.✳
Bald Mt.
Wilton

27
27
16
16
16
16
16
16
142
4
142
4
4
17
17
142
156
156
2 27
2
4

Titcomb Mountain Trails

West Farmington

Ski or snowshoe. Fee. Lodge with food service. Rentals and lessons.

Overview: Titcomb Mountain Trails, Farmington Ski Club. 16 kilometer trail system groomed for classic and skate technique. Night skiing on 2.3k lighted trails—only lighted groomed trails in Maine at this writing. Choice of level, moderate, or steep terrain. Cross-country trails open for snowshoeing, as are summer mountain bike trails—but please walk single file on one side of groomed ski trail, and away from set tracks.

Summit views north toward Mount Abraham and the High Peaks, and east over the Sandy River Valley toward Bannock Mountain and the ridges that lie west of the Kennebec River.

Somewhat of an unknown to first-time visitors to Maine, Titcomb is very popular with local people because of the high quality of the trail network, and ease of access—just a 5 minute drive from U.S. Route 2. This Nordic ski, Alpine ski, and snow-board center is owned and managed by the Farmington Ski Club, a loyal and hard-working group of people from the region who love skiing in all its forms. The Club organized in 1939, opened its first lift, a rope-tow, in 1942, and now has two-T-bars. The area is named for John "Jack" Titcomb of Farmington, who served in the US Marine Corps, and died in the Pacific Theater in World War II.

In the mid-1900s Northern New England was dotted with small, local ski operations like Titcomb. Local townspeople cleared a suitable hill for skiing, installed a rope tow—often powered by an old truck engine—and away we go! At Titcomb, initially Alpine skiing and tobogganing were the draw. There was a ski jump here until the 1980s. In the late 1960s and early 1970s Nordic skiing grew in popularity in the US, and the Farmington Ski Club began clearing cross-country trails. While many other local ski operations in Maine and New England closed in the 1980s and 1990s as large resort areas expanded, Titcomb, supported by a large, loyal volunteer network, has thrived.

Trailhead: Ski Slope Road, off Morrison Hill Road, off Maine Highway 43 to Temple from Farmington. To reach the Morrison Hill Road/Route 43

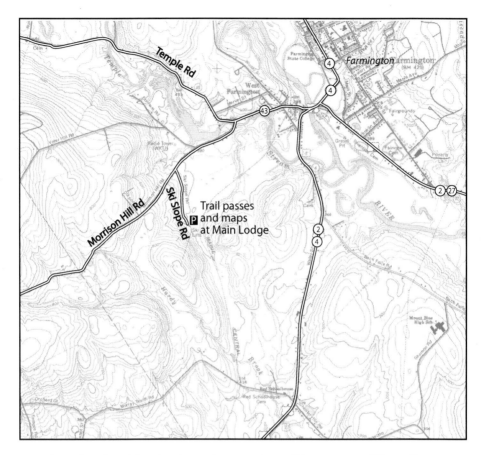

junction, head for the 4-way intersection of Route 43 and Town Farm Road, in West Farmington, west of US Route 2 Center Bridge. West Farmington Post Office is just off this intersection. From this intersection go west on Route 43 for 0.3 miles; turn left onto Morrison Hill Road at bridge over Temple Stream; travel 0.6 miles to Ski Slope Road.

Nearest Towns: West Farmington Village; Farmington

Maps: Delorme *Maine Atlas* Map #19, 5-D;
Titcomb Mountain Trails Map—available at lodge.

Elevation Gain: Varies from zero to 200′

On Trail

I begin my ski outing with a warm up on the Airport Loop, George's Woodlot, or both. These are level trails that start on the east side of the parking area. Ski from the front door of the lodge, head left past the equipment sheds, to reach these trails. The Woodlot Loop circles through a low, mixed growth woodland of red maples, alder, and cedar. Airport Loop is a long, flat, wide-open trail—good to practice technique, or simply to enjoy the ease of travel and the long views.

From here I head back towards the equipment sheds to the cross-country-Nordic "Stadium" (the broad open area used for start and finish of Nordic ski races) then left on the Cedar Swamp Trail—the first of Titcomb Nordic trails to have lights for night skiing. Cedar Swamp leads me to Turnpike, longest trail in the system, at 1.7 kilometers. Turnpike heads southwest, mostly level, with some gentle uphill and downhill, to reach the ski area southern boundary at a 90-degree turn uphill. Turn around to retrace the route back toward the Lodge, or continue on a hill climb up the west ridge of the mountain, towards the summit. The summit route begins on Ridge Road, and continues as Stonewall Alley.

I usually do the climb, using herringbone technique at first. The terrain moderates and I then either stride in classic technique, or skate. This is my favorite section of the Titcomb trail system. High white pines rise along the ridge to my right. An old rock wall borders the trail to my left. This was once farmed ground! In late afternoon the winter sun, low on the horizon, throws a rich golden light upon the trees. Long shadows reach over the snow. Stillness prevails. This is a favorite place.

After passing a number of intersections along this wooded route, and an Adirondack-style shelter rest stop, I ascend to the higher points on the mountain. Near the summit the Nordic trails are just a few steps from the top of the Alpine slopes—which offer long views to the north and east. There are two view points, one at the top of the Bunny and Beagle Alpine Trails; the other at the top of the "Main". Both are worth a visit, as the views are a bit different from each.

The open summit on the northern horizon is Mount Abraham (Abram), 4050′ elevation. The three low, rounded mountains closer and to the northeast are the New Vineyard Mountains. More directly east lie the Sandy River Valley and the town of Farmington. Beyond these a series of north-south ridges divide the Sandy River watershed from that of the Kennebec River, 25 miles away, and out of sight.

More choices. One is to continue northward past the Bunny/Beagle slopes T-bar, on the Upper Wild Acres trail, which offers the longest continuous straight downhill run on the mountain, followed by winding trail connecting to Lower Wild Acres and the route back to the Lodge. Another is to take this same northward route and at the first intersection, climb back up on Ramdown to the top of the Alpine slopes—then retrace the earlier ascended route: down along the stonewall, to Turnpike, and back to the Lodge. Another choice is Roller Coaster, which parallels Stonewall Alley but has more up and down terrain before it reaches an intersection with a series of zig-zag routes down the east side of the mountain—and back to the Lodge.

These are a few of many choices. I do enjoy skiing amidst those high pines up top, with west-lying sun beaming rich light across the snow. Remember the night skiing! Visit Titcomb Mountain to find your own favorite routes!

Powder House Hill Trails, Flint Woods

Farmington

Snowshoe; ski on ungroomed terrain. No fee.

Overview: Wooded ridge-top trail system with loops, and look-out points, convenient to downtown Farmington. Fine get-a-way spot for skiing or snowshoeing, to start the day, to end the day—or have a break in the day. Wear a headlamp and come for a snowshoe trek or ski outing on a winter evening.

Known locally as the Flint Woods or the Village Woods, the Powder House trail system combines both tracts and covers 83 acres of high ground on Box Shop Hill, Powder House Hill, and the connecting ridge. Add in the nearby Bonney Woods and the total reaches 93 acres.

Views extend to Mount Blue, the Sandy River Intervale, toward the west, and the mountains of New Vineyard and Strong to the north—Herrick, Pratt, and others. A major draw is the serene setting of these woods. High pines, both white and red, rise on the ridge, neighbored by great hemlocks. The light-filtering canopy of these magnificent conifers shades the forest floor year round and provides both a cathedral-like feel, and fairly long views through the forest itself. Some folks make daily visits year-round to this serene spot for a morning walk, or an afternoon trek.

Trailhead: The Powder House Hill Trailhead is at a plowed parking area, well-signed, on Anson Street 0.5 miles east of Main Street. (Turn at the corner intersection at the County Court House with the clock tower.) A trail kiosk provides a map display, and paper trail maps may be available at the kiosk. I recommend bringing a map along on the first few outings, to become familiar with the many trails, and with the location of look-out points and other features. If the map box is empty, you might sketch a map of your own from the display. (A notebook and pen are a standard part of my hiking gear.)

Nearest Town: Farmington

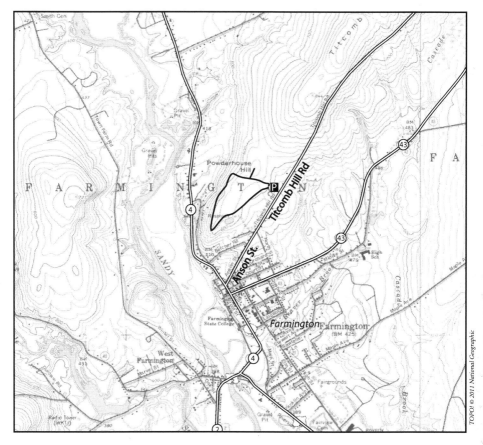

Maps: Delorme *Maine Atlas* Map #20, 1-C;
Delorme *Maine Atlas* Town of Farmington Map, A-1 (See oval of former reservoir; to the right of that, Flint Woods, off Anson Street.)

Elevation Gain: less than 100'

On Trail

On day following an 8˝ fresh snowfall, I head out on snowshoes along the East trail intending a counter-clockwise loop, to take in the three viewpoints of Powder House Hill, The Flint Woods Lookout, and Box Shop Hill. All are noted on the map. High hemlocks droop with snow-laden branches. Slight breezes come and go, dislodging snow above me, scattering snow flurry bursts as I pass. Save for the soft rush of these intermittent flurries, the prevailing sound is that of silence. The late afternoon sun slants in through occasional gaps in the canopy. This is a place of remarkable beauty. On this fresh-powder day I am reminded of scenes from the children's classic *The Snowman.*

Others have gone before me. I see snowshoe tracks before me, which eventually will diverge in another direction. A set of ski tracks crosses my path, as someone has chosen to make his or her own way, rather than follow the trails. That can be done here. It would be difficult to get lost, with streets on two sides, a long ravine on a third, and a stone wall along the final side.

Trail distances are short in the complex, and in under 10 minutes I reach the end of the East Trail, where that stonewall marks the northeast boundary of the trail complex. A route continues from here for a short ascent of Powder House Hill, moving out of the conifers into a more thinly wooded mixed hardwood-softwood growth. I head in that direction to see what views await, reaching the top in 5 minutes.

This is a stopping point with some curious, personalized history—perhaps a tradition. Mementos left by past visitors, including a very large mouse trap and a small string of Christmas lights hang from a small white birch by the summit. The high ground offers views through the trees to the northeast where rise the foothills of New Vineyard and Strong. There was a time when this was open ground, and Powder House Hill offered a 360-degree view of Farmington and the surrounding foothills. It is pleasant enough on this day, even with its tree growth. I linger, imagining how Farmington residents have walked to this spot for a few moments of peace and beauty for decades—more than two centuries, actually!

I retrace my steps to the stonewall, re-enter the trail complex, and move along the Lookout Trail which slabs the north rim of the ridge that falls away to the Sandy River valley. No one else has passed this way since the recent snowfall. I break trail in the fresh, light, snow, and easily so. Next, I pass through a small clearing just below the Flint Woods Lookout, knowing that eventually I will hike to that point.

Another visitor to the woods sits on a wooden bench at the lookout, taking in the view. We nod and maintain the silence, as I pass about 10 yards below. I continue westward, using the Flint Connector, to reach the summit of Box Shop Hill. Here a viewpoint with a log bench looks over the Sandy River intervale towards Mount Blue. The intervale and river are in shadow at this hour, but the heights of Mount Blue glow in the afternoon sun.

From here, I angle past the reservoir, rimmed by a high-rising stand of Red Pine, distinctive by the red, scaly bark. This is the appropriately named "Tall Pines" section of the trail complex, which borders the old reservoir. From here I cut over to the Flint Woods Lookout, where a short side trail ascends a rise, opening to a striking view of Mount Blue perfectly framed by an opening in the trees. Log benches await the visitor who wishes to linger here. For all the beauty of this entire trail complex, this for me is the most beautiful spot of all.

For my route back to the trailhead I make my way to one of two small ponds within the trail complex. A plaque there honors the late James Flint who gifted this portion of the forest to the community. Mr. Flint visited here regularly on walks with his dog, and wished that others might discover its wonder and beauty as did he. Remarkably, though this is a cold mid-winter day with temperatures well below freezing, water runs steadily from a seep to enter the pond. I watch as a steady trickle of water drops toward the ice-covered pond, exposing a bit of green moss on this otherwise snowy terrain.

As I near the trailhead a cross-country skier glides soundlessly through the trees in the distance. My own outing on snowshoes has lasted only an hour, and I have seen much in that time. There are many trail options. A person could step into the woods for a few moments of enjoyment, or make one's way along a combination of trails to spend the better part of a morning or afternoon here.

I shall return—on skis, on snowshoes, and in warmer months, on foot, to enjoy this compelling woods.

Sandy River Intervale

Farmington

Snowshoe or ski on terrain both ungroomed and groomed snowmobile trail for part of the route. No fee.

Overview: 1.5 mile ungroomed loop for snowshoeing or cross-country skiing around broad bottomland on the east side of the Sandy River. Access from downtown Farmington. Long views north toward Mount Abraham and the High Peaks Region. Views up and down the Sandy River. A snowmobile trail along the east edge of the field is groomed, and frequent use by those on skis or snowshoes, usually presents a packed route. If breaking trail is necessary, the terrain is essentially flat.

Good choice for a short outing, or when in the immediate Farmington area and seeking a nearby spot with long views, and no significant driving time. When the outing is over, it is a short walk into town for a bowl of chili, soup, or chowder, and a hot drink.

Trailhead: Off Front Street in Farmington, in vicinity of the Narrow Gauge Movie Theater (Narrow Gauge Square). Parking in movie theater lot is for movie customers only (enforced). Some parking in the nearby area is reserved for local business. If no parking available, there are additional spaces across Front Street, and down Front Street (south).

Carry gear towards the "Snack Shack" refreshment stand for University of Maine at Farmington athletic events. This is located on the former railroad bed berm that cuts across the intervale. On the far side of the Snack Shack a path leads to the right, down to the Varsity Soccer Field. Head north along the east side of the field by a snowmobile trail, pass through a perimeter fence, and enter the intervale. Continue 0.1 mile to enter the broad "cornfield". No trail sign. The way should be obvious—around the perimeter.

Travel the loop in either direction. I usually head left (west), towards the river, to circle the field clock-wise—for no other reason than wanting to approach the river bank early in my outing to look for signs of waterfowl at open water, or tracks of mammals on their way to the water for a drink. Either direction is fine. Often I will travel the loop twice,

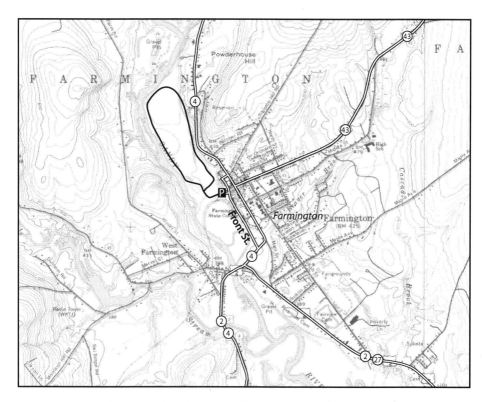

reversing direction for the second loop, for the different perspective that affords.

Nearest Town: Farmington

Maps: Delorme *Maine Atlas* Map #20, 1-C; and Delorme *Maine Atlas* Town Map for Farmington—look for Sandy River, Front Street, and Narrow Gauge Square.

Elevation Gain: None.

On Trail

Afternoon mid-winter sun plays brightly on the broad, snow-covered hay-field on the Sandy River Intervale. Far to the north, the multi-peaked high ridge of Mount Abraham (Abram to locals) rises, snow-capped purple against the sky. Before me stretches the far-reaching loop that swings west to the banks of the Sandy, north to just short of the far tree line, arcs back along a field-edge brook to approach my starting point.

Let's go! A good friend starts nearly every day here on skis, wearing a head-lamp in the early hours of the morning, circling the great bottomland accompanied by his dog. Today my wife and I are on snowshoes, and we head left (west) to trek along the banks of the Sandy, past Red Maple and Sumac, the latter with maroon-red bobs a contrast to the surrounding snowy white. Quick water has opened a breech in the ice-pack. Dark, dark blue waters rush by, highlighted in the sun, plunge out of sight under thick mid-winter ice.

At the upper end of the field we swing over the outer end of the loop, turn south to pick up the well-packed snowmobile trail, and pass near a snow-covered stream at the edge of Powder House Hill. A hundred feet above us, light traffic travels by, but in curious quiet, as the sound simply passes high over our heads. We hear little other than the draw of our own breathing. Wizened-brown Gold-enrod and field grass poke through the snow at the edge of the field. To the south the tops of the town's higher buildings rise above the trees. The courthouse clock rings the 2 o'clock hour. It is like a scene by Currier and Ives!

The day is so clear, the going so much at ease, that we reverse direction to hike the loop again, gaining more long views to the High Peaks, and another look at the Sandy River. Start, end, or celebrate your day here!

Make-Your-Own Routes

Abandoned roads, snowmobile trails, open fields, woodlots—these provide opportunity for winter outings. When the land is private property, I ask permission of the landowner. I have never been turned down and landowners appreciate the courtesy.

I describe travel on snowmobile trails, abandoned woods roads, bushwhacking over fields or through woods, and night travel.

Note: Safety considerations and Self-Rescue considerations are all the more vital on make-your-own routes. As always, inform a responsible person in writing of where you are going and what time you plan to return. Leave a map of your itinerary with this person.

Snowmobile Trails

Maine has an extensive network of snowmobile trails, primarily maintained by local snowmobile clubs. Some of these trails are part of regional state-to-state and international trail systems, and some are local. Some are maintained by the Maine Bureau of Parks and Lands.

These trails are usually open to use by those on snowshoes or skis—I have yet to encounter a snowmobile trail closed to those on foot. They often provide access to terrain difficult to reach in winter, when some access roads are not plowed.

Cautions

Be alert for approaching snowmobiles—stating the obvious, which cannot be overstated.

It is a misconception that snowmobiles produce so loud a sound that there is ample time to collect a group and move out of the way. Newer machines run more quietly than older models. Approaching snowmobiles project little sound forward. In snowfall, and in the woods, what sound there is may be muffled.

Wear visible clothing. Have a headlamp at the ready at night and in low-light conditions.

Keep a group together. Do not string out, or block the trail. Proceed single file or not more than 2 people abreast.

Dogs on leash.

Be a Good Trail Neighbor

I wave to snowmobilers as they pass. If there is an opportunity, I stop to talk, exchange trail information, and welcome visitors to the region. Particularly in backcountry foot travelers and snowmobilers may be vital resources to one another in the event of a mishap.

Each year I make a donation to a local snowmobile club for trail maintenance.

A beaver lodge in winter.

A Favorite Snowshoe Hike – Using Snowmobile Trails

On Trail

Not far from my home a snowmobile trail crosses the road, to climbs a series of ridges before dropping down to a lake about 5 miles away. By combining the snowmobile route with an old, largely abandoned road, I can make a big loop back to my house. In a typical winter, I may make this hike once a week.

One winter morning, my Chocolate Labrador with me on a leash, I hike to the trail crossing, put on my snowshoes, and head north over a groomed snowmobile trail to climb to a north-south running ridge topped by a hayfield. The first section through which I pass was logged about 10 years ago, and is now filled with new growth—fir, birch, young maples, and a few pine. After crossing the old log yard, level terrain, I ascend steadily, warming quickly. I have trekking poles with snowbaskets. These help me to maintain balance, and hold traction in slippery spots.

Soon I leave the logged area for a predominantly hardwood forest, with rock maple, beech, ash, and white birch, still on the trail. After 20 minutes of travel I reach the high hayfields on the ridge, stepping away from the groomed trail to head for a rock outcrop that affords a view to the west of Mount Blue and Bald Mountain near Weld. To the east runs a series of low hills and ridges dotted by farmland. I return to the trail, make my way over the ridge and down its north side, crossing from one stone-walled field to another, before bottoming out not far from a country road.

Here the trail climbs again, and again I make some of my own warmth, keeping a steady pace up a hill on my way to a prized viewpoint—a lookout to the high peaks far to the north. To reach this point the trail follows an old woods road that connects one hayfield to another. In the nearby woods, largely covered with snow, lie remnants of farm work past: a rusting truck, a wheel-less manure spreader. Farmers cleared this well-draining, sun-warmed high ground in order to extend the growing season by 2–3 weeks.

Through an opening in the trees I spy a north-lying mountain, step out into the next hayfield—and there rise the high peaks of Western Maine. The Saddleback Range, Mount Abraham (Abram), Spaulding, and Sugarloaf Mountains—there they are! To the west, Mount Blue rises impressively, with its symmetrical summit cone.

This is one of the finest views in Western Maine—to be found along a snow-mobile trail not far from downtown Farmington. It is a good example of the discoveries that await those who make their own routes, whether on snowmobile trails, or on old roads, or by bushwhacking. I find a rock, brush off the snow, put down a small closed cell foam pad I carry to sit on, and enjoy lunch and hot tea. Life is good.

I continue across the open fields of this high ridge, enter yet another hayfield with views north toward the Bigelow Range, and follow the snowmobile trail up and down its ridge-way course. When the trail meets a road to continue on to the lake, now about a mile away, I check my time. Some days I climb over the lake-side ridge to drop down to the lake itself. Other days I follow a short spur trail to an abandoned road that will bring me down to the road where my house is located. Follow that road and cut through familiar woods, and I trek right up to my back door.

Snowmobile maps are readily available at Town Offices, snowmobile dealers, and wilderness outfitters. Discover routes that work for you!

Bushwhacking

Bushwhacking is the making of one's own trail over un-groomed terrain. This may be done either on skis or snowshoes, with snowshoes usually the better choice for uneven or steep terrain. However, there are cross-country skis designed for bushwhacking, and these can work well.

Maine has a good many abandoned roads, woods roads, and farm roads that remain unplowed in winter. I have received permission from multiple neighbors to snowshoe about on their property. Some of us have made cross-country ski trails on pasture and hayland, or on old woods roads, and welcome our neighbors to enjoy these. Park lands, local and state, may offer untracked terrain. Even if the parks are not officially open in winter, access may be available.

A few phone calls and you should be good to go.

Gear

The usual gear and clothing guidelines apply, but I add the importance of *eye protection*. Bushwhacking may literally be making a way through brush or thick woods. The leafless branches on hardwoods, and needle-less lower branches of softwoods may be difficult to see. If following another person there is the chance of a branch whipping back to catch the face.

I advise bringing *a compass*—which may already be in your "ready bag" of items you carry on every outing. A handful of times over the years I have been exploring new terrain, including frozen swamps and bogs, and heavily forested lowlands, and suddenly not been quite sure where I was. Sure, I could follow my tracks back out, retracing my route, but at least once I was nearing the end of a 2-hour hike, and did not want to have another 2 hours ahead of me when I knew I was close to my end point. It was an overcast day. The sun was not a help in determining direction. But I had a compass, knew where I was in relation to a road I planned to reach, and I made my way out. A topological map is also a good idea, for both navigation, and identification of landscape features.

Snowshoeing on an Abandoned Woods Road

Overview: The Western Mountains of Maine hold many an abandoned road that offer fine snowshoeing terrain. Time spent looking at topographic maps, and speaking with local people, can yield good leads about such roads. Much of this region was farmland between the late 1700s and the early to mid 1900s. Some roads provided access to farms. Others linked farms. Yet others served as direct routes between village settlements, routes now surpassed by other routes as some settlements have grown into town centers, while others have disappeared from the map. Now, traces of the former roads remain.

The following is a description of a favorite snowshoe hike. Discover your own new-yet-old roads and paths!

On Trail

One bright morning after a fresh snowfall, I call our Chocolate Labrador Retriever "Moose" and head out on one of my favorite snowshoe hikes to an abandoned road about a half mile from my home. I snowshoe across our back pasture, making fresh tracks on unbroken snow, and bushwhack through familiar woods to pick up the road. The old road climbs through a mixed growth forest of softwoods and hardwoods, levels out to pass stone walls constructed a century or more ago, skirts a great marsh, and climbs again to a stony brook draining a high wooded hillside. Quite varied the scenery for a road that is about a mile and a half long!

What a day! The bright sun rides low in the southern sky, throwing a rich golden light across the snow. Yellow birch turn amber in this low, glowing, light. The deep green of the pine, fir, and spruce, shimmers in the sun. A clearing-out northwest wind rushes through the bare hardwoods. Sugar Maples sway and creak. Aside from my own breathing, the soft crunch of snowshoe on snow, and the occasional call of a Chick-a-dee, it is the wind that offers the prevailing sound of the day.

The old road lies before us, unblemished. I am the first human to be out that day, but we are hardly alone. Distinctive two-plus-two tracks of snowshoe hare—also known as varying hare, for their seasonal change of color—cross our path. Two small front paws, two large hind paws. Deep, plunging tracks of deer cross our path. I marvel at how deer navigate the woods in winter with their slender legs and small hoofs. Of course at times the snow becomes too deep, and the deer remain in a deer-yard, chosen for good browse, and protection from wind, and wait for the snow to draw down.

We ascend for a mile, pass an old cellar hole. My, my. People once made a home here, worked the stony soil. Good site for a home: southern exposure, just enough of a brow of nearby hill to protect from the harshest northwest winter winds, and those of wild nor'easters. The cellar hole commands a level spot among hilly ground, and lies not far from the brook—our destination.

The brook is largely snow-covered, but in a few spots, is still open. Streams in winter fascinate me. Even on the coldest of days I may come across a brook that runs, no matter how many degrees of frost.

Moose the dog, and I, descend into the snow-filled draw where the brook runs. The wooden bridge that once spanned the short reach is long gone. A blow-down has fallen by the stream, dropped by the force of the wind, who knows when? I brush the snow off, make a seat for myself. Then the fun begins. I watch, listen, sniff the air.

Lace-like ice has formed between the open water and solid ice at the edge of the stream-bed. Sunlight sparkles on dark water that runs out from under one brook-spanning snow bridge, to disappear under another. A Pileated Woodpecker, out of sight, breaks the silence, rattling away. The crisp air has a distinctive clean smell. More deer tracks. These lead to the water; the stride shortens up, as when the deer paused to drink, then head across the brook to disappear into the woods beyond.

It is always good to have a seat in the woods, open up the senses. It never fails that I will see, hear, or smell something that I might have missed, had I not taken the time to stop and draw silent.

I rise to head for home, following my now-tracked snowshoe trail. One of the benefits of returning by the same route is that the trail is well packed! There are more discoveries. The downhill stretch of the road offers a fine view to Mount Blue, sunlit on the far horizon.

Such a day! No fees, no driving, no crowds, no noise—but rather, the simple gift of a winter snowshoe walk with our dog, in the Maine woods.

Night Travel

On Snowshoes by Moonlight

Overview: Take a walk in the moonlight—in mid-winter! The Maine skies in the Western Mountains are so clear that our family plans a number of a moonlight outings on snowshoes or skis every winter. I do bring a head lamp because I *always* bring a head lamp as a safety measure, but rarely need it. Eye protection is a good idea, as low-hanging branches and un-protected eyes are not a good combination. Remember that with 2–4 feet of snow on the ground, branches that are overhead in summer, may be at eye level in winter!

I make sure that I know where I am going—because landmarks can be missed. The route is either one I have taken often, or else I have a detailed map and have studied it well. Unfamiliar bodies of water are off-limits, even on the coldest nights, as springs and underwater currents can weaken ice in unexpected ways and places.

Remember the outdoor safety rule: Tell a responsible person where you are going, and when you expect to return. Better, show this person the route on a map.

Maine's moonlit winter nights are the closest phenomenon we have to a "white night"—the summer nights above the Arctic Circle when the sun never sets. They truly are not to be missed. To glide over an open field, or step through the woods on snowshoes, surrounded by silence, illuminated by the light of the moon—not to be missed.

Our family has a tradition of inviting friends to an annual moonlight snowshoe or cross-country ski outing. We begin with a pot-luck meal, then head out across nearby fields and into the woods, over trails I have laid out in the preceding days. There is much light under the moon, and even cloudy nights offer light when the moon is nearly full.

On Trail

By the light of a nearly full moon, I make my way on snowshoes across our back yard, toward pasture edged by a stand of high pine, spruce, and fir. Fresh powder snow from a storm of the day before gives way gently beneath my feet as I break trail and head for the nearby woods. Long, soft-edged, shadows run at length into the snow-covered fields, luminous in the bright moonlight. Sweeping gusts from a clearing-out northwest wind buffets the tree-tops, which respond with a low symphonic roar. In between the gusts, the prevailing sound is no sound—of sheer silence.

I am in for quite a treat this night—to witness to an event that I have rarely encountered in the outdoors. That event is the sudden, collective settling of a build-up of snow, following a storm. Snow once fallen, enters a process known as "sintering", by which separate snow crystals bind to other snow crystals. At some point this forms enough mass that great expanses of snow collapse under their own weight.

Often this happens as a quiet settling process. Think of it as the collective weight imperceptibly lowering ever so slowly, onto the snow base below. But at other times, conditions combine that there is a sudden *Whump!,* and a great expanse of snow will drop at the same time. Similar to the triggering of an avalanche, this abrupt and dramatic settling may be set off by a small movement—such as a snowshoe falling on snow to upset a delicate balance of snow on snow.

That is what was about to happen to me. As I make my first steps in the moonlight from yard to pasture: *Whump!* Startled, I stop in my tracks! *Whump!* became *Whump! Whump! Whump!* Tremors reverberated across the field. Those many inches of fresh powder snow dropped at that very moment, fell into itself.

Snow conditions have to be just right for this to happen, and, of course, someone has to be there for the instant when it does happens. For my sake, I was! The last time I recall witnessing this phenomenon was high country mountain skiing in the Colorado Rockies some 30 years ago. As mysterious and awe-striking as all this is, imagine what it is like to be present for this moment of winter moments, under the light of the moon.

Still marveling at that experience, I make my way well into the woods, following an old twitch trail that runs along a stone wall. Even in the woods there is light enough to make out the distinctive lobbed leaves of a small red oak tree fluttering with a papery sound in the breeze. Oak clings to its dry leaves well into the heart of winter.

Farther along I stop to inspect the distinctive furrows of a black ash, and the rough scales of a red spruce. In full daylight I might have passed them by. In the moonlight the fact that I can see any detail to them at all, causes their familiar bark to become a new discovery.

Plunging deer tracks cross my path, along with two-plus-two paw prints of snowshoe hare. In the woods in the winter such signs provide evidence of life here, largely out of human sight. I pass a fresh blow down, a dead fir broken off about three feet up the trunk. It will moulder into the soil, add to the soil, and continue the cycle of life in the woods.

The twitch trail drops down a short hill. I make a few surfing steps on the snowshoes, glide a bit over the powder snow. Beyond, I enter a stand of spruce, rising like great pillars in the moonlight. Then—what's that sound? The bellow of a fawn in distress!

Again, I stop in my tracks—this time to listen well. I know of a deer yard up in this area, and I am purposely well away from that! Could a fawn be out on a night such as this? The joke is on me! Not far off to one side and into the stand, a dead tree leans across a spruce limb a good ten feet from the ground. The spruce sways in the wind, the two trees scrape against one another, and like a great bow running over the string of a bass fiddle, the result is a long, bellowing sound!

I move on, shaking my head at how familiar woods offer such wondrous experiences on a night hike in winter. It is an old saying, but so true, that familiar things look quite different when seen in a new light.

A spring trickles from the base of a small hillside boulder, to become a small stream trickling off into the woods, making its way down to a small swamp a hundred yards or so away. It is a cold night, temperatures in single digits, but flowing water is powerful force.

For a good hour I snowshoe my way through the woods, across a snow-covered swamp, up and down low ridges, through various stands—one dominated by white birch, another by thick, tall pine, others the familiar mixed growth that characterizes much of the woodland in this part of the country. All takes on a shadowy glow. I trek through a great black and white photograph!

To be on snowshoes—or cross-country skis—in the moonlight is a quite special opportunity available to those of us who live in the North Country! Keep an eye on the calendar for the phases of the moon. Take note that very early morning, as well as evening, can be a time to be out in the moonlight. One day I go out an hour before dawn and enjoy beholding the setting moon drop through trees on the western skyline.

Expand what there is to see and hear! Head out on a moonlit night!

Your Own Field and Forest Route

I have tracked a ski trail around hay fields near my home, and extended the trail into fairly level ground in nearby woods. The overall distance is not great, but I enjoy the convenience of skiing without having to drive. I just walk out the door, make my way to where the trail begins, and ski as many loops as I wish.

Usually I begin the trail-making process by tramping out the route on snowshoes. Next, I go over the packed surface on skis. At the outer limits of this ski trail, where it borders on more uneven terrain, I bushwhack on snowshoes to create farther trails for snowshoeing only. The result is a near ski loop, and a far snowshoe loop. One of the joys of having a nearby, homemade, route is the opportunity to observe wildlife, wildlife signs, and subtle indicators of the change in seasons as winter progresses. Tracks, scat, food remains, even the imprint in the snow of the wings of a prey-seeking owl or hawk—these are in the woods for the viewing.

What is there to be seen and heard on my bushwhack? Hardwoods creak in the wind, as they sway on a below zero day. Low angle winter sun throws an amber glow on the bark of a yellow birch. A small seep releases water into the head of a small brook, even at subfreezing temperatures. The remains of a well-chewed cone from a white pine tell of the work of a red squirrel. Stomped snow near a thicket of young fir indicates the lair of snowshoe hare. The plunging tracks of deer lead from the woods to a hayfield where deer have brushed away the snow to feed on the grass underneath.

Oh, the simple joy of breaking trail. The quiet. The bright beauty of sun on new snow the morning after a winter storm. Your turn!

Long Distance Trail Systems

Maine Huts and Trails

This book describes day trip approaches to the four huts (full-service lodges) of the Maine Huts and Trails (MHT) System open as of this writing. The 80 kilometer trail system connects the huts, making it possible to have multi-day outings that include overnight stays at one or more huts. There is no fee for trail use at this time. Some day visitors purchase a modest Day Membership in consideration for trail maintenance, but there is no requirement to do so as of this writing.

Some parties start at one end and ski or snowshoe for succeeding days to the other end, using a passenger shuttle either for drop-off or pick-up. Others start at one end, ski to the most distant hut, then reverse direction—negating the need for a shuttle. There are many options, including using one or more huts as a base camp for multiple daytrips; and visiting two or three huts instead of all four.

Consult with MHT to determine what itineraries are suited for your party's size, interest, mode of travel (ski or snowshoe) and experience. Reservations are required for all hut stays. MHT staff will advise prospective visitors of clothing, gear, and safety recommendations.

Appalachian Trail

Day hikes in this book over portions of the Appalachian Trail (AT), include the Piazza Rock, Ethel and Eddy Ponds hike; and Little Bigelow Mountain. Occasionally I receive inquiries about distance hiking the AT in winter.

I do not describe hikes to the higher Appalachian Trail peaks in the region and neither do I describe AT overnight hikes. While I have hiked and camped on the AT in winter, I caution interested hikers that winter conditions on these high peaks can be extreme and the routes can become hazardous. Parties who undertake such travel should be well-experienced in mountain winter-camping, have winter wilderness first aid and medical training, have sound navigation skills, and be well-conditioned. Those who wish to gain winter camping experience may consider obtaining the services of a Registered Maine Guide with winter camping and foot travel expertise.

Recommended Reading

Forest Trees of Maine, Centennial Edition, 1908-2008. Augusta, Maine: Maine Forest Service, 2008. This is the best resource I have found for identifying Maine trees, understanding their annual rhythms, appreciating their use. Color photographs of bark, leaves or needles, buds, cones, seedlings combine with a crisply written text. The compact size, with a spiral binding, is convenient for the daypack. Available in bookstores and at www.maineforestservice.gov.

Tracking and the Art of Seeing: How to Read Animal Tracks and Sign, 2nd edition. Paul Rezendes. New York: HarperCollins, 1999. Winter is an optimal time to observe tracks and sign. This superb guide has color photos of North American mammals and birds, and our one marsupial, the opossum. Scat and other frequent signs that can be difficult to identify, are here in full color. Graphics of track patterns supplement photos of tracks. Ample text explains creature habits and how to interpret creature behavior from the evidence left behind.

Winter World: The Ingenuity of Animal Survival. Bernd Heinrich. There is much creature activity in the woods in winter! Heinrich, a wildlife biologist who has lived in the foothills area of the Western Mountains for decades, details winter life for creatures small and great—insects, moths, and frogs, to moose and black bear.

Woodswoman: Living Alone in the Adirondack Wilderness. Anne LaBastille. New York Penguin. 1976. Written nearly 40 years ago, this classic describes year-round life in a north woods cabin, with compelling observations of the sights and sounds of winter. The author followed this book with a Woodswoman series. Most recent title, *Woodswoman IIII,* was published in 2003.

Trail Maintaining Organizations Mentioned in This Book:

Quick Reference

What are the trail conditions? Are conditions more favorable for snowshoeing or for skiing? Is the parking lot plowed? What is the local weather forecast?

It is a good idea to contact the organization that oversees the chosen terrain and trails, to plan an outing. Changes are continually made to trails and trail systems. Some parking areas are regularly plowed, while others are not. Weather events and seasonal variations in snowpack can affect terrain conditions and access.

Special events may be scheduled, such as snowshoe rallies, organized ski tours, and moonlight outings. Instruction and rentals are available in some locations. Fee structures apply for some organizations.

Maine Huts and Trails, Kingfield, Maine: 207-265-2400;
<www.mainehuts.org>

Maine Bureau of Parks and Lands, including Bigelow Preserve
Western Regional Office in Farmington: 207-778-8231;
Augusta Headquarters: 207-287-3821;
Mount Blue State Park, Weld: 207-585-2261;
<www.maine.gov/dacf/parks>

Rangeley Lakes Heritage Trust, Oquossoc-Rangeley, Maine: 207-864-7311;
<www.rlht.org>

Rangeley Lakes Trails Center, Dallas-Rangeley, Maine: 207-864-4309;
<www.rangeleylakestrailscenter.com>

Sugarloaf Outdoor Center, Carrabassett Valley, Maine: 207-237-6830;
<www.sugarloaf.com>

Titcomb Mountain Ski Area, West Farmington, Maine: 207-778-9031;
<www.titcombmountain.com>

Contact the Author

How was your snowshoe hike or cross-country ski outing? Has a weather event changed the nature of a trail or route? Do you have an equipment or clothing tip to share? Perhaps you have a favorite winter destination you would like to see described in a future edition of this book?

There is a long tradition among outdoor persons of swapping information. Join that tradition!

Send me an email: <footandpaddle@gmail.com>.

I look forward to hearing from you!

— Doug Dunlap

All photographs by Doug Dunlap.

FIELD NOTES

One More Time – Be Safe!

Always let a responsible person know where you plan to go,
and when you plan to return.

Bring water, food, a headlamp, a whistle,
and a warm layer to put on at break time.

Carry a map and a compass and acquire the skills to use both.

Cold temperatures shorten battery life in cell phones—
save them for emergencies.

Enjoy the Maine winter—and be safe!

Set in Adobe Minion type
by
Michael Höhne
of Höhne-Werner Design
Wilton, Maine
in
2016